Pegasus
the Seminal Early Computer

with best wishes
Hugh McGregor Ross

ALSO BY HUGH ROSS:

George Fox speaks for Himself

George Fox a Christian Mystic

The Gospel of Thomas
Newly presented to bring out the
meaning, with Introductions,
Paraphrases and Notes

Introducing the Gospel of Thomas

Thirty Essays on the Gospel of Thomas

Jesus untouched by the Church
His Teachings in the Gospel of Thomas

Spirituality in the Gospel of Thomas

Also the websites at
www.gospelofthomas.info
www.gospelofthomas.net

Pegasus
the Seminal Early Computer

by Hugh McGregor Ross
and Colleagues

A Bright Pen Book
an imprint of Authors Online

Published 2012

Copyright © Hugh McGregor Ross 2012.

Catalogue records for this book are available from the
British Library and the Library of Congress.

Typesetting and illustration by Hugh Ross
using Garamond font and Apple-Mac Pages.
Cover and Annexes done by Mono Studio, Stroud.

ISBN 978 0 7552 1482 2

Authors Online Ltd
19 The Cinques,
Gamlinglay, Sandy,
Bedfordshire SG19 1NU, England

Printed and bound by Lightning Source.

Acknowledgements

Amongst the photographs copyright is acknowledged: At the Museum of Science and Industry Ferranti documents/archive, in document DC10A pages 12, 14, 25, 26, 38, 41. And in document DC45 pages 5, 7. (I wrote both those documents.). And on pages 78 and 79 of this book.

At the ICL Archive, the photograph on page 116 of this book.

On page 134 of this book, Professor Simon Lavington.

Amongst the Annexes copyright is acknowledged: Institution of Engineering and Technology Annexes 2, 3, 4 and 8. And the Science Museum Annex 9. And the Computer Conservation Society Annex No 10.

Other sources are acknowledged in footnotes.

It is regretted that no photograph of Bernard Swann has been identified, nor has it been possible to get in touch with his sons Humphrey and Peregrine.

I am grateful to my surviving colleagues George Felton and Ted Braunholtz for reading through and commenting on a draft for this book.

The other book about Pegasus is *The Pegasus Story, a history of a vintage British computer* by Professor Simon Lavington ISBN 1-900747-40-5

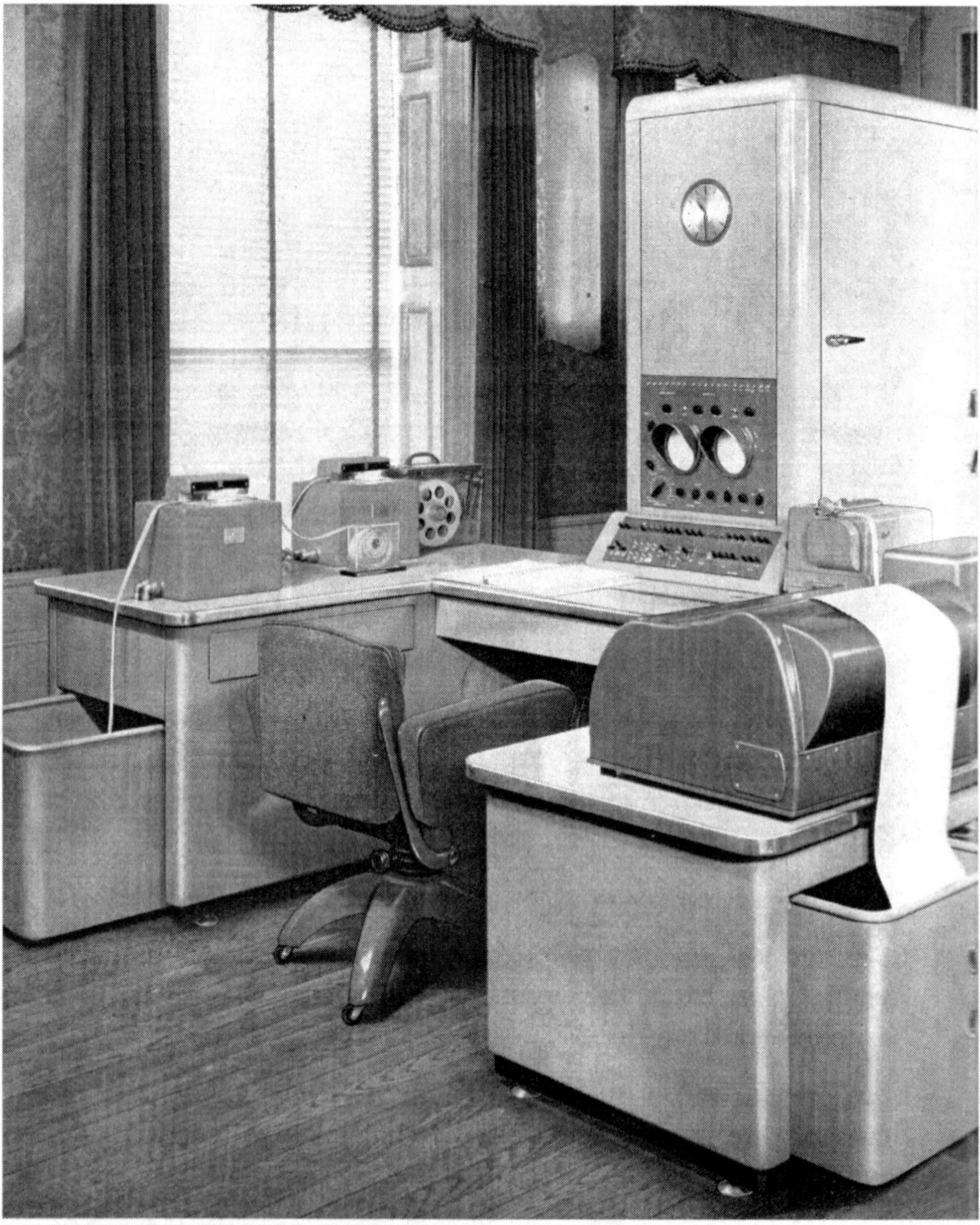

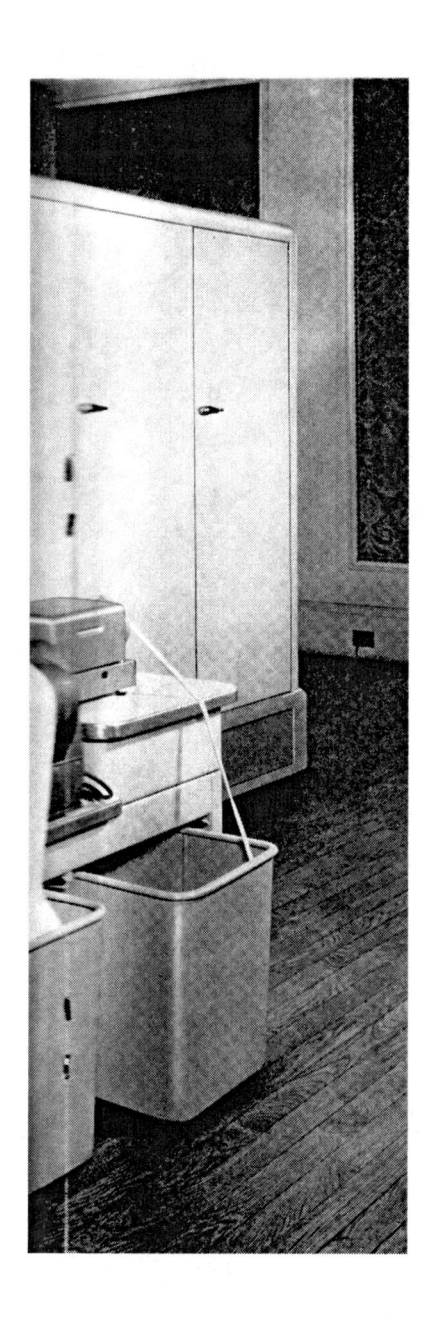

The first Pegasus computer, the main subject of this book. In its Rolls-Royce quality cabinet it was fitting that it was built and used in the elegant ballroom of a Nash London palace. There it comprised the first Computer Centre

Contents

Preamble	Page	1
Nicholas and the Elliott 401		3
The migration from Elliotts to Ferranti		9
Conditions of Work		13
Simplification of Programming		16
Support for Programmers		25
Machine Errors and Reliability		33
Combatting Machine Errors		36
Self Checking		47
Handling Input and Output		
Punched Tape		51
Punched Cards		54
Printers		57
Data Input		60
The Ferranti Common Interface and Autonomous operation		62
The Magnetic Tape System		65
Data Links and Data Transmission		70
Quantity Production		76
The Pegasus Costing Muddle		82
Marketing		85
New Applications Devised with Pegasus		93

Contents

Descendants of Pegasus
    Computer for British Ordinance Survey   101
    Three Proposals for Data Processors   104
    Proposal for an Enhanced Pegasus   107
    The Converters   111
    Pluto   113
    Perseus   115
    Pegasus 2   121
    FP6000   127
    The ICL 1900 Series   131

Epilogue   133

Annexes—

No 1   Elliott's first document on packages   135
No 2   Elliott and colleagues describe Pegasus   138
No 3   Fairclough on the basic delay-line store   147
No 4   Merry and Maudsley on the magnetic drum   153
No 5   Braunholtz describes Pegasus   158
No 6   Emery describes Pegasus   164
No 7   Braunholtz & Hogg on the magnetic tape system   170
No 8   Scarrott & Naylor on enhanced delay line store   176
No 9   The Common Input/Output Scheme   188
No 10   Merry extols the designers of Pegasus   198

Preamble

In the early part of the twenty-first century it is difficult to visualize that the computer revolution—later styled the information technology revolution—only came about, at least within Britain and other countries of Europe, through the labours of quite tiny groups of workers. Each member of these groups worked with extreme dedication and innovation, in virtually an obsessional way. Further, each group was centred on a particular individual who not only had drive, technical brilliance and creative abilities but was also an inspiring leader to the other members. This leadership led to deep loyalties. Those loyalties were the crucial catalyst for the enthusiasm which started that revolution and forged its progress.

Pegasus represents the quintessence of this environment, and is a prime example of the achievements thus made. It holds a special place because it and all its supporting activities embraced so many different strands of the computer revolution. This all took place within just the few years of its commercial life-time.

Furthermore, many of these developments, whether they took place wholly or partly within Pegasus, were carried forward to later computers and computing techniques.

The leaders who inspired their groups were W. S. (Bill) Elliott for the distinctive objectives and nature of its electronic and mechanical equipment, later called hardware; Christopher Strachey and Stanley Gill for the quality and versatility of its programming, later called software; and Bernard Swann who established and guided the marketing and customer support.

PREAMBLE

Another remarkable feature was that we were all *so young*. At the time of the creation of Pegasus, with the single exception of Bernard Swann, all the chief players were only in their late-thirties. Furthermore none of us had received any formal training or experience in management nor the financial aspects of running a business.

Enthusiasm was predominant.

Nicholas and the Elliott 401

The Elliott Research Laboratory was set up in 1946 as part of the effort to capitalize on British technological developments during World War 2. It was attached to the long-established company Elliott Brothers (London) Ltd which had a reputation for high-quality electrical and mechanical instruments. Its Director was John F Coales, an inspiring leader. He placed emphasis on his Laboratory being multi-disciplinary.

One of the departments, led by William S Elliott[*] (Bill) was developing digital electronic circuits, especially those potentially applicable to computers. Annex No 1 gives the original paper discussing Elliott's work on assembling digital electronic circuits into modules, each carrying out a specific logical function. The electronic circuits themselves were the responsibility of Charles Owen.

At that time the most crucial factor in the design of any digital computer was the technique to be used for the high-speed store. Elliott had read in an American journal that nickel possesses magnetostrictive properties. It is not known whether that article proposed, or Bill Elliott conceived, the idea of exploiting this effect to make a digital delay-line storage unit. In this transducers were placed at each end of a nickel wire and arranged with a circuit to inject a pulse at one end, with a valve amplifier to return the pulse from the transducer at the receiving end to the driver transducer,

---

[*] The similarity of name between the company an the individual is merely a coincidence.

thus giving a recirculating digital delay-line. Annex No 3 gives an original document discussing a later version of this type of delay-line store.

This design had advantages over the mercury delay-line store with piezo crystals used in EDSAC at Cambridge University and in the Pilot ACE at the National Physical Laboratory. It permitted the transducers and the ending of the delay-line to be independent, it minimized reflections at the ends, it avoided the task of machining the ends of a long tube parallel, and the problem of obtaining mercury in much larger quantities than for any previous purpose.

Nicholas* came out of a contract placed in late 1951 by the Royal Aircraft Establishment that involved much calculation. It was valued at £20,000. It was initially thought that the project would be done using hand calculators of the Munro or Brunsviga type. However a mathematician, Bruce Bambrough, realized that the sum could be better used to develop a computer utilizing the logical circuits established in Elliott's department of the Laboratory together with a storage system based on nickel delay-lines.

So the three-man team of Ed Hersom, Charles Owen and Bruce Bambrough set about designing the computer. The electronic circuits were to be the second generation of those devised by Charles Owen. These are described in Owen's document 'Three standard circuits for digital computers' *Elliott Research Laboratories Report no. 301, 2nd Sept. 1952*. However, at a crucial moment in the Nicholas project Owen fell ill with mumps, and was off work for three weeks. During this time he devised the complete logic design for the computer, together with the order code. His logic design, on a single large sheet of paper, is still in existence.

---

* A fuller account of Nicholas and its creation is given by Ed Hersom in *Computer Resurrection* issue 27, Spring 2002.

NICHOLAS AND THE ELLIOTT 401

What became known as the Nicholas computer thus comprised a test bed for nickel delay-line storage together with a practical machine to carry out the work of the Government contract. It went on to provide a useful computing facility for eight years.

George and Ruth Felton worked on the programming of Nicholas. They report that it was user-friendly from the programmer's point of view. Ruth Felton wrote the programmers' manual and fortunately a copy of it still exists. At that time matrix mathematics had begun to be applied to practical problems, and George Felton wrote an embryonic matrix interpretive scheme to assist their use in Nicholas. A particular applications of this was by Peter Hunt of the de Havilland Aircraft company, for the design of the Comet aircraft, the first civilian jet-engined 'plane. Because of the very limited storage of Nicholas, he had to idealize the whole aircraft into only ten elements.

The National Research Development Corporation (NRDC) was set up to exploit, on a national scale, the British technological advances arising from World War 2. It was funded by the tax-payer, but was expected to recover its costs from royalties on patents e.g. the cathode-ray tube store invented by Professor Williams at Manchester University, and by pay-back from sales of sponsored projects.

By the early-1950s its Director was Lord Halsbury. He had great foresight, and was supported by a tiny group of very talented men. It must be presumed that Bill Elliott, supported by John Coales, persuaded him to sponsor a real general-purpose computer based on the techniques established in Nicholas. A contract was placed, and it was given the Laboratory cost-collection number of 401.

Years later, Bill Elliott's wife Betty told me she would sometimes find Bill had been working obsessively all through the night, and the floor was littered with discarded papers. My surmise is that he was experimenting on paper with the selection and arrangement of basic logical elements in order to arrive at groupings that would provide the minimum number of types of standardized packages. These might have been for the 401, or when optimized for the later Pegasus as described in Glyn Emery's formal paper reproduced in Annex No 6.

For the 401 Bill Elliott assigned the responsibility of specifying the logical connections of the Charles Owen packages to Hugh Devonald. He also carried out the necessary basic programming of the 401.

Apart from the nickel delay-line storage, the most crucial component of the Elliott 401 was the magnetic drum store. Its importance lay in the provision of a clock track to control the timing of signals throughout the computer. A crucial feature of the circuits devised by Charles Owen was that within each digit-period, typically 3 microsec long, the signals were strobed or gated by a shorter, sharply defined signal derived from the drum. This permitted substantial tolerance against distortion of the waveforms associated with the functioning of the machine.

The drum also provided a backing-store of a really useful capacity.

The Elliott Laboratory was well equipped to provide this drum, with a highly competent mechanical department, accustomed to precision work. The importance of the drum is evidenced by the fact that it still exists as an exhibit in the Science Museum, London.

As the work progressed Bill Elliott conceived the ambition to display the machine at the Physical Society Exhibition, held annually in London. During W.W.2 and subsequently, this was the paramount occasion for displaying novel technological developments. This spurred on his obsessional manner of working, which he communicated to the tiny group of men assisting him.

In the event, he achieved that ambition. It created a real stir, for at that date very few people had even seen a digital computer, and it was the first time a practical digital computer had been transported and got into working condition for such an occasion.

It will be recounted in the next chapter that at about that time John Coales found it necessary to resign as the Director of the Elliott Laboratory, and Bill Elliott (and myself) chose to do the same. Both Coales and Elliott moved to Cambridge University. The NRDC, who owned the 401 computer, decided that it should go with them. Accordingly, it was transferred to Cambridge. Bernard Swann's *History of the Ferranti Computer Department** records that "Strachey did a considerable amount of redesign work" on it there, employed by the NRDC. It is apparent that Lord Halsbury combined his insight that computers would be important for British industry with an appreciation that Christopher Strachey and Bill Elliott as a pair were of exceptional value in achieving that objective. It must be assumed that Strachey was carrying out programming studies to investigate features that would be desirable in a computer, and discussing with Elliott the practical implementation of them, using the logical design facilities offered by the packages carrying the circuits devised by Charles Owen.

In support of this, Hugh Devonald who had been deeply involved in the design and construction of the 401, was engaged by NRDC to work for two or three days a week to complete the development of it and to make sure it was bought up to a high degree of reliability.

At that time it was not appreciated that the hardware of a computer had to be complemented by a substantial amount of software. What is most probable is that when the machine was at

---

* Written some years after ICT had taken over the commercial business of the Department, but never published.

Cambridge Christopher Strachey assisted by Donald Gillies did a significant amount of software experimentation and development on the 401.

After some time at Cambridge, the NRDC decided to donate it to the Rothampstead Agricultural Research Station. For a substantial number of years it did much useful work there, especially on the statistical analyses of experimental results.

The Migration from Elliotts to Ferranti

This chapter recounts and reflects the intense personal loyalties that lay at the heart of the vitality of the early computer scene.

In addition to what has already been told about the Elliott Research Laboratory some more needs to be written. Having been set up in 1946, by the early 1950s it had grown to over 450 persons. One of the qualities of its founder John Coales was to establish a direct and personal relationship with the more senior members of staff, who regarded him with great respect. While in practice almost independent, at least at first, it was beneficial to be attached to the long-established and highly regarded company Elliott Brothers (London) Ltd.

During 1947 Leon Bagrit became managing director of the whole company. He was an outstanding entrepreneur, with a conviction that extensive automation including computers would be introduced into industry. He also had much financial skill. For all technical decisions he relied implicitly on his colleague Dr Ross.*

During 1952 there were signs that the difference of Coales' emphasis within the Laboratory and the implementation of Bagrit's vision were beginning to create stresses. By the autumn although merely a group leader at the third level of the hierarchy, I saw that Dr Ross would require John Coales to go. It was a strange little incident. As part of Coales' policy all staff shared one canteen for lunch. One day I noticed Coales and Dr Ross come in, and Dr Ross

---

* The similarity to the present author's name is pure coincidence.

handed his coat and hat to Coales as one would do at a club cloakroom.

As foreseen, John Coales announced his resignation by the end of 1952, and it became clear he would go to Cambridge where he took up a professorship. At about the same time W S Elliott offered his resignation, but delayed leaving until the 401 computer had been exhibited in working order at the Physical Society Exhibition in April 1953. These resignations disturbed NRDC who had funded the development of the 401 computer under Bill Elliott. They arranged for the 401 computer to be moved to Cambridge together with Bill Elliott. Harry Carpenter and Hugh Devonald, still employed by Elliott Brothers, worked on the machine there from time to time.

By February 1953 I began discussions to join up with Vivian Bowden, in the Ferranti Computer Department. I had known and worked with him for a number of years previously, applying scientific method to the making of cinema films in studios. I joined Ferranti in July 1953.

In furtherance of Lord Halsbury's conviction that there was a commercial future for computers, NRDC arranged for Christopher Strachey, assisted by Donald Gillies, to work with Bill Elliott to develop further what had been established in the 401. Strachey was engaged in the capacity known later as an independent computer consultant. Gillies was a very bright computer theoretician from Illinois University.

As the work of the Elliott/Strachey/Gillies trio progressed, NRDC approached Ferranti with the proposal to sponsor the manufacture of a batch of ten computers to their design. Bowden and Swann had seen the 401 at the Physical Society Exhibition and been impressed by it. It was a major struggle to sell the large Ferranti Mark 1 Star computer, and there was a serious need for something more marketable. NRDC were pressing us to take on a commitment to make and market a batch of ten successors to the 401. Elliott himself was becoming established at Cambridge university.

Although it may have been in accord with what was planned by others, my recollection is that I suggested to Bernard Swann that we should try to enroll Bill Elliott who I had known and respected at the Elliott Laboratory, even though not being in his group there. This was a somewhat oblique suggestion, because being an engineer he would come into Brian Pollard's jurisdiction, not Swann's. Pollard was chief engineer and also general manager of the whole computer department.

This potentially difficult situation called into play one of Bernard Swann's outstanding capabilities. He had not for nothing risen, at an early age, to be an Under-Secretary for State. Such a British civil servant has to have the skill to resolve impossible situations proposed by his Minister. On this occasion he devised the plan that Bill Elliott should have his own development laboratory in London, an adequately safe distance from Pollard's empire in Manchester. Swann merely records that Eric Grundy, the engineering director senior to Pollard, agreed.

Accordingly, Elliott's embryonic team of engineers occupied a whole floor of the newly-opened Portland Place Computer Centre. There they started to build the first Pegasus computer.

This had a further highly beneficial effect. It created close relationships and understanding between Elliott's engineers and the other members of Swann's department. In the early years of Pegasus it meant a mixed team of engineers, programmers and salesmen could meet a customer. In Pegasus's later years it meant that every enhancement of the computer proposed by engineers was soundly based on customers' needs.

MIGRATION FROM ELLIOTTS TO FERRANTI

As Bill Elliott joined Ferranti, he brought with him Charles Owen and Hugh Devonald from his previous team at the Elliott Laboratory.

At much the same time, it became clear that substantial programming support would need to be given to the new Ferranti machine, and I suggested that George Felton and his wife Ruth be invited to join the company. Felton had worked with me on an analogue computer at the Elliott Laboratory before moving over to digital machines; he and Ruth had done the main programming on Nicholas.

Related to these migrations was that Peter Hunt, employed by the de Havilland Aircraft Company, had worked with George Felton to carry out calculations on Nicholas for the Comet aircraft. Due to the tiny size of the store of Nicholas, the structure of the aircraft had to be idealized into only ten elements the numerical values of which were analyzed by matrix algebra (the 'flutter calculation'). I had also got to know Hunt, and later together with Felton we encouraged him to join the Ferranti programming team. Hunt made invaluable contributions to the programming of Pegasus, and later went on to become responsible for the administration of all software support for ICL systems.

Conditions of Work

The conditions of work in our part of the Ferranti company had a significant effect on the creation and life of Pegasus.

The company had been set up by Sebastian de Ferranti towards the end of the nineteenth century for the invention and manufacture of electrical engineering products. It established a high reputation for innovation and quality. By the 1950s it was run by Sir Vincent Ferranti, of the second generation. Sir Vincent had had the foresight in taking on the re-engineering of the first Manchester University computer to recognize that there was a commercial future for computers. He had an amazing grasp of situations within the company. Thus I recall that at any moment he might turn up at the Portland Place Computer Centre to find out about progress, and after seeing Bernard Swann might burst into my office to enquire where I had got to on some project or other.

This vitality carried through to everything. It encouraged the engineers to be innovative and to give their labour without stint. Everyone working on computers knew we were breaking new ground, exploring in a territory without any antecedents to guide us or to limit our activities.

Time-keeping was determined by the needs of the job, not by the clock. Two word-pictures may help to convey the situation. First. On leaving my office in the Computer Centre I had to pass Swann's office, which had glass walls. Often he would call out "Hugh, may I mention so and so?" In consequence I learnt the quickest way to run from the Centre to the station for my commuters' train,

CONDITIONS OF WORK

choosing relatively empty roads to avoid being delayed by traffic. Second. One afternoon at home I reclined in the sun on a deck chair watching 'planes draw vapour trails across the blue sky. Suddenly I realized that it was the first time for two years that I had had that luxury.

Likewise payments were on a strictly salaried basis. There was no overtime pay or bonuses, no commissions, just annual pay reviews with modest increases.

A little feature turned out to be important. At the Computer Centre was a tea room, and staff and visitors were encouraged to take their morning and afternoon breaks at the same time. This resulted in an informal interchange of information about new projects, about progress or difficulties, and it created something of an academic atmosphere. It minimized the need for much in the way of progress meetings with their greed for time for the writing and reading of reports.

One consequence is that there is no recollection of any member of staff leaving to join a competitor in Britain. Just the major exception of Bill Elliott being enticed to go to IBM with the prospect of setting up a new research and development laboratory. He took Charles Owen, Ian Merry and John Fairclough with him

From a business point of view there was another side to these somewhat idealistic conditions of work. Very little attention was given to financial aspects of the activity. There was nothing like business plans; perhaps this was inevitable because one cannot plan a project to explore in unknown territory. Nor were there budgets, with regular reviews of keeping to the budget. Innovative schemes could -be approved purely on their merits—like mine for a quarter-scale model of Pegasus to show at exhibitions. It was made by Bassett Lowke the foremost makers of model railway engines.

When one of Bill Elliott's engineers needed a component of some unusual value he would walk during his lunch break to

CONDITIONS OF WORK

Webb's Radio in Soho, the Mecca of all electronic enthusiasts, and would be reimbursed from a petty-cash account.

There was no awareness, within Ferranti nor any other computer company at that time, that the cost of software would be significant relative to the cost of the hardware.

One of Bill Elliott's outstanding qualities was to be able to select capable colleagues. Thus he started out in his London Laboratory with only a handful of staff, yet within three years he had over one hundred. At no time during the span of Pegasus were more than 10 to 15 of those working on Pegasus, the others worked on military projects, supervised by Peter Dorey.

Bernard Swann records that his group in the London Computer Centre started with 20 staff, and a decade later had grown to 60. Interviewing people for these new positions had an interesting aspect. I did much of this, assisted by George Felton or Peter Hunt if software was to be a major rôle. There was no reservoir out there of people with experience of computers. Everyone was coming new to them. It was no use trying to explore what previous computing capability they had. I found it best to enquire whether the applicant enjoyed playing chess. After the initial amazement—"is this a firm that pays you to play games?"—had worn off, this usually led to revealing the innate capability for our kind of work. For the more senior positions, the applicant was then interviewed by Swann.

Simplification of Programming*

Design of the machine

Pegasus was the first computer in which the simplification of programming had been a primary objective of the design. This was the great, creative, contribution of Christopher Strachey.

Christopher Strachey Courtesy B Halpern and M Campbell-Kelly

---

* Major contributions to this chapter have been made by T.G.H. (Ted) Braunholtz.

SIMPLIFICATION OF PROGRAMMING

The programmer of any computer at that time had to have a clear visualization of the structure and functioning of the computer. It is therefore appropriate to describe in terms he, or she, would have understood, the main contributory factors of that simplification.

At that date any person intending to program a computer had to grasp certain concepts: that numbers were represented in binary form, and held in registers; that a program comprised a sequence of instructions; that these instructions also took the form of patterns of bits held in registers; and that the instructions were obeyed sequentially.

The computer itself could thus be represented as in the diagram on the following page. For a programmer at that time familiarity with such a representation was absolutely vital for his thinking.

In the first computers the results of each instruction (add, multiply, OR, etc) were put in a register called the accumulator, or the contents of the accumulator were put in a register, and so on.

The foremost novel feature of Pegasus was to provide seven accumulators. In a program some could be used to store intermediate results. This saved a lot of moving numbers to and fro from the accumulator.

Pegasus used the combination of an immediate-access store, comprising 32 single-word nickel delay-line stores, with a main store implemented on a rotating magnetic drum. This basic arrangement was recognized as the optimum, at economic cost, for fast processing together with substantial storage for program, data and results. However, what was crucial to the programmer were the facilities for inter-relating these two stores. Those provided in Pegasus were particularly effective.

A characteristic feature of applications put on a digital computer, or of the mathematical formulation of any problem, was the

SIMPLIFICATION OF PROGRAMMING

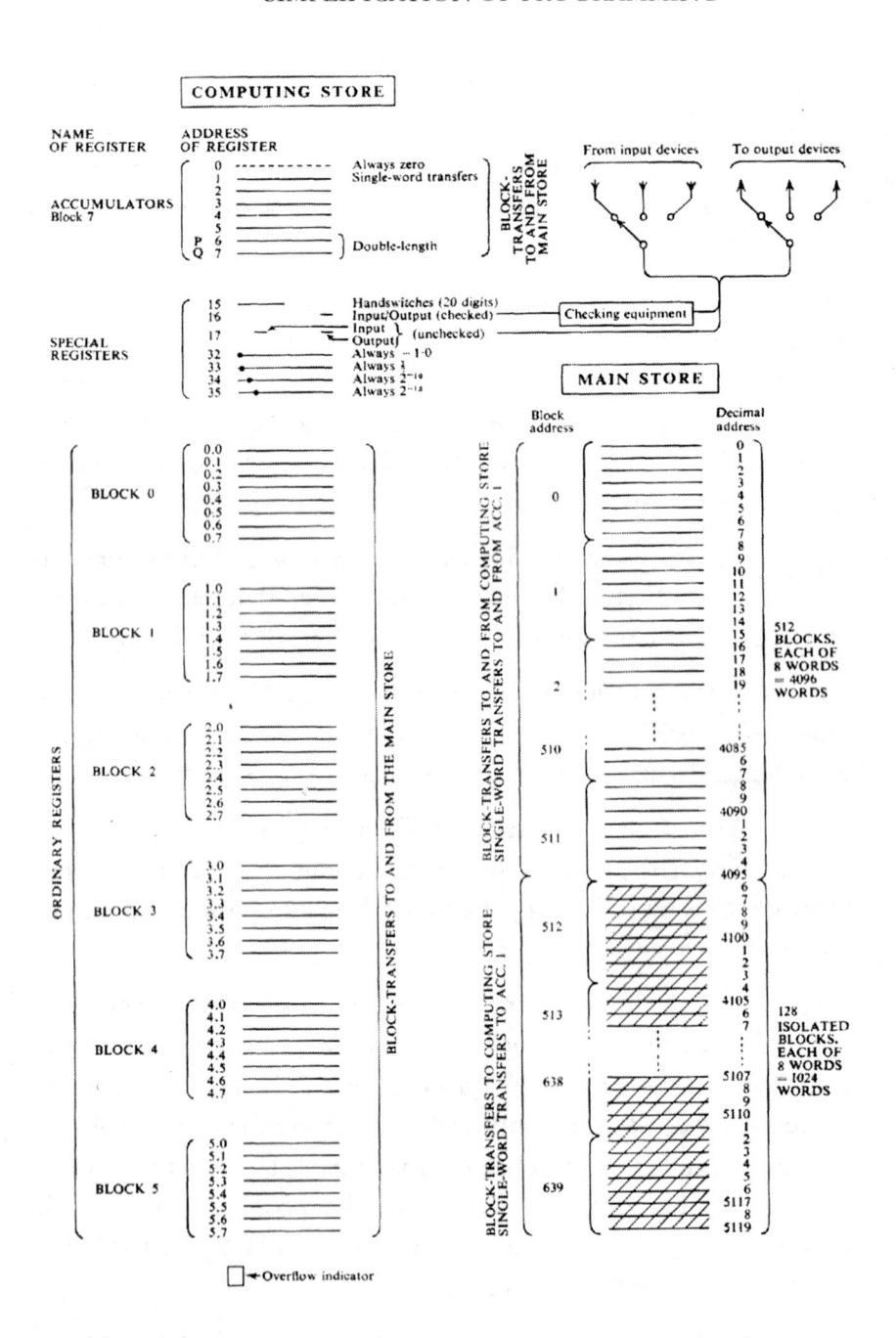

Representation of Pegasus

SIMPLIFICATION OF PROGRAMMING

repetition of a group of instructions, termed a loop.

A loop was formed by including in the program a jump instruction, which had the effect of altering the normal uniform sequence to make the operation go back to an earlier instruction. (Jumps could also go forwards.) The jump was conditional on the contents of an accumulator used as a counter, or on a test for zeros. Pegasus had an exceptionally comprehensive set of jump instructions.

A further important feature that contributed to the ease of programming Pegasus was that part of an instruction could be used to modify the address of the register specified in the instruction. Merely by changing the modifier, the program would work through a whole series of items held in the registers. This modifier facility was first used in the Ferranti Mark 1 computer, and in Pegasus it was more sophisticated, being suited to each type of instruction.

These features were provided in the computer in what was called 'the Order Code'. This was the great creative achievement of Christopher Strachey. It is shown on the following two pages.

Taking all these features together, it was possible for me to write (in italics for emphasis) in a contemporary document (List DC 10A) *"We see therefore how Pegasus has been conceived as a whole, how every aspect of it fits in with the others, and so each part can only be considered in the context of all the rest. For many applications, the features of the machine combine together to make it very nearly equivalent to one with an immediate-access computing store of over 4000 words, thereby approaching the ideal."*

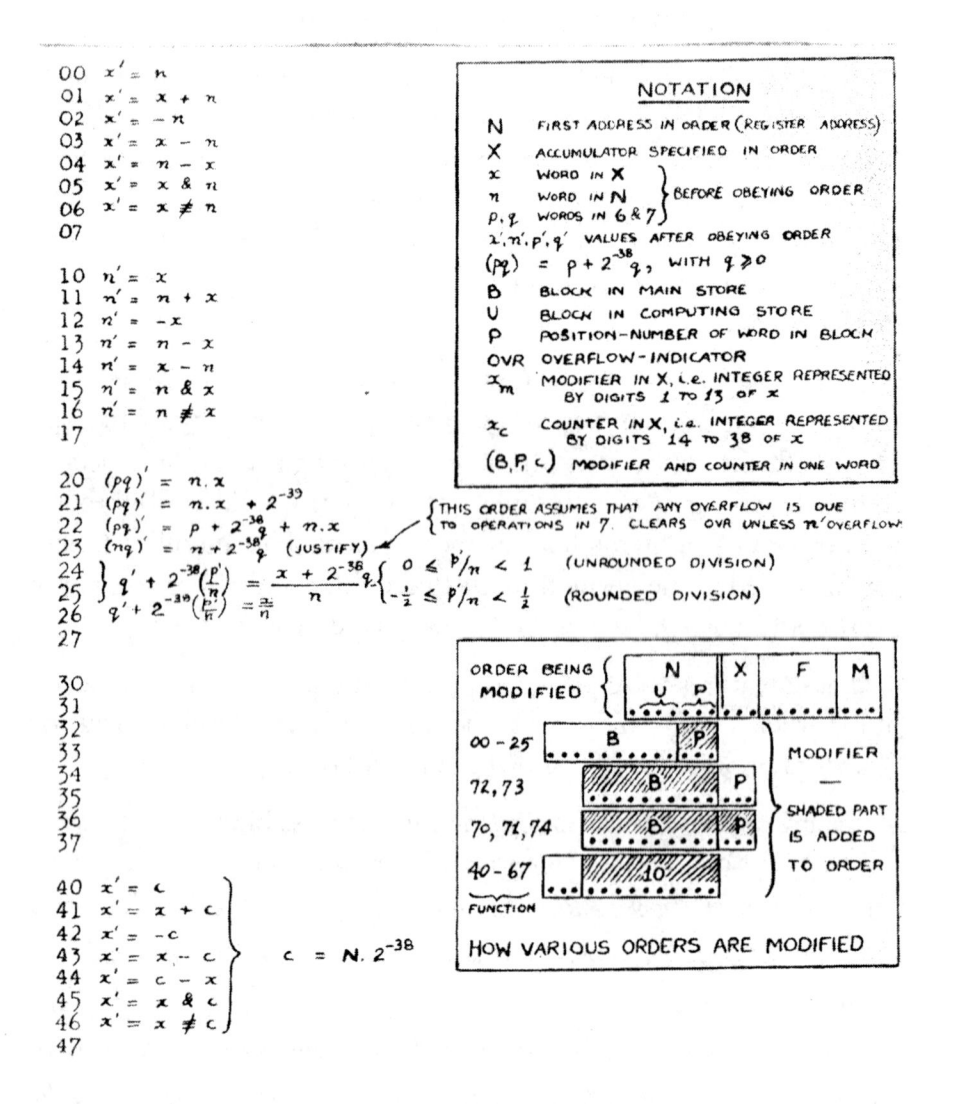

SIMPLIFICATION OF PROGRAMMING

```
00  x' = n
01  x' = x + n
02  x' = -n
03  x' = x - n
04  x' = n - x
05  x' = x & n
06  x' = x ≠ n
07

10  n' = x
11  n' = n + x
12  n' = -x
13  n' = n - x
14  n' = x - n
15  n' = n & x
16  n' = n ≠ x
17

20  (pq)' = n.x
21  (pq)' = n.x + 2^{-39}
22  (pq)' = p + 2^{-38}q + n.x
23  (nq)' = n + 2^{-38}q   (JUSTIFY)
24  q' + 2^{-38}(p'/n) = (x + 2^{-38}q)/n   { 0 ≤ p'/n < 1 }   (UNROUNDED DIVISION)
25
26  q' + 2^{-38}(p'/n) = x/n                { -½ ≤ p'/n < ½ }  (ROUNDED DIVISION)
27

30
31
32
33
34
35
36
37

40  x' = c
41  x' = x + c
42  x' = -c
43  x' = x - c     c = N.2^{-38}
44  x' = c - x
45  x' = x & c
46  x' = x ≠ c
47
```

NOTATION

- N — FIRST ADDRESS IN ORDER (REGISTER ADDRESS)
- X — ACCUMULATOR SPECIFIED IN ORDER
- x — WORD IN X ⎫
- n — WORD IN N ⎬ BEFORE OBEYING ORDER
- p, q — WORDS IN 6 & 7 ⎭
- x', n', p', q' — VALUES AFTER OBEYING ORDER
- $(pq) = p + 2^{-38}q$, WITH $q \geq 0$
- B — BLOCK IN MAIN STORE
- U — BLOCK IN COMPUTING STORE
- P — POSITION — NUMBER OF WORD IN BLOCK
- OVR — OVERFLOW-INDICATOR
- x_m — MODIFIER IN X, i.e. INTEGER REPRESENTED BY DIGITS 1 TO 13 OF x
- x_c — COUNTER IN X, i.e. INTEGER REPRESENTED BY DIGITS 14 TO 38 OF x
- (B, P, C) MODIFIER AND COUNTER IN ONE WORD

THIS ORDER ASSUMES THAT ANY OVERFLOW IS DUE TO OPERATIONS IN 7. CLEARS OVR UNLESS n' OVERFLOW

ORDER BEING MODIFIED	N / U P	X	F	M
00 – 25	B P			MODIFIER
72, 73	B P			—
70, 71, 74	B P			SHADED PART IS ADDED TO ORDER
40 – 67	10			
FUNCTION				

HOW VARIOUS ORDERS ARE MODIFIED

SIMPLIFICATION OF PROGRAMMING

50   $x' = 2^N x$ ⎫   NOTE :—
51   $x' = 2^{-N} x$ (ROUNDED)   ⎬ SINGLE-LENGTH ARITHMETICAL SHIFTS $x' = x$ IF $N = 0$.
52   SHIFT x UP N PLACES   ⎭
53   SHIFT x DOWN N PLACES   } SINGLE-LENGTH LOGICAL SHIFTS

54   $(pq)' = 2^N (pq)$ ⎫   NOTE:— $p' = p$ AND
55   $(pq)' = 2^{-N}(pq)$ (UNROUNDED) ⎬ DOUBLE-LENGTH ARITHMETICAL SHIFTS $q' = q$ IF $N = 0$.
56   (NORMALIZE) $(pq)' = 2^\mu (pq)$; $x' = x - 2^{-38} \mu$ ⎧ EITHER(i) $\frac{1}{4} \leq (pq)' < \frac{1}{2}$ AND $-1 \leq \mu \leq N-1$
57   ⎨ OR (ii) $-\frac{1}{2} \leq (pq)' < -\frac{1}{4}$ AND $-1 \leq \mu \leq N-1$
                                                                         ⎩ OR (iii) $-\frac{1}{4} \leq (pq)' < \frac{1}{4}$ AND $\mu = N-1$

60   JUMP TO N IF $x = 0$
61   JUMP TO N IF $x \neq 0$
62   JUMP TO N IF $x \geq 0$
63   JUMP TO N IF $x < 0$
64   JUMP TO N IF OVR CLEAR ; CLEAR OVR
65   JUMP TO N IF OVR SET; CLEAR OVR
66   (UNIT-MODIFY) $x'_m = x_m + 1$.   JUMP TO N IF $x' \neq 0$ (MOD 8)
67   (UNIT-COUNT) $x'_c = x_c - 1$.   JUMP TO N IF $x'_c \neq 0$

70   SINGLE WORD READ TO ACCUMULATOR 1. $1' = S$
71   SINGLE WORD WRITE FROM ACCUMULATOR 1. $S' = 1$
72   BLOCK READ FROM MAIN STORE. $u' = b$
73   BLOCK WRITE INTO MAIN STORE. $b' = u$
74   EXTERNAL CONDITIONING.
75
76
77   STOP.

	SPECIAL REGISTERS
15	HANDSWITCHES $H0, H1, \ldots, H19$
16	CHECKED INPUT/OUTPUT TAPE READER $\to 16_c \to X$ $X \to 16_c \to$ OUTPUT PUNCH
17	DIRECT INPUT/OUTPUT TAPE READER $\to 17_m \to X$ $X \to 17_c \to$ OUTPUT PUNCH
32	-1.0
33	$\frac{1}{2} = (512.0, \; 0)$
34	$2^{-10} = (1.0, \; 0)$
35	$2^{-13} = (0.1, \; 0)$

THE ORDER-CODE OF THE FERRANTI PEGASUS COMPUTER.

Oct. 1955
M.M.G.

CD 11777

George Felton

Efficient Programming

At the start of the twenty-first century the concept of efficient programming scarcely exists. Programs can be of megabyte size, and computing power is so great that it is wantonly wasted—in almost all personal computers or those attached to networks the actual processing function operates only for a tiny fraction, perhaps even less than one per cent, of the time

When Pegasus was developed fifty years earlier efficient programming was a major objective of its designers, both the equipment designers and also the software designers.

Primarily it was an attitude of mind to write programs that were efficient. This stemmed from Christopher Strachey, and was carried forward by George Felton. Felton had learnt his programming skill

SIMPLIFICATION OF PROGRAMMING

on Nicholas, with which a program had to be highly efficient, especially with respect to the demand for storage, to be able to do anything useful at all. Felton inculcated this approach to programming amongst all who learnt from him, and hence those who subsequently learnt from his colleagues.

Such efficiency was compounded of two factors. First, to make effective use of computing power. This was a precious commodity, rare and expensive. This was affected by the nature of the instruction set, specially the instructions used in the inner loops of a repetitive process, and by the organization of transfers between the fast and backing stores. The fundamental design of Pegasus, devised by the Elliott/Strachey/Gillies team, gave programs in which the user was not troubled by timing problems such as those associated with long recirculating delay-line stores ('optimum programming'). It was an important advance to be able to use a recirculating store with the 'random access' capability of a cathode-ray-tube store.

The second factor was to permit programs to occupy the minimum amount of storage space, specially for the inner loops held in the fast store which at that time had to be so small. This was specially influenced by the instruction set.

In Pegasus both these factors were particularly affected by the provision (due to Strachey) of the seven accumulators each of which could also be used as a modifier. This enormously reduced the number of steps in a program.

A related practice was the way in which data was handled in Pegasus, especially in connection with its input and output. A numerical quantity was recorded on an input or output medium as a series of coded decimal digits, and the size of the field—the number of digits—was no larger. Within the computer each such quantity was converted to binary, and stored as a single word or, in the case of multiplication or division, as two words.

SIMPLIFICATION OF PROGRAMMING

Alpha-numeric quantities were handled in the same way, the number of coded characters being no more than those in the item. Within the computer such characters were packed into words.

These techniques meant that the space required for storage was minimized, and the technique was termed 'variable-length coding'. It contrasted with the alternative practice, derived from punched card usage, where each item of data was allocated a specific number of columns on a card, termed a field, with blanks either at the more-significant end of integer numerical quantities, or at the right-hand end of alpha-numeric quantities. It also meant that there was no bias towards working with groups of 80 characters, this being the capacity of a punched card—60 years later several elements of computing systems optimize at 80 characters in a line of text.

As a consequence, the computing efficiency of Pegasus in practical applications was greater than could be expected from a mere study of its parameters. As users began to try out their practical applications on the machine at the Computer Centre, and went on to report what they achieved with their own machines, this became a significant element in its commercial success.

This approach to efficient programming was carried forward into later Ferranti machines, and when the ICL 1900 series was subsequently evolved the same approach was used in their basic operating systems, termed George III. It contributed significantly to the efficiency of those systems. I well remember the contrast between running, one and a half decades after Pegasus, the same application on an ICL 1900 which appeared nimble, and on an IBM 360 which seemed to spend most of its time running round its operating system rather than doing the actual work.

Support for Programmers*

New Concepts

Pegasus represented, and even constituted, the transition of computer business from an engineering activity to a true combined hardware and software activity.

Just as Pegasus pioneered the concept of simplifying programming, it also introduced another related concept. This was that a viable computer business required the provision of both hardware (the equipment) and **also** a comprehensive range of supporting programs, later to be termed software.

This novel feature had to be learnt the hard way, with many hesitant and tentative steps. To begin with its need was not recognized. No specific financial provision was made for it. There was no precedent for it, either within Ferranti or any other computer company. It was alien to the management of an electrical engineering company.

The contemporary situation is well illustrated by the groundbreaking book *Faster than Thought* published in 1953 by Vivian Bowden aided by Bernard Swann and others. This was based on experience gained with the Ferranti Mark 1 computer at Manchester. It describes a large and varied number of applications of computers. But close study of it shows these were all potential applications that

---

* Much of this chapter has been contributed by George Felton.

the authors had envisioned, and it is completely silent as to who would provide the programs for those applications.

To be a commercial success Pegasus had to break out of this situation. How was it done?

Programmers' Training Courses

During W.W.2 Bernard Swann had been responsible for introducing punched card systems for statistical work for the British army in India, and later other systems for demobilization. He had found that it was much easier to learn the techniques for using card systems than to learn about the statistical work itself. The problems lay round the treatment of exceptional cases.

With the advent of Pegasus at the Ferranti Computer Centre in London, this led to a major activity in providing programming courses. The objective was to train up a substantial body of users who in turn would develop programs for an increasing number and variety of applications.

The concept lying behind this was that it would be easier for people to learn to use Pegasus, than for specialist programmers to learn the practical applications with all their exceptional cases.

These courses were begun after the design of the machine had become stabilized, but before it was fully operational. They were conducted by George Felton and Peter Hunt. On the first course they found they were following the classic academic practice of writing each chapter of the programming manual just in time for the next day's lectures!

When the machine became available, participants on the courses found they could write and try out on the computer their own programs within the first week. The availability of Pegasus in the London Computer Centre was invaluable in permitting this 'hands-on' experience.

SUPPORT FOR PROGRAMMERS

These courses were highly successful and Swann records that ultimately they were being attended by 240 people per year. In a contemporary document I recorded that about 800 new programs for Pegasus were being written each year.

The Initial Orders and Assembly

In any computer there is the requirement to start in a pre-determined manner when first switched on. It is done by hardware. In Pegasus a couple of hardwired instructions bring in a block from the drum and jump to it, the computer then obeying instructions from that block.

This is augmented by a group of subroutines to check input data, to assemble numbers and convert to binary, or to store alphabetic characters. It contains facilities to help the user detect errors in his program. It also controls output.

The Initial Orders included Assembly, to assist incorporation of subroutines into the user's program.

The Library of Subroutines and Programs

A particularly valuable means to simplify programming had been devised at Cambridge University. It comprised relatively short programs to carry out specific tasks, which a user could incorporate into his specific program. Typical examples were subroutines to calculate trigonometrical functions, logarithms or square roots. Stanley Gill had become familiar with this technique, and on joining the Ferranti team greatly assisted in developing it on Pegasus.

Much of the early programming work done on Pegasus had, of necessity, an investigative element. Because of that, and with the co-operative attitudes that grew up between staff and those attending the programming courses, something akin to an academic atmosphere developed, with a remarkable absence of financial or commercial restraint. Accordingly, many subroutines were contributed by others.

However, it was found that these contributions had to be thoroughly tested and often improved to make them generally usable in the Library. This work was done primarily by Derek Milledge.

The Library was implemented on a punched tape mounted in the second tape reader. After a user's own program had been read in, the Library tape was scanned, and the required subroutines were automatically incorporated into the user's program, with all the required links.

In due course programs of increasing complexity entered the Library.

To give an idea of the nature and comprehensiveness of this Library a summarized index is shown on the following page. For this, the number of subroutines under each heading is shown, as at 1961. As an extension of the Library no less than 36 complete programs of general usefulness were included in it, with the convenience of being instantly available. For these complete programs, in particular, comprehensive descriptive and instructional documents were provided.

Matrix Interpretive Scheme

When Pegasus became available considerable progress had been made in evolving mathematical techniques using matrices, and, in particular, applying them to specific types of practical application. Much of this had been done at the National Physical Laboratory, at Cambridge University and at Government research laboratories.

SUPPORT FOR PROGRAMMERS

Library of Subroutines & Programs

```
Class          Type
```
Output   24 items
        Output of numbers
        Non-numerical output

Input   23 items
        Input of numbers
        Non-numerical input

Functions   22 items
        Roots and powers
        Exponentials, logarithms, etc
        Circular and hyperbolic functions and inverses
        Other functions of one variable
        Other functions of more than one variable

Operations   19 items
        Quadratures and differentiation
        Inverse interpolation and curve fitting
        Power series

Differential Equations   9 items
        Ordinary differential equations, first order
        Ordinary differential equations, linear (not first order)
        Ordinary differential equations, other
        Partial differential equations

Linear Algebra   18 items
        General purpose schemes (including matrix interpretive scheme)
        Linear equations
        Eigenvalues and eigenvectors
        Other special-purpose matrix operations
        Linear programming

Programmed Arithmetic   7 items
        General-purpose aids to coding (including Autocode)
        Floating-point, single-length
        Complex numbers (including floating-point)
        Multiple precision (including floating-point and complex numbers)
        Subroutines used by programmed arithmetic routines

Data Processing   13 items
        Conversion
        Sorting and merging
        Standard processes
        File organization
        Subroutines used by data processing routines

Applications   5 items

Individual Pegasus users' private routines

Miscellaneous   24 items

Isolated routines   18 items
character-shapes were on a series of disks

SUPPORT FOR PROGRAMMERS

Digital computers are particularly suited for carrying out calculations expressed in matrix form, a matrix comprising quantities arranged in rows and columns. Accordingly, during the early 1950s much attention was given to developing matrix algebra and in expressing practical applications in this form.*

Ferranti computers with their facility to modify the address in an instruction were particularly suited to this form of calculation. The program was written with one loop for locations in the rows, within another loop for locations within the columns. Merely by adding unity to the modifiers each time round the loops the whole matrix was processed.

Dr D G Prinz and Dr John Bennett, working in Ferranti Manchester, developed programs for processing matrices. George Felton evolved the matrix interpretive scheme for Pegasus.† In effect, this was an early program compiler, for a specific class of work. It was easy to use and was free from defects. All calculations were carried out in double-length arithmetic to ensure accuracy. It was very extensively used, especially for design of aircraft and other complex structures, and in the flow of electric currents or liquids in networks.

The Pegasus Autocode

An Autocode was a master program that provided for a very simple form of program-writing for a particular class of application. The first one had been devised by Tony Brooker for the Ferranti Mark 1

---

* This contrasted with my own experience, of studying engineering at Cambridge University just before W.W.2. The course had a particularly strong emphasis on mathematics, yet matrices were never mentioned!

† It was first described in the Ferranti document CS 135, 1957.

computer at Manchester University. Brian Clarke and George Felton prepared an enhanced version for Pegasus. A user could write a series of instructions in a form that appeared natural to him, and the Autocode program converted this into machine code, introducing the necessary individual instructions and allocating all the required storage locations.

The emphasis was on ease of use, rather than speed of processing. The initial idea was that it might be used for one-off calculations, where the overall combined time and cost for writing the program plus the calculation might be minimized. However, in practice it was found so useful that much work at each Pegasus installation was done with Autocode.

Benefits

Great benefits accrued to a programmer from the simplifications of the matrix interpretive scheme and the Autocode:

- There was no need to consider the schematic representation of the computer with its distinctions between the accumulators, the fast store and the main backing store.
- Specially for matrices there was no need to set up the modifications, and the repetitive loops with their counting down and testing.
- When using subroutines there was no need to set up the links and parameters.
- With these schemes it was simple to provide text and annotations in the results.

The Outcome

Despite its very tentative beginning, this programming support for Pegasus became substantial. The work was done in Swann's Sales Department, where the close contacts between users, sales personnel, programmers and the development engineers for Pegasus existed. Apart from the software contributions by users, it was funded partly from the fees for the programming courses but primarily by sales of machine-time on the Computer Centre's Pegasus. In itself this became a significant business activity. Alan Bagshaw managed it competently.

Machine Errors and Reliability

In the twenty-first century even an inexpensive computer will work without hardware errors for perhaps several years on end. It is therefore extremely difficult to visualize how at the start of the computer revolution machine errors or malfunctions presented very severe problems to users, and their reduction was a major challenge for computer engineers.

The contemporary situation may be well illustrated by two examples. Bernard Swann has recorded that in the first months of the use of the first Ferranti Mark 1 computer at Manchester University—MADM, a fully engineered machine, not the prototype made by Professor Williams and his University team upon which it was based—tension developed between Vivian Bowden and Swann, on the Ferranti side, and Professor Williams because users were wanting the machine to work for more than a few minutes without a machine error. Professor Williams regarded this as an improper request. Perhaps he considered that in ten minutes the computer would do as much work as could be done on a hand machine in several weeks. Furthermore, it was normal practice, and an essential requirement, when using manual calculators to introduce cross-checks, primarily to pick up faulty keying or errors when copying figures from the machine onto paper, and other mistakes. It was up to programmers to introduce equivalent checking procedures into their programs. For longer calculations it could be considered entirely reasonable to split them up into sections each of which could be done and checked singly. (In practice this was difficult on that machine because at first the output and input routines were not well suited to handle intermediate results.)

It was decided that rather than the principals in this quarrel being involved, Mary-Lee Berners-Lee of Ferranti should discuss the problem with Tom Kilburn, Professor William's chief engineer. She recalls that he did not wish to argue the point, and she felt indignant that he was dismissing her as a mere woman. At a reception some years later, and fortified by a glass of wine, she tackled him on this point, but discovered that he had secretly agreed with the Ferranti objective.

What actually happened was that John Bennett, of the Ferranti team, gave Mary-Lee the assignment to write a general-purpose diagnostic routine. This used a punched tape which was read in after any program-tape, that identified points in the program where the contents of the accumulator or any register could be punched out for subsequent printing. It thus permitted the user to trace where malfunctions had occurred and whether they were due to machine errors or program errors.

As the second example, John Bennett conceived the idea that the MADM computer could be used for survey traverse calculations in map making. The technique then and since Roman times was to use a theodolite, a telescope with cross-wires in the field of view mounted above a protractor scale, to measure the angles between triangular sightings. Together with a base line measured with a chain of 22 steel links—the length of a cricket pitch—all dimensions and shapes for an area of a map could be worked out. The calculations used trigonometrical tables and their limited four-figure accuracy resulted in a 'closing error' at the end of the computations. The subtlety of the process was, by successive iteration, to reduce this error.

[I learnt to do this, and do the calculations, when at college, and drew a map of a bit of Cambridge for the umpteenth time.]

MACHINE ERRORS AND RELIABILITY

Examples of practical surveyors' data were obtained from the Ordnance Survey (O.S.), responsible for Britain's maps. Harry Cotton helped to write the programs for MADM. He recalls that when ready to demonstrate the work, a representative from the O.S. was invited to Manchester. An officer in military uniform arrived. That day, however, the engineers failed to make the computer work at all. Instead of the hoped-for order of a computer, the O.S. decided to automate their work with a punched card system.

These episodes occurred in 1952 or 1953, and were typical of those well known at the time. This was the environment in which Bill Elliott was striving to devise means to overcome such incidence of machine errors, initially in the Elliott 401 and consummated in Pegasus.

Combating Machine Errors

At the time Pegasus was developed the incidence of machine errors was a major limitation in the use of computers. One of Bill Elliott's paramount design objectives was to reduce these errors, to provide means to detect them, and to speed up their rectification. The techniques evolved and built into Pegasus had a major influence on all later computers.

While it is well known that at that time the scale of many applications was limited by computing power and, to a greater extent, by storage capacity, in fact a more sinister limitation was the likelihood of an occurrence of a machine error. This made it impractical to run lengthy applications, or made it necessary to complicate the program to introduce checks against such errors, together with restart points.

In general, machine errors did not lead to a total outage of those early computers. Most often, and more troublesome, the defect only related to a single bit or a small group of bits. If these errors occurred in a data register the calculation was corrupted; much more significant was when the defect occurred in a register holding an instruction, or in the circuits of the 'mill'—where the arithmetic and logical functions were carried out—for these corrupted the sequential nature of the program. Very often such defects were transitory; these were exceptionally troublesome because it would be so difficult to find out where they occurred and to establish what was the cause.

Another source of machine error—midway between total outage and transitory errors—was trouble in the magnetic drum or disk, or in transfers between that and the central processor.

There were several classes of machine error, and various techniques were used in Pegasus to combat them:

Variance in component values

Charles Owen had found by experiment with the Elliott 401, that the characteristics of valves were very different from the published figures, and also in other experiments that these were very variable. This second effect was minimized by choosing only types of valve that had large production runs.

At that time resistors were usually far off their nominal values, plus or minus 20% was normal and only more expensive 'high stability' resistors were better. Further, a resistor by its nature generates heat in use; this and the thermal stresses when a component was soldered in, resulted in further deviations, often progressive. Capacitors also deteriorated to some extent.

Deterioration of valves

The performance of thermionic valves at that date gradually deteriorated, primarily through contamination of the caesium emitting surface of the cathode, which was run at near red-heat. This deterioration was in general unpredictable.

Tolerancing

Charles Owen devised mathematical techniques to determine the effect of deviations in the characteristics of valves and the tolerances of other components on the functioning of logic circuits. This permitted circuits to be better designed, and was a major contribution to the reliability of Pegasus. He is reported to have said, when it was finished, "The whole design of Pegasus is merely a matter of tolerances, tolerances, tolerances." Bill Elliott and Charles Owen later carried these techniques into the first of the IBM 360 series (360-40).

Critical machine operations

Two machine operations were particularly likely to cause machine errors: transfers between the fast store and the drum backing store; and complex operations within the 'mill' such as multiplication or division.

These errors typically only affected a single bit. Therefore in Pegasus a parity bit was added to every word and was checked by circuits at every transfer to or from the drum or at every operation of any of the accumulators.

Failure of such parity checks stopped the computer and prompted the user to call the maintenance engineer. Facilities were provided to help the engineer determine where in the machine the malfunction was.

Connector errors

It was well known at the time that plugs and sockets (now called connectors) and plug-in valves were a likely source of errors. This led some other engineers to question seriously the validity of the plug-in package concept. The problem was due to oxidation of the contact surfaces. For Pegasus these were silver-plated and, in addition, Brian Maudsley used a distinctive form of socket-element which scraped a tiny layer from the plug-element each time they were mated. The silver layer nevertheless was made thick enough to ensure a long life for the connectors. (After fifty years they are still usable in the London Science Museum Pegasus.)

Bad soldering

'Dry joints' were a major contributor to the malfunction of computers of the time, these being constructed from a multitude of discrete components. The package technique provided a ready means to employ flow soldering of all the connecting leads of components, passed through holes in the plate. Further, the high degree of quality control in the Ferranti factory and rigorous testing of packages and back-wiring harnesses, resulted in only few dry joints in machines after delivery—a contrast with other computers of the time when dry joints cropped up 3, 4 or even 6 months after delivery.

Logical design errors

Logical errors occurred when the design of the logical units was wrong or they were not inter-connected correctly. When Pegasus first became operational, Christopher Strachey spent many hours testing that every function of the machine behaved correctly, particularly when dealing with exceptional cases.

Data sensitive errors

More difficult during the testing of a prototype was to identify design defects which only showed up with particular patterns of data. The prolonged use of the prototype Pegasus in the Computer Centre by potential customers, using real data, was a major factor in overcoming this class of error.

MACHINE ERRORS AND RELIABILITY

Marginal testing

Bill Elliott and his team had found, probably on the Elliott 401, that the effects of deterioration of components, specially the valves, could be predicted by reducing the positive high-tension voltages and the negative bias voltages by a significant amount. This was called 'marginal testing'.

Pegasus was designed so that each morning the resident engineer would reduce the voltages and run programs to test every function of the computer—a not inconsiderable task in itself. The package containing any valve that had started to deteriorate to a significant extent would be identified, and the whole package replaced by a good spare. The machine could then normally be relied upon to run for the rest of the day without machine failures. In fact it was rare to have a catastrophic failure of a valve, i.e. the performance falling below an acceptable level—this being the bane of all other contemporary computers.

George Felton recalls how some of the users of other computers, who came to try out Pegasus at the Computer Centre, were amazed to find that their previous significantly complex fault-detection features in their programs were no longer required.

The maintenance scene

At the time when Pegasus was devised it was normal for every computer to have a maintenance engineer in attendance all the time. The idea that a computer could go to a purchaser without an engineer was beyond imagining. One consequence was a major burden on a manufacturer to train up each maintenance engineer and then lose him.

There was a further consequence in that computers were operated for long hours in each day, with a succession of programmers or machine operators, often working well outside normal hours. This sometimes necessitated more than one maintenance engineer at a site.

It was normal for each computer to be given one or two hours 'preventative maintenance', usually at the beginning of the morning. Then it would be handed over to users. With Pegasus and its package concept the engineer—if not called on for an emergency—could during the remainder of the day test individual packages and rectify any faults that were discovered.

When a Pegasus computer had been in use for some years, it was found adequate that the engineer was available on call, not resident.

The package concept

The package concept, conceived by Bill Elliott and implemented initially by members of his groups in Elliotts and in Ferranti—Charles Owen, Andrew St Johnson, Lawrence Clarke, Hugh Devonald, Harry Carpenter and Brian Maudsley—was of extreme significance for the success of Pegasus and many later computers.

It had the following objectives and consequences:

a) *Unification of design.* In all other computers at that time each major functional unit was of purpose-made design, usually on a single chassis. This can be seen very vividly in the replica of the first computer now in Manchester.

With the package concept sub-functional units were devised in such a way as to limit the number of types of such unit. In Pegasus there were 20 types. However all the logical functions were carried out by only five of them, the analysis of these many different functions into only so few types being a testimony to Charles Owen's brilliance. These five types comprised 314 out of the total of 444 in the machine.

MACHINE ERRORS AND RELIABILITY

This permitted a major simplification for manufacture. Each type could be made in quantity (relatively speaking), and without regard to the individual machine in which they would be used. Stock-holding of spares was greatly reduced.

b) *Simplification of testing.* Test rigs were devised which permitted each package to be comprehensively tested as a sub-unit. and tested independently. These rigs were used in the factory, and also by each on-site engineer.

c) *Simplification of error diagnosis.* When a machine error was detected, the maintenance engineer could run a test program which only had to identify the package in which the defect occurred, rather than having to identify the actual defect and the defective component.

d) *Rapid rectification of defects.* A defective package having been identified, it was replaced by a good and tested spare. Then the machine could be quickly returned to the users.

Each engineer had on site a simplified test rig which would enable him to identify a faulty component for repair, or to return the package to the factory.

A particularly important factor in the design of the Pegasus packages, due especially to Charles Owen, was identifying the logical functions that should go in each type of package. This is undoubtedly the crux of the matter, and the key to its success.

MACHINE ERRORS AND RELIABILITY

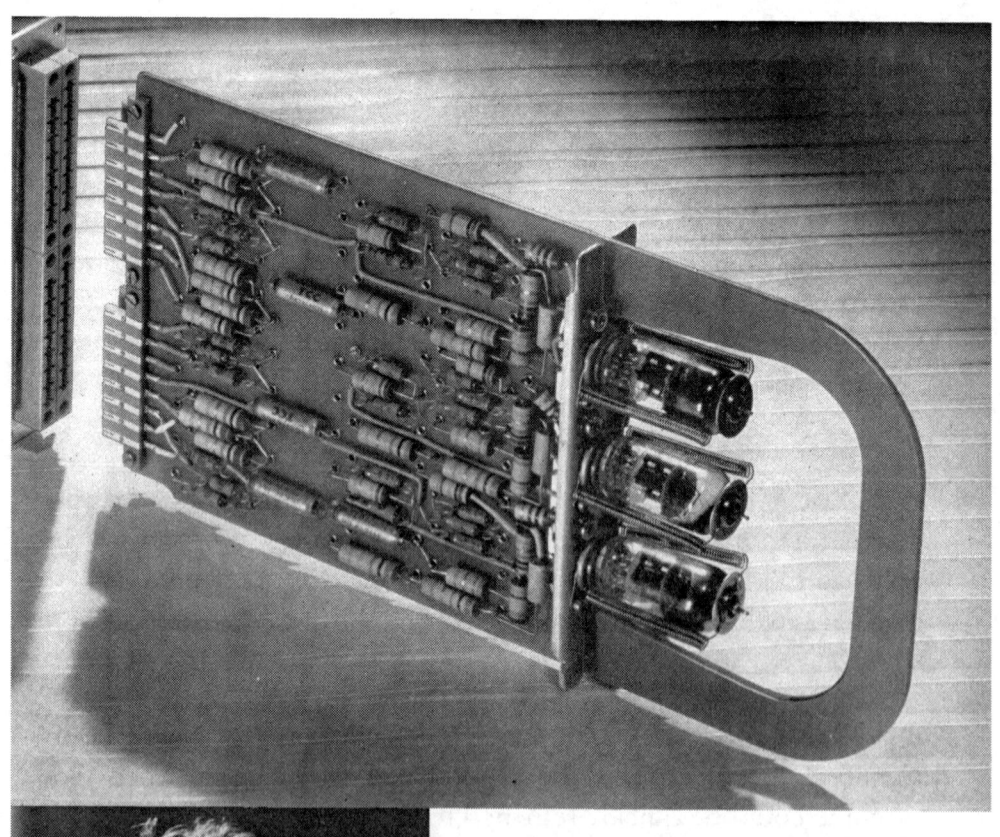

A logical package and Hugh Devonald the leading logical designer.

MACHINE ERRORS AND RELIABILITY

Basic single word delay-line package. 37 bits. Nickel wire, longitudinal pulses

MACHINE ERRORS AND RELIABILITY

The magnetic drum

Self-Checking

A most important design concept was incorporated in Pegasus. It is the facility for self-checking against machine malfunctions.

Although it is not known for certain, it may have been due to Bill Elliott or to Dr John Bennett. Certainly once it had been introduced it spread throughout the engineers of Bill Elliott's London Laboratory until they, and anyone else taking a technical interest in Pegasus, considered it was merely the sensible thing to do.

It involved a way of thinking that was contrary to the main thrust of a development engineer's efforts at that time. It was certainly not used in traditional steam engineering, nor in automobile engineering then—only later the ABS automatic braking system used a form of the concept. Servo systems, which were being used in aeronautical engineering, and negative feedback used in analogue electronic systems were only related to it. It was not used in horology, and it was alien to, and absent from, punched card technology.

It is relevant that every one of the descendants of Pegasus described in a later chapter that reached maturity utilized the concept. But, on the other hand, all those that omitted to use it remained only suggestions on paper.

In digital technology it was primarily implemented by the use of a parity bit. With Owen's logical units grouped on packages it was easily done. Thus in Pegasus a parity bit was added to every word, and checked whenever a word was processed or transferred between the computing store and the magnetic drum.

SELF-CHECKING

If the check failed the computer stopped. The situation has been described * in February 2012 thus:

Normal Practice on receiving an indication of a Pegasus computer Parity Error.

An alarm would sound and a lamp would light on the console to indicated whether it was a 'Computing store error' or a 'Drum parity error'.

The engineer would take over the machine. He had means to restart the machine and determine what caused the problem. He would trace it to a particular nickel delay line or to a drum read/write package. He would possibly reseat the line or package and test it manually and run test programs to determine the machine was working properly before handing it back to the operator.

Computing store parity failures did not occur often. Drum parity errors were extremely rare.

The practice of the operator or programmer was to restart the program in which the error had occurred.

Programming practice at that time was to write intermediate results to the drum or to punch them out so that the program could be restarted from the section that failed. This was always the case with long-running programs of several hours. Shorter programs of a few minutes duration would just be restarted after the engineer had cleared the problem.

Another form of the concept used in Pegasus was the code used in the punched tape. On the 5-track tape there were only 16 combinations of the punched holes that had odd parity. The tape code ingeniously allocated these to numerals and the important delimiters used with numeric quantities. On Pegasus 2 7-track

---

* By Len Hewitt leader of the Pegasus Working Party for the resurrected machine at the Science Museum London.

SELF-CHECKING

punched tape was also available and the larger code used one track for a parity check on every character.

In either case the parity was checked on reading tape, and an error stopped the machine.

By July 1955 in the proposal* written by Dr John Bennett for a computer for life insurance work, which ultimately became Perseus, the concept was developed and exploited to a high degree. This is apparent from the following quotation from that report:

A notable feature of this computer is the provision made for built-in checking devices. These reduced very considerably the number of program checks required. They are:

(i) <u>Printing</u> Here, numerical information is in a self-checking code, so that the possible transposition of one bit in any one character from a zero to a one or vice versa will not cause the printing of one decimal digit for another. This means that in the rare instance that any such transposition escapes detection elsewhere in the computer, a printing error results which can be readily detected by eye.

(ii) <u>Magnetic Tape</u> Information is placed on the tape a character at a time and a check sum is automatically placed at the end of each block. Thus any error occurring during writing, storage or reading, will be detected. Access to check sums is available in special registers.

(iii) <u>Card Input</u> Double sensing stations are provided, and a facility for comparing 8-word lines is available: unsuccessful comparison results in the setting of a staticizer which can be tested by program.

(iv) <u>Card Output</u> A post-punching sensing station will be available; this when combined with the 8-word comparison

---

* This is the third of the Laboratory reports referred to on page 104

SELF-CHECKING

facility mentioned above, provides the check required.

(v) <u>Tape Input</u>   Two tape readers are available. One possibility is that tape will be fed through these in turn, and a comparison instruction is available which can be used to ensure correct input. Alternatively, as the editing punches permit two tapes to be punched with the same information at once, one of these tapes can be fed to each reader. With both tape and card input it is assumed that care has been taken to ensure correct punching.

(vi) <u>Storage and Transfer Within the Computer</u>   Each instruction has an imparity bit, which is used to ensure that it has not been changed in the working store. All arithmetic and transfer instructions, except those designated in the instruction list as being non-arithmetical, result in the information on which they operate being checked character by character for imparity as this information goes to the arithmetic unit. If the check shows that a bit has changed the machine will stop. During transfers of numerical information from the arithmetic unit, imparity digits are automatically supplied,

(vii) <u>Addition and Subtraction</u>   These operations are checked by carrying out the reverse operations and comparing the result with one of the original numbers. Thus $(A + B) - B$ is compared with A. Failure causes the machine to stop.

(viii) <u>Multiplication and Division</u>   As these operations are effected by a combination of addition and subtraction operations their checking is an extension of the processes just described.

(ix) <u>Collation</u>   Facilities are provided to check the correct operation of logical 'And', 'Or' and 'Negation'.

(x)   No built-in checks, however comprehensive, can provide a complete guarantee of the absence of undetected errors. Some provision should be made for the normal accounting checks to be carried out by program as well.

Handling Input and Output
Punched Tape

The peripheral devices supplied with the first Pegasus computers for input of programs and data and for output comprised two paper tape readers, with photo-electric reading, and one paper tape punch. Typically the second tape reader was used for the Library of subroutines and master programs.

Such devices had the merit of simplicity. They operated one character at a time, and could start or stop on a single character under computer control. The computer was fast enough to keep the tape readers running at their full speed of 300 characters per second. The software accepted characters as coded characters or as binary, thus permitting programs or intermediate results to be handled in binary form for compactness.

The tape reader had been developed by Ferranti for the Mark 1 computer and exploited the feature that the drive roller was on one output shaft of a differential gear; both output shafts carried brakes energized by one or the other of a pair of thermionic valves.

A tape punch was a much more complex machine. Its action relied on a clutch being engaged or disengaged from a constantly-running motor. The design of punches was a very specialized matter, derived from long experience of telegraph machines.

It has to be realized that at that time the potential market that could be foreseen for computers was totally inadequate to justify the development of new electro-mechanical equipment for their use.

HANDLING INPUT AND OUTPUT

All that could be done was to adapt devices made for some other purpose.

A wide range of equipment was evolved from existing units to permit the preparation and use of the punched tapes for input of programs and data. An important item was a tape comparator, which enabled the manual keying to be duplicated, preferably by a second operator, and the previous and new tapes to be compared automatically as a check against errors.

This tape editing equipment was inexpensive and very widely used by organizations to prepare punched tapes to be run by the computing service we provided on the Pegasus at the Computer Centre in London.

At first the output punch on Pegasus ran at only 25 characters per second (later 33 ch/sec). This was a significant restriction on the practical use of the computer, which is reflected in the commonly-used phrase that Pegasus was one of the computers intended for 'scientific' work.

That tape punch was made by Creed and Co, the British firm making telecommunication devices. At a later stage the American Teletype Corporation evolved a tape punch operating at 60 characters per second. This came about as part of the evolution of an enhanced telecommunication system that superseded telex. It was quickly adapted for use with Pegasus, (it is shown as the free-standing cabinet on page 123). Further, by 1959 Creed had been prevailed upon to develop, primarily for Pegasus, a paper tape punch that ran at 300 characters per second.* It incorporated an integral check reading station. It was a major achievement, but it was a complex machine and inevitably expensive. A particular problem

---

* A document I wrote on this tape punch has been deposited in the Archive of the Institution of Engineering and Technology, London, ref NAEST 176/3.

with a tape punch was that the 'chad' that had been punched out had to be thrown clear, otherwise it would interfere with the photoelectric reading. This called for development of special paper for tapes, done by Waterlows using esparto grass.

To begin with, results obtained from Pegasus were printed on Creed teleprinters, operating at 7 characters per second. These were telegraph machines with minor modifications and because of their long period of development were highly reliable. The printers were operated from a paper tape reader, thus taking advantage of the fact that results often came out of the computer in intermittent bursts. It gave an 'off-line' facility. Later the Flexowriter, developed by Freiden Ltd, was adapted for use with Pegasus in a similar rôle. It had enhanced features and superior print quality.

Handling Input and Output

Punched Cards

Some general-purpose computers of the period used punched cards for input and output. An example was the English Electric DEUCE computer, developed from the ACE computer at the National Physical Laboratory which had extensive experience of using punched cards for mathematical work. This was a simple use of punched cards.

On balance, however, for technical applications, and in terms of convenience, speed of operation, and cost, punched cards and punched tape were fairly evenly matched,

For commercial data processing applications the situation was entirely different. For many years the punched card companies had been evolving highly sophisticated ways of mechanizing the processes of commercial offices. This was done by using electro-mechanical machines, some significantly complex.

The arrangements in the early years for the supply of punched card machines for Pegasus can best be described as absurd. A great deal of frustration resulted.

During the 1950s two punched card companies were active in Britain, Powers-Samas and British Tabulating Machines. They were bitter commercial rivals. Both saw that their future products would need electronic capabilities. Brian Pollard, the general manager of the Ferranti computer department agreed to work with Powers-Samas to develop some enhanced systems. Powers-Samas were intensely secretive about their development activities, and in the event nothing materialized.

Furthermore, an agreement was made that Ferranti would not attempt to market Pegasus for data processing applications, leaving it to the Powers-Samas salesmen. Again, in the event that considerable sales force could not achieve even a singe contract.

This situation was allowed to continue until, for other reasons, the British government stepped in and forced the merger of the two companies, to form International Computers and Tabulators (ICT). The technology of British Tabulating Machines became dominant in the combined company. This brought about a much more effective co-operation with the highly competent ICT development engineers.

It will be described later how, from a very early stage in the evolution of Pegasus, engineers in the Ferranti London Laboratory had visualized the addition of punched card facilities to Pegasus. This, however, was done within the thinking of the incorporation of self-checking against errors, a very cardinal feature of Pegasus.

In conventional punched card usage, the concept of self-checking was absent. Instead, good practice involved a variety of other checks to identify errors, which were not infrequent, and to permit remedial action before the consequences became serious.

The machines that were manufactured by ICT had a modular feature, in that each machine had a card track comprising a series of pairs of rollers, with an ingenious card-feed mechanism at one end, and punching or reading units. It was possible for Ferranti to obtain machines that provided a post-reading station in a punch, or two reading stations in a card reader. Together with storage for the card image in the electronics, and checking circuits of the two card images, this permitted the checked operation required for Pegasus. These machines are shown in the photograph on page 133

HANDLING INPUT AND OUTPUT

Some other computers of the time, typically the NPL Pilot ACE and its derivatives Deuce and LEO, and some American machines, used punched cards for input and output of data and programs. The card engines were of large size, and their design perfected over many years. In operation, each card was released by engaging a clutch. For reading, the card travelled broadside passing under a row of 80 reading brushes; for punching it passed step by step through a single punching station. This mode of working was fundamentally different from the character-by-character use of punched tape, and necessitated significantly more electronics to convert the signals and to provide a buffer to hold each card-full of data.

This form of card engine were made by IBM and BTM. A third form, made by the British company Powers-Samas operated on a complete card at a time, reading by means of pressing spring-loaded prods onto the card, or punching it in a big die. There was intense competition between these card companies, their practices being in general non-interchangeable, so that a user was tied to a particular supplier. This greatly complicated the whole matter of attaching punched card facilities to Pegasus, with arguments based on technical points, commercial considerations, personal preferences and emotion. It was only when Pegasus 2 was developed, four and a half years after the original Pegasus, that punched card input and output became available. Even so, the punched card engines required an extra cabinet full of electronics,

Handling Input and Output

Printers

At the time of Pegasus all printing in the office was done on machines that had raised character shapes that were struck onto the paper through a carbon ribbon. This had the advantage that by interposing a thin sheet coated with carbon duplicate copies could be obtained, in special cases up to five copies.

The character repertoire was severely limited, being confined to the numerals zero to nine, just a few symbols, and the 26 letters of our alphabet, only as capitals. This led to the practice, still sometimes continued 60 years later, that names and addresses on cheques for example, are printed in capital letters only.

The usual character spacing along a line was one-tenth of an inch. This led to very condensed shapes for the letters M and W, and the need for numeral one and capital letter I to have exaggerated serifs. The usual vertical spacing on the page was 6 lines per inch.

When Pegasus was used for technical calculations it was adequate to print the results on a teleprinter, even at the slow rate of 7 characters per second. Layout of the text was obtained by repeated Spaces horizontally, and repeated Line Feeds vertically. Because the actual output of the computer was to a tape punch and was usually in intermittent bursts, in practice it was seldom that the slow speed of printing was itself a limiting factor.

When Pegasus was considered for commercial data processing, the only options were to use a printer derived from the tabulator of punched card systems. In conventional punched card systems of the time the most important machine was the tabulator. This had arithmetic capability, some logical capability and, in particular, a printer for results. There were three types of printer. The first used vertical type-bars carrying the raised character-shapes, one for each character-position along the line. They were raised to the appropriate position for the required character and the paper was struck against them by a line of hammers. The second kind, favoured by IBM, used a continuously moving horizontal chain carrying repeated groups of the raised character-shapes that were struck against the paper at exactly the right moment by a row of hammers. This had the advantage that each line of printing was uniformly straight. In the third kind, favoured by the French company Bull, the raised character-shapes were on a rotating drum across the page, and the paper was struck against them by a line of hammers at exactly the right instant. In all these machines, after impact the hammers had be withdrawn instantaneously to avoid blurring of the printed characters. They were inevitably noisy and had to be enclosed in sound-deadening cabinets.

An important feature for commercial data processing was the use of pre-printed stationery. This required precise feed of the paper, which was attained by using sprocket feed, engaging with holes punched near each edge of the sheet. This feature was combined with a fast paper throw, controlled by a loop of plastic tape. The loop was specific for each layout of document.

Because these printers were an integral part of every punched card system they were highly developed and rugged machines capable of hard usage. The printing unit of a tabulator could be obtained as a directly driven output printer for a computer. They were known as line printers.

HANDLING INPUT AND OUTPUT

A considerable amount of design and development work was involved in connecting such a printer to Pegasus, even taking advantage of the logical design capability provided by the packages.

Part-way through the life of Pegasus the Powers-Samas company came up with the Samastronic printer. This had a significant amount of electronics built into it. It was utilized with several Pegasus systems. It had an ambitious performance, printing 300 lines per minute, with 140 characters along each line.

Its method of printing was to employ a row, right across the page, of 240 fine styli, each operated by a solenoid, to strike against an inked ribbon and the paper. These were used to draw out, in the form of a matrix of dots, the shape of each character. A guide plate with the whole set of styli oscillated to give th columns of the matrix. The paper moved in tiny jerks during the printing phase, to give the rows in the matrix. This gave the appearance of continuous movement.

Bernard Swann wrote of this product:

This was an ambitious development which took time to get working but proved to be reliable.

Still later the Creed company evolved a printer that operated at 100 characters per second.* It had a single print head that moved across the page. This carried a matrix of printing styli which were actuated hydraulically from pulsing devices in the base of the machine. A few of these were used with Pegasus, being very easy to connect and operate, but they were not fully developed and tended to leak the hydraulic oil onto the pages.

---

* It is described in the same document I wrote for the Creed 300 character per second tape punch, deposited in the Archive of the Institution of Engineering and Technology, London.

Handling Input and Output

Data input

Throughout the 1950s virtually all data—whether for calculations or for commercial data-processing—was prepared by hand for input to computers. This operation was so much slower than the processing speed of any computer that it was done as an off-line process.

For the original Pegasus (and earlier Ferranti machines) it was done on a machine derived from telegraph practice comprising a keyboard and a paper tape punch. For punched card systems, although some powered machines were available, it was often done on a very simple card punch with only 12 keys; this was exclusively muscle-powered and, furthermore, for alphabetic data the operator had to do the code conversion mentally and depress two keys at the same time. It was amazing the skill attained by an experienced operator.

The great problem with either of these schemes was the detection of operator's errors. The practice was to key all data a second time, preferably by another operator. This was done on a verifier, which read the initial punching as the data was re-keyed, compared the two character-by-character, and any discrepancy locked the machine. When the error had been identified, and the correct character identified on the source copy, erroneous holes would be covered over, or extra holes punched in, both by hand—although alternatively a complete card could be repunched. It will be realized that throughout this verification process it was vital to

HANDLING INPUT AND OUTPUT

maintain everything in the correct sequence—woe betide anyone who dropped the pile of source documents or a stack of cards!

For error detection when punching programs it was usual to make a print-out as the tape was punched, and do proof reading against the programming sheet. Programmers usually punched their own tapes, finding the practical work a welcome change from the pen and paper writing.

Ferranti called such a suite of machines a tape editing set. Because these were quite inexpensive and on short delivery most users of a Pegasus, and any group awaiting delivery of their own computer, would posses several sets. They did not go wrong, nor need maintenance.

The Ferranti Common Interface and Autonomous Operation

The connection of a computer to a peripheral device, usually for input or output of data or results, is no simple matter. Almost always such devices are of electro-mechanical nature requiring electrical signals to start, stop and control the mechanism, as well as those to transfer the data itself. There are further requirements to inter-relate the different operating speeds of the computer and the device.

On all early computers the electronic circuits for effecting all this were designed specifically for each type of device, this being the most efficient method technically.

As the first Ferranti Mark 1 computer in Manchester University gradually attracted more users with new applications, a need arose for different types of input and output equipment, other than the paper tape devices.

This particularly applied to the work of the Imperial Chemical Industries Central Research Laboratory, also in Manchester. Their Gordon Eric Thomas (known as Tommy) had previously worked with F C Williams, Tom Kilburn and Dai Edwards and understood the functioning of that machine. Wishing to connect other types of peripheral devices, and realizing that it would be impractical to arrange for the computer to be modified for each one, he devised the concept of a general-purpose interface.

Such an interface is an imaginary surface across which data-signals are transferred, under the control of extra signals to carry out the transfer, all specified by what was later termed a protocol. In itself it does not comprise equipment, other than a connector. On either side of the interface logical units and electronic circuits of appropriate types carry out the conversions to conditions specified at the interface.

Such an approach requires, for any single peripheral device, more equipment and more complication than a scheme specific to that device. But for any variety of devices it offers a great overall saving. Furthermore, it permits the equipment on each side of the interface to be developed independently.

The computer at Manchester University was modified to provide such an interface, and the University and Ferranti personnel assisted in making the scheme work. The concept and the scheme has been applied to countless other computer systems, the most widely known being the RS 232 interface to connect a modem for data transmission over telecommunication lines.

This interface was adopted as a standard in subsequent Ferranti computers. This included the enhanced form of Pegasus 2. The specification for it is given in Annex No 9. The concept has been adopted for many other computer systems, with increasing comprehensiveness and effectiveness.

Autonomous Operation

In early computers all the logical processes required to make a peripheral device operate were carried out by the central processing unit. This occupancy of the CPU interfered with the main processing task. With paper tape devices this did not matter much, for they were simple to operate. However, as more complex devices were considered the occupancy of the CPU would be of significance.

FERRANTI COMMON INTERFACE

To tackle this problem the concept of autonomous operation of all the equipment on the peripheral side of the interface was devised. In effect, a whole series of logical operations akin to those that could be done in processing were carried out in circuits dedicated to the peripheral unit. In Pegasus these circuits took the form of packages, and usually these occupied most of a extra cabinet.

This feature can be thought of as a rudimentary form of time-sharing or simultaneous processing, with the difference that the sequence of operations on the peripheral side of the interface was controlled by wired logic, not by a reloadable stored program.

The Magnetic Tape System

By the early 1950s recording of audio signals on magnetic tape had become well established. But, at least within Europe, recording of digital signals was not yet successful, although several companies were experimenting with it.

Bill Elliott's foresaw the importance of magnetic tape for Pegasus, and it became the first development to reach commercial status. His policy was to buy in equipment for his computers, whenever this was available, and he identified that a tape transport made by the Electrodata branch of the American Burroughs Corp[n] would be suitable for Pegasus.

This used a half inch wide mylar based tape, coated with iron oxide. This became standard for all subsequent computer systems.

At that date, it was widely recognized that magnetic tape was the optimum means for providing a substantially increased storage capacity for a computer. For Pegasus it was also established that an appropriate way to use it was to regard it as equivalent to a greatly enlarged drum store. That is to say, recording words of binary digits, arranged in blocks of 16 or 32 words.

The first experimental system, comprising a tape control unit and two Electrodata tape units is shown on the next page.

This was connected to the Pegasus computer in the Computer Centre in Portland Place, London. This made it very convenient for the development of the programs in the Library that were an essential, even vital, part of the system.

THE MAGNETIC TAPE SYSTEM

The first Pegasus magnetic tape system

The technique used in Pegasus* was to provide a separate tape control unit, which could serve 4 tape mechanisms. This contained a buffer store made of 32 single-word delay lines. A special order in the instruction code exchanged at high speed any 8-word block of binary data between the computing store and the buffer store. Subsequently the contents of the buffer store were transferred to or from the tape.

---

* The definitive paper on the Pegasus magnetic tape system is given in Annex No 7 It is written by two of the engineers involved, and discusses factors that affected the design.

THE MAGNETIC TAPE SYSTEM

It is apparent from the schematic diagram on a following page that the buffer store and its relation to the fast computing store was equivalent to an extension of the main store on the drum. And the tapes themselves provided an unlimited storage beyond that.

Pegasus used magnetic tape that had been pre-tested and formatted with 16- or 32-word blocks, each one addressed. This was the first stage in overcoming errors in the recording/reading process, by avoiding blemishes in the tape.

In the use of magnetic tape for commercial data processing—a major objective and attraction—one of the most useful processes would be to update the items in a file. It had been established that the optimum way to do this was to run the master tape through one tape unit and in another tape unit run the updating data; (alternatively, the updating data could be in the main store on the drum.) On the computer finding an item to be updated it would be amended and recorded on a third unit. However, all the unamended items would be merely copied over unchanged.

It is apparent that the plain copying would be much more frequent than the amendments, typically by a factor of 250 for daily updating. This requirement necessitated an unprecedented degree of error-free operation. Nothing like it had been required before.

In the Pegasus system great attention was given to this error-free requirement. It was all done in the equipment, without placing any burden on the programmer. Thus:

- the parity bit on every word was tested;
- in every block on tape the binary-ones on each track were added together and the sum recorded after the block;
- two recording/reading sets of heads were provided. On recording these provided a post-check, on reading a pre-check;
- there were numerous checks that the tapes were running truly past the heads; and that the electronics were operating correctly.

This combination of checks against malfunction may be regarded as the most sophisticated and comprehensive implementation of the concept of self-checking.

Thus the magnetic tape system could be used in three ways:

i To provide the storage needed by very large calculations;

ii As a means to link Pegasus to other equipment, especially for input of data and output of results; this was first implemented in the Converter described in a later chapter;

iii As a means to carry out the processing associated with commercial data processing with its immense files of data.

When the magnetic tape system was attached to Pegasus, none of the previous programs were affected. This was an early example of attaining pre-compatibility in system evolution. However, a substantial number of new programs were written and added to the Library, to make best use of the magnetic tape system. These included checks that the operator had not made mistakes that would cause errors.

In the event, the magnetic tape system on Pegasus, which became operational in March 1957, was the first successful one in Europe. Together with its target for error-free operation, it set the pattern for all subsequent magnetic tape systems in Ferranti computers.

THE MAGNETIC TAPE SYSTEM

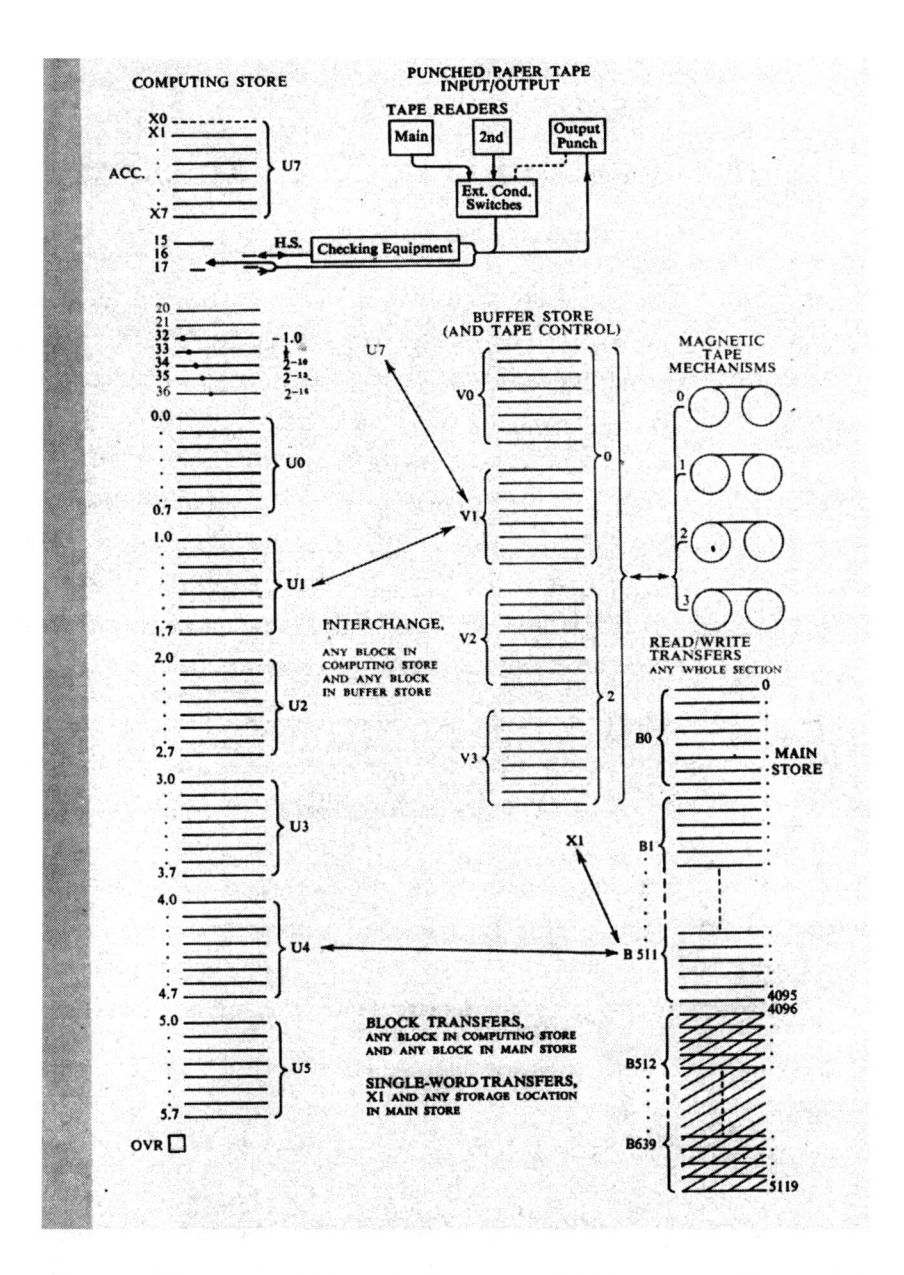

Representation of Pegasus with Magnetic Tape

Data Links and Data Transmission

At the time of Pegasus there were two telecommunication facilities: telegraphy and telephony. They each had distinctive characteristics, and were very different from each other. In U.K., and in most other countries, they were managed by the Post Office—it was before BT was created. Their engineers developed a very high degree of specialist skill, which was not shared out with other branches of engineering. However, in the process of installing the most modern form of telephone system in the Portland Place Computer Centre I had established good relations with individual engineers that turned out to be of extreme, even vital, benefit in subsequent events.

Taking telegraphy first. This was a digital system. The bit-rate was 50 bits/second. Items of equipment used a synchronous motor, locked to the 50 c/s mains supply, which drove a commutator to create data signals. These were grouped into 7½ units to establish characters. A skilled telegrapher using the keyboard of a teleprinter maintained an even keying speed of 7 characters/second, thus utilizing the full capacity of the system. An 'auto-transmitter' that read punched tape and sent signals to line did the same

The telegraphy system was available in two forms: using switched connections within the network, called telex; and using 'tied lines', connections permanently routed between two stations. The latter was much more expensive to hire, and on economic grounds was only infrequently justified. It did however permit the higher signalling rate of 75 bits/second. At that date virtually every office

DATA LINKS AND DATA TRANSMISSION

and factory was equipped with telex, and in some it was very extensively used.

In telex, calls were set up using a rotary dial that emitted pulses to operate the circuit switching equipment. However a feature of the system was that certain characters had specific functions. The most notable was the 'Who Are You?' character that activated an automatic device within the receiving teleprinter to return a distinctive identifying sequence of characters thus permitting the sender to check the call was correctly established. Other characters set the Figures Shift or Letter Shift of the teleprinters.

Because the 5-track punched tape used with Pegasus for input and output, it was apparent that the telex facility could be used for sending data and results in character-coded form. However, a more crucial requirement was to be able to send program tapes, especially during the program development phase. Although these were prepared by punching the characters written on a programming sheet, at an early stage in the process they were converted to binary form, primarily because it was much more compact. This required every possible combination of bits to be transmitted—a practice that became known as 'code transparency'.

When I discussed this requirement with a Post Office engineer, Alan Croisdale, he stated that by removing a link within the equipment the in-built code-sensitive features could be inhibited and code transparency attained.

Thus the first practical telecommunication facility for use with computers was born. In Ferranti we called them data links. They comprised modified teleprinters or telegraph tape readers (auto-transmitters) as senders, and teleprinters with tape punches as receivers.

There were no specific error detecting features built into these simple data links. Once a call had been set up, the telex system was inherently reliable, and at least adequate for its widespread use.

DATA LINKS AND DATA TRANSMISSION

For numerical data and results the built-in parity checking of the Pegasus character code would suffice. For alphanumeric data or results the redundancy of language and spelling would be adequate. For programs in binary form the practice was established that a copy-tape would be returned to the sender (simultaneously by the same equipment) for the sender to pass through a tape comparator or to check visually by holding the original and copy-tapes to the light. The error-detection built into the Pegasus basic software would provide a further check.

In the event, these telex data links were very successful. Their equipment was inexpensive and required little maintenance. They permitted a form of remote usage of Pegasus, because we provided as part of our Computer Centre activities for our staff to run the transmitted tapes on our Pegasus computer.

They were used to such an extent that in 1962 I could write "One Ferranti computer installation where about 1.5 million characters flow each day in and out of the computer installation on such data links; about half the traffic is incoming, and about half outgoing". Also, in January 1962 I presented a paper to the Institution of Electrical Engineers entitled 'Data Links for Use with Computers, with Particular Regard to Applications in Banking'. This was based on our experience of using telegraphic data links and applying them to this class of work where freedom from errors was crucial.

Turning now to the telephone facility. This was an analogue system, transmitting sinusoidal signals in the frequency band of about 100 to 2000 hertz. It was also available in two forms: either subscribers being connected via switching centres in the network, or it being possible to hire a fixed connection, 'tied lines'. The former relied on the use of a multiplicity of electro-mechanical relays. The contacts of these were in the open air which inevitably resulted in erratic poor connections that could be heard as clicks and crackles. The latter were more

DATA LINKS AND DATA TRANSMISSION

expensive to hire, and were only seldom justified. Communication in the network between switching centres was done by multiplexing the audio signals onto high-frequency carriers.

Being a world-wide system, everything was determined by rigorous standards, these being evolved and regulated by the authority CCITT in Geneva. (This acronym being formed from the initial letters of its long title in French.)

To permit this facility to be used with computers the first requirement was to evolve a standard to permit them to be connected. By this time I had established good relations with more senior Post Office engineers, and was invited to join the U.K. delegation to a CCITT meeting called to consider this requirement. I was strictly instructed to speak only if called upon by the head of the U.K. delegation, and was pleased to hear the chairman of the meeting (also from the U.K.) state that the U.K. delegation included a computer engineer, the first one!

The standard that was evolved was related to the interface that had first been devised for the Ferranti Mark 1 computer in Manchester, and developed in Pegasus for connection of peripheral devices. It relied on the exchange of a series of electrical signals (we called it 'hand-shaking') to permit the transfer of a group of data signals in parallel representing a coded character. I and an American engineer worked late into the evenings writing this standard. It became RS232 and is the basis for the connection of all digital telecommunication facilities today.

The second requirement was to evolve a standard to permit the digital computer signals to be converted to the analogue signals in the network. This was done by specifying a modulator/demodulator device, which became the first of the 'modems'. Essentially, a digital one created (or sensed) a tone of one audio frequency, and a digital-zero created (or sensed) a tone of another frequency. The modems also serialized the bits of the character coming over the interface. I was closely involved in all this standards-making.

The successful use of the telegraph-based data links with Pegasus prompted me to encourage the engineers in the Ferranti Bracknell Laboratory, the successors to those who created Pegasus, to develop a data transmission system using the telephone network. Because this was the adaptation of an analogue telecommunication system for digital use it was inherently more error-prone than the earlier telegraph data links. Accordingly, the engineers evolved a system akin to that used for the Pegasus magnetic tape facility. Blocks of data were read from a punched tape reader into a store, whereupon a parity bit was added to each character plus a summation character added at the end of the block. This gave lateral and longitudinal checks.

At the receiver, if any of these checks failed the whole block of data was retransmitted. Only those blocks that passed these tests went to the paper tape punch.

By this date the Teletype punch operating at 110 characters/second had become available, thus providing a substantial improvement over the earlier data links. The photograph on the next page shows the data terminal. The electronic equipment is in the cabinet on the left. This gave a high-performance off-line data transmission facility for Pegasus.

The equipment was designed on a modular basis, which made it practical to provide it in three forms:

DL2, one-way transmission, either from A to B or from B to A, using the switched telephone network

DL3, both-ways transmission, simultaneously and independently. This used tied lines.

DL4, connected directly into an Atlas computer, which offered either-way transmission over the switched telephone network. This worked into the 'Supervisor', which allocated jobs and facilities as required for the application.

After the take-over by ICT, the last-mentioned became known as the ICL 6000 data link, and was very extensively used with the University and Government Atlas computers.

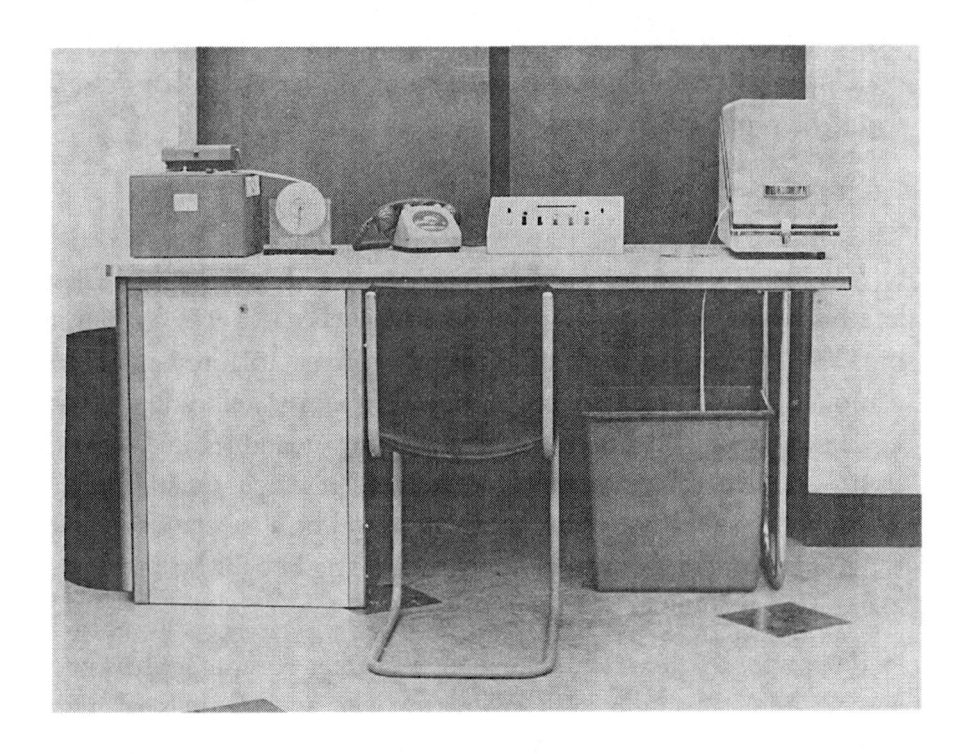

The fast punched tape data transmission terminal, 110 char/sec over switched telephone lines, either way. Very sophisticated error control.

Quantity Production

[Although the paper referred to is dated April 1956, this is written from the viewpoint of 1953 when Pegasus was conceived, for I am convinced that Bill Elliott envisaged from the very start that Pegasus would be produced in quantity.]

The original definitive paper describing Pegasus has the title '. . . Pegasus, a quantity-production computer'. It was by Bill Elliott and his senior colleagues. At the time when Pegasus was conceived, mid-1953, it was the work of a major visionary to foresee that any computer would need to be produced in any significant quantity. Earlier computers had been made in only tiny quantities, and most of them taken up by universities or military research establishments. There was no evidence then that there would be a substantial market for computers, for this would imply their being bought by companies in industry or commerce.

Furthermore, the manufacture of all earlier computers had been a very time-consuming task calling for the special skills of what became known later as commissioning engineers; often they had to be assisted by the design engineers. Although the main assemblies could be constructed each from a multitude of components, when the whole computer had been put together there was a long and expensive period during which everything was made to work correctly. During the testing whenever a fault was found a very high degree of skill was needed to identify the cause of the fault and put it right.

QUANTITY PRODUCTION

A further complication related to the high-speed store, which lay at the heart of any computer. The cathode-ray tube store, originated by Professor Williams and his colleagues at Manchester University, while being a most noteworthy development, was not at all easy to make to work properly. It was difficult to make tubes without imperfections in the coating of the fluorescent material of the screen, and the signal derived from secondary emission of electrons from a stored one-bit were very weak. Further, the large metal collecting plate adjacent to the screen was very susceptible to stray electric fields from adjacent parts of the computer; this necessitated heavy screening with mu-metal, which was expensive and difficult to fabricate. Mercury delay-line stores as pioneered by Professor Wilkes at Cambridge University and used in EDSAC and at the National Physical Laboratory for ACE (and later LEO and DEUCE), were difficult to construct and for any quantity production would have required more liquid mercury than existed in the world.

The nickel delay-line store, which Bill Elliott and colleagues had devised and which relied merely on a length of nickel or hard-drawn steel wire, was eminently capable of being made in sufficient quantity.

However the most important contribution to the potential for manufacturing Pegasus in quantity lay in the design of the circuits and their packages by Charles Owen. His achievement covered two aspects. First, he analyzed the logical functions that had to be carried out and devised a very small number of sub-groups, each of which could be implemented on a package. In fact, despite the very comprehensive set of instructions in Pegasus he came up with only five types of package required for the logical functions, 314 out of a total of 444 in the whole machine.

Secondly, he devised mathematical techniques to accommodate the variability or tolerances of the various components, particularly the valves. The consequence was that packages could be made independently of the whole machine. When the whole computer was assembled from its pre-tested packages, the commissioning time, effort and expense was greatly reduced.

The early packages were made with connecting wires between the components on the reverse of the plastic plate. This was superseded by printed circuit boards. Later still, the teams perfected the technique of flow-soldering the whole package, thus giving a major reduction in the amount of manual soldering required.

Assembly of Pegasus packages. About 22,000 of them were made, a remarkable achievement. Courtesy UMIST

QUANTITY PRODUCTION

Final assembly and commissioning. <small>Courtesy UNIST</small>

At that time the only practical form of electronic backing store was the magnetic drum. (At the Elliott Research Laboratory a magnetic disk had been made but it was not superior.) The problems lay in the low signal-level when reading, from cross-coupling between write and read heads, and the need for a very tiny gap between the surface of the drum and the read heads. Earlier drums had used ball-races to carry the rotating drum with their inevitable tiny clearances, and adjustment of the position of each head was extremely tricky without clashing on the surface of the rotating drum and ruining it. Brian Maudsley adapted a superior form of bearing, used in precision machine tools. Ian Marry contributed to enhanced magnetic materials. Brian Nolan devised enhanced magnetic heads and their associated circuits. Although the drum on the first Pegasus machine took a considerable time and effort to bring to its full performance (the read-only clock track which provided the timing signals for the whole computer had been available earlier) the final design and construction was certainly capable of production in quantity and at an economic price.

A further factor in Bill Elliott's reasoning, in which he was fully supported by Christopher Strachey, Donald Gillies, NRDC and Ferranti, was that Pegasus should be a truly general-purpose computer. This meant that it should have the capability, merely by reading in and storing different programs, of being suitable for many different applications. This contrasted with several other machines of the time, and even later, which used computer-like techniques for a limited type of work. For example, the American ENIAC and the Elliott 503 and 504 machines were to solve sets of differential equations for guided-weapon trajectories; and, a little later than Pegasus, punched card companies developed electronic digital machines to replace, with enhancements, the functional processes of tabulators. At that time no single type of application had been envisaged that would require computers in production quantity.

Bill Elliott attached so much importance to the possibility of quantity production for Pegasus that he strove to have the production facilities under his control. Only in this way, he considered, could the necessary close contact be maintained between the development engineers and the production engineers and their teams. However this clashed with Ferranti company policy which located manufacture in Manchester—whereas Elliott and his development laboratory were located in London. Further, the overall management of the Computer Department lay with Brian Pollard who was based in Manchester.

QUANTITY PRODUCTION

Elliott's anxieties were realized in practice, for it took a considerable time and effort to get the production of early Pegasus computers going smoothly, and early delivery dates could not be met.

In the event, Bill Elliott's initial objective came near to being achieved. It has to be kept in mind that at that time sales measured in tens counted as ambitious, and production of say one hundred machines was scarcely even thought of. Forty Pegasus computers were sold in all. However at a critical stage in their commercial life Brian Pollard ruled that completing orders in progress or quoting for new orders must be held up. Bernard Swann, the sales manager, was convinced that, without this impediment, a total of eighty Pegasus computers would have been sold.

The Pegasus Costing Muddle

A Pegasus computer was first offered to customers for £25,000, in 1952 money. Conversion to the modern value of money will show this to be a substantial sum. However, at the time it was extremely attractive, being about one quarter of the price asked for a Ferranti Mark 1 Star.

This was for a basic machine, its peripheral equipment comprising two high-speed paper tape readers, one medium-speed paper tape punch and one teleprinter for results.

Such machines were from the first batch of ten, which had been promoted by NRDC. In fact, NRDC did not provide a grant for them. Rather, it undertook to pay for their manufacture in this quantity, but required a proportion of the selling price of subsequent machines to be refunded. This repayment was a bone of contention with Brian Pollard, overall manager of the Ferranti computer department.

At the time the price was first established Bill Elliott had substantial experience of the problems or simplicities of making the various types of package, knew about making the drum store, knew the cost of making the structure and cabinets, and could assess the amount of labour involved in putting the whole machine together and making it work. He was fully confident about the tasks of making the machine, as he was in every other aspect of Pegasus.

That data was used by the normal Ferranti costing department. The practice was to apply a mark-up on the basic component and manufacturing costs to cover overheads, with a further contribution for development costs. Since NRDC were a semi-government body, and the whole project was being monitored by their John Crawley who was very competent and thorough—for, after all, it was their money at stake—it must be assumed NRDC must have been satisfied with regard to the estimates and the on-cost for overheads.

As manufacture progressed, reports were heard that the uplift for overheads were inadequate. This manufacture attracted the same figure for overheads as applied throughout the Moston factory of Ferranti. Some mystery attaches to these. Suffice it to say that they were established for the supply during W.W.2 for the products made for and supplied to the Government under the 'cost-plus' scheme. There was long-established agreement that they were appropriate.

The practice derived from the Moston works was to allow an uplift of 10% on the loaded factory costs for marketing. While appropriate for the traditional products of the works, later experience in the computer field was that a figure more like 30% would have been realistic.

It also has to be said that throughout all the Ferranti computer activity at that time very little regard was generally paid to the financial aspects. While there was no opportunity for extravagance or wasted work, the objective was always to do a good job and make good equipment without the individuals concerned having to consider the finances.

When the first few sales of Pegasus showed that it could be marketed, the price was increased to £35,000, and this is the figure that is usually referred to. If, as was often the case after the first few machines, there were additional peripheral equipments, these added to the cost for a system. Each system was being quoted for individually, depending on its complexity, under the careful supervision of Trevor Buckley who was based in the Manchester factory and in a position to see what was going on. No distinction was made for a customer's ability to pay, nor for favoured customers, nor for 'loss-leaders'.

There was another aspect of this whole matter. For Pegasus and its Ferranti derivatives, the basic system software, the operating system and the library of subroutines and the general-purpose application programs—which later made a fortune for Microsoft—were developed as part of the marketing activity under Bernard Swann. The costs of these were largely covered by the income derived from users hiring time on the machine in the Computer Centre; in this way the combined costs were kept within the 10% 'marketing' target. Although Swann kept his own accounts of the costs of this work and also the direct marketing expenses, these were not brought out separately nor accepted within the company. Furthermore in about 1995 Swann admitted to me, as his deputy, that he had never been allowed to know the costs formally attributed to the running of his own department.

Marketing

Pegasus was the first computer, certainly in Europe, to be promoted and marketed actively in the sense that is currently understood. Previously, computers had been purchased almost exclusively by universities or by military authorities. These were organizations who had already recognized their needs for larger-scale calculations than could be done otherwise. Thus it would be true to say that those computers were sold to purchasers who already knew they had overriding needs for calculations, rather than their being marketed.

However there was a very important difference from the situation sixty years later, in that at that time no market for computers existed. In essence, the marketing activity for Pegasus comprised the creation of the market for electronic digital computers. The situation then may be appropriately illustrated by three examples:

i) When Ferranti Ltd had been authorized to make the Mark 1 computer for Manchester University, Sir Vincent Ferranti had the acumen to recognize that there might be a commercial future for computers. It is not known whether anyone else had had that foresight at that time. In about 1950 he engaged Vivian Bowden (later Lord Bowden) to investigate this possibility. (Bowden had a wry sense of humour and mockingly styled himself as "The world's first computer salesman".) Soon after, he met in a London street Bernard Swann who was a friend from earlier years, and prevailed on Swann to leave a high position in the Government Civil Service and join him. It was told, much later by Bernard Swann, how Bowden went to Sir Arthur Vernon Roe, who ran the distinguished aircraft manufacturers AVRO, also in Manchester and a friend of Sir Vincent, to interest him in the potential value of a computer for design of aircraft. Sir Vernon responded "Discuss it with my chief designer". Bowden did this and reported "Your designers see no value in having such a machine", to which Sir Vernon responded "Tell them they must have one". Although the order was delayed, this became the sixth Mark 1 Star to be built.

ii) In early-July 1953 Shell Transport and Trading placed an order for a Ferranti Mark 1 Star, for optimizing the loading and movements of their fleet of oil tankers. That is thought to be the first truly commercial sale of a computer, perhaps anywhere in the world. Previous orders had been from government establishments or firms working on government-funded contracts. The sale was achieved by the development within the group under Vivian Bowden of the 'linear programming' technique for solving a large number of simultaneous linear equations—it is thought primarily by the mathematician Dr Dietrich Prinz, with Dr John Bennett and Cyril Gradwell, possibly assisted by members of the Manchester University group and even the Shell mathematical team.

iii) The Lyons Catering Company had the particular production requirement of making foodstuffs of a perishable nature, typically cakes and ice-creams, the demand for which was very variable, depending even upon the weather. In the early 1950's their directors had the foresight to consider that a computer might be used for what was later called data processing. However at that time the market for computer-based data processing was so non-existent that no machines were available. Accordingly they resolved to make their own, which was based on the Cambridge University EDSAC, being developed primarily by Dr John Pinkerton and his small yet very capable team. It became the LEO series of machines.

This was a scene that can hardly be visualized from the viewpoint of the early twenty-first century. It can be summed up by noting that

MARKETING

there was then scarcely a director on the board, nor a managing director, of any company or organization, who could see the potential usefulness of a computer or would support its purchase.

While the primary initial task for Bowden and Swann was to identify applications for which a computer might be used and the relevant organizations in industry or commerce, Swann recalled an experience when he served with the British Army in India, and was assigned the task of introducing punched card systems into their administration. He had found that it was much easier for an Army man to learn to use punched card automation, than for a punched card expert to learn Army administration. The problems lay principally in coping with exceptional cases.

Therefore it was resolved that the most promising way to market computers would be for Ferranti to set up a computer in a service centre at which potential users could learn computing techniques and make trials to determine how their own practical applications could be tackled.

Bowden and Swann also realized, from their early attempts, that it would be difficult to get decision makers from potential customers to make the 200 mile journey to Manchester to see a machine so unfamiliar and of such little interest—the centre had to be in London.

So I was sent to London to start Ferranti computer activities there. I was soon joined by Conway Berners-Lee and Harry Johnson. Chris Wilson was recruited shortly after. Each was given a segment of the potential market, so they might gain familiarity with its distinctive requirements. Within a matter of months a building with a room large enough to house a Ferranti Mark 1 Star computer had been found, an eighteenth-century grand residence, and conversion to office and computer work begun.

However, while that was still in progress the proposal from NRDC for Ferranti to make and market ten computers to the

MARKETING

Elliott/Strachey/Gillies design was received, so it was decided the first should go in the London Computer Centre. This became Pegasus.

The marketing of Pegasus laboured under two particular difficulties. The first was that whereas the overall management of the Computer Department came under Brian Pollard he had no sensitivity for the requirements of marketing, and even an antipathy towards the contributions that were made from the marketing experience; secondly, the marketing scene was gravely complicated by relations with the punched card companies. These factors constituted a veritable mine-field through which Bernard Swann, the sales manager, had to tread.

Swann could rely on his many contacts with senior people in British industry from his earlier experience in the Board of Trade. Through this he could follow up with the ultimate decision takers the openings that the members of his team made.

A significant early development was that the Society of British Aircraft Constructors set up a committee to investigate the ways in which the new computers might be used for aircraft design, and to encourage development of relevant mathematical techniques. There is indirect evidence that the initiative for setting up this group came from Vivian Bowden, while it was supported by the mathematical group in the National Physical Laboratory (were the Pilot ACE had been made) under Wilkinson and Woodger. I represented computer interests on this, aided by colleagues with more mathematical and programming knowledge, Derek Milledge among them. A similar group was later set up by SBAC to cover use of computers for design and testing of aircraft engines.

Through the SBAC activity the Hawker Aircraft Co (makers of the wartime Hurricane), the Armstrong Whitworth Aircraft Co, Vickers Aircraft Ltd (makers of the Spitfire) and the de Havilland Aircraft Co (makers of the Mosquito and the Comet) became

MARKETING

interested in Pegasus, and were the first to use the Computer Centre. Hawkers were the first purchasers of a Pegasus, and the Vickers Viscount aircraft is thought to be the first European aircraft to be designed largely using computer techniques.

All early marketing, based on the concepts Bowden and Swann had decided upon, depended on building up the techniques for using computers. Suitable mathematical methods were being established in universities: the concept of subroutines to provide complex functions within programs, pioneered by Maurice Wilkes, David Wheeler and Stanley Gill with EDSAC at Cambridge and enhanced by Christopher Strachey; the so-called linear programming to solve large sets of simultaneous equations; iterative use of matrix algebra. All this was brought into the basic programming for Pegasus. It constituted the indirect component of the marketing activity. The same approach was later used very successfully for marketing the more powerful Mercury computer, especially for atomic energy applications, under Chris Wilson. He was singularly successful in marketing Mercury to the atomic energy industry but, because of its close association with military activities, little record of that work is available. Nevertheless his achievement enhanced his self confidence so that he became an extremely determined and successful salesman for Pegasus.

A major part of the direct marketing activity was giving presentations on the nature and the capabilities of Pegasus. Each of us became adept at giving lectures. Another major component was running training courses for those who had embarked on learning to use Pegasus. George Felton led this work, and with Peter Hunt wrote the programming manual.

Another component of marketing, that might be regarded as a hybrid between indirect and direct, was the documentation support. When I had previously been at the Elliott Research Laboratory the director John Coales had impressed on me the importance of writing up new work. (Bill Elliott likewise, who with his named colleagues, published formal technical papers on Pegasus, see Annexes Nos 2 to 4). Therefore as a contribution to the marketing effort I encouraged members of staff, and also visitors, to write up some account of any new achievement. The distinctive quality of each resultant document, after editing by myself or Peter Young or Joy Williamson, was that it carried the authority of the person doing the actual work described. This extensive series of documents, 460 in all, comprise a most striking record of the creation of the market for computers, showing the identification of new application areas and the evolution of techniques and new equipments to exploit them. This practice was taken up subsequently in the remarkably comprehensive documentation of ICL computers.

A further component of the marketing, which was very valuable with certain customers, was the very close and harmonious co-operation between the Pegasus development engineers of Bill Elliott's laboratory and the whole department under Bernard Swann. On the one hand this covered presentations on the engineering features of the machine—for at that time some customers were concerned about, and took a substantial interest in, the relative technical qualities of different machines—and on the other hand a willingness to provide for special items of equipment that were requested by customers.

All this marketing activity was done by staff paid on a salary basis, the exact opposite of a commission basis (as used by the punched card companies). This resulted in close working relations between the selling staff and the programming staff, and in fact also with the engineers in the London Laboratory.

These approaches to marketing had two particular merits. First, that their cost fitted in well with the general Ferranti policy that these should not exceed 10% of the selling price. It was much more economical to maintain contact with potential customers—a vital component of the long-drawn-out nature of marketing computers at that time—by encouraging them to come to the Computer Centre, rather than have a large sales force going out to the customers. Secondly, it suited organizations interested in breaking out into new activities or willing to make some fairly radical change to their techniques, whether technical or administrative. In a sense this was the essence of the computer revolution.

However it contrasted with the marketing approach of the punched card companies which at that time provided for the mechanization of administrative activities in commercial organizations. These companies provided an overall service, and IBM excelled at this. During the mid-1950s Ferranti attempted to establish a working relationship with the Powers-Samas company. Because of contradictory attitudes towards innovation, marketing and the relation between development engineers and sales staff, this ran into severe difficulties. One objective was to develop a Pegasus computer with Powers-Samas card engines which Powers-Samas would market. It was called Pluto but Powers-Samas never managed to sell even one system, it was left to Harry Johnson of Swann's group to sell it to Martin's Bank. Thus it was the first Britishbank to use a computer system for its main work.

By 1958 a much upgraded system named Perseus had been announced, although arrangements with Powers-Samas prevented it from being intensively marketed in Britain. However Johnson sold two systems abroad.

At a later stage in the life of Pegasus, and when the dead hand of the arrangements with Powers-Samas had been lifted, to make more marketing progress in the data processing field the highly successful Pegasus 2 system was developed. This used card machines of the Hollerith type, usually from BTM, together with magnetic tape for file storage and with a line-at-a-time printer.

The Outcome

This marketing activity resulted in the sales of forty Pegasus computer systems, and the situation was just beginning to snowball. This is a feature of the selling of any innovative product, and it can place severe stresses on production.

At this stage the aggregate financial commitment of outstanding orders was becoming severe. Combined with the uncertainty over costing, this caused Brian Pollard to rule that no orders in progress of negotiation could be carried to completion and no new orders could be quoted for.

This had a catastrophic effect of the selling situation. At that time the sale of any computer was a long drawn-out affair. From a first contact, through to convincing the customer's technical people that a computer would be useful and that Pegasus would be suitable, and then for them to persuade their managers and directors that the money should be spent, took at least one year, usually two and sometimes three.

Although the ban was lifted after seven months it was very difficult to regain the sales momentum, and Bernard Swann, as sales manager, considered that forty prospective opportunities were lost. This tumult continued until Pegasus was beginning to reach the end of its commercial life with the prospect of a transistorized version, the FP6000 developed by Gribble and others in the Canadian subsidiary of Ferranti, coming on the scene.

New Applications Devised With Pegasus

At the time Pegasus was devised, except for military applications which of course were secret, practical applications for such a computer were the realm of imaginative, even visionary, workers. Vivian Bowden was near to publishing his book *Faster than Thought*, but although that refers to a great number of practical applications a careful reading will reveal that all were merely proposals.

This theme is explored more thoroughly in a presentation I made to the Computer Conservation Society of London in 2005. A transcript together with the tables to illustrate the situation may be easily found on its website *

This aspect of Pegasus was dealt with in the first place by Christopher Strachey, Bill Elliott and Lord Halsbury. A significant contribution came from Bernard Swann whose experience introducing automated processing (admittedly using punched card systems) for the British army in India convinced him that work on applications had to be led by persons familiar with the the practical knowledge of each type of problem. In consequence establishing new applications with Pegasus was synonymous and intertwined with our marketing activity.

Pegasus excelled for the work of establishing new applications for several reasons:

i) Its ease of programming (compared with other computers of its time)

---

* Go to *Computer Resurrection* issue 36

ii) Its reliability, so that when developing a new program the user could be confident that any malfunction had to be remedied solely within his program;

iii) The extreme attention we gave to training new users and supporting them in their work;

iv) Our employment of persons already skilled in the main fields of new applications.

In practice the new applications were largely developed under the guidance of individual members of our staff.

Thus I inherited the activity previously established by Vivian Bowden for applications in the aircraft industry. In doing this much support was given by Peter Hunt who came from the de Havilland Aircraft Company, and by Derek Milledge who came from Westland Helicopters. In practice much of this work was tackled by the use of matrix arithmetic, so that George Felton's matrix interpretive scheme was a major contribution to its rapid progress.

To begin with, this work, guided by the Aircraft Design Panel of the Society of British Aircraft Constructors focussed on structural design of aircraft, and their vibration under aerodynamic forces. There were applications for fixed-wing and also for helicopter aircraft. Experts from the National Physical Laboratory provided much of the theory.

Later, an Engine Panel was set up. This led to applications for vibration in multi-disk turbines where gyroscopic effects dominate, and to optimization of flight paths.

Both of these led to applications for recording and processing of test data, from transducers in wind tunnels and engine test beds.

In my employment before joining Ferranti I had many contacts with the optical industry, especially the leading British company. Taylor, Taylor and Hobson. It was a time when zoom lenses and also non-spherical lens surfaces were being pioneered. To design these a computer was required.

Conway Berners-Lee

Conway Berners-Lee was exceptionally innovative for the applications he brought to Pegasus. He came to us from a background of operational research, and statistics.

He provided simulation projects. An example was the optimum scheduling of jobs in an engineering workshop. Jobs would come in requiring the use of a variety of machines for different lengths of time. These needed to be scheduled in a specific way to optimize the profitable use of the machines.

Another application was the cutting of sheet material, tinplate or sheet glass. The aim is to minimize waste while cutting the different sizes and quantities of finished items required for orders, especially when there are defects in the parent sheet.

His published paper on optimizing production planning gives examples of finding the least-cost mix of ingredients for the manufacture of food for animals; of plant loading in an automobile factory; on applications in oil refining (which had great financial benefit); of problems arising in discontinuous manufacture; and of optimal sequencing of the stages of a production process.

Berners-Lee invented a sorting method that was likened to imagining monkeys on a monkey-puzzle tree and bringing them down in order. The process later turned out to be useful in assessing the performance of large storage systems.

Another innovation he dealt with related to typesetting. At that time the type for printing any document was set as a series of individual metal letters and signs. When an author made the inevitable alterations on a proof copy, great trouble and expense ensued in altering all the lines to the end of the paragraph. Berners-Lee's program permitted that complex alteration to be automated, the result being fed to a basic type-setting machine. This had the distinction of being one of the earliest non-numerical applications of a digital computer.

Bill Payne established a number of practical applications on Pegasus relevant to the general engineering industry. There were two that were very widely used. First, programs for the stressing of structures comprising complex frameworks. In some of these the joints between members were regarded as pin-joints, in others which are more difficult the joints were regarded as rigid, as in welding.

A second class of applications was equally important. They related to the stresses in complex pipeworks. In such systems expansions due to thermal changes and also those due to pressure changes can give rise to substantial stresses. The whole system, being three-dimensional and usually with rigid joints made an important application of Pegasus.*

---

* This group of applications is summarized in a Ferranti document DC24 *Computing Stresses in Pipesystems*.

NEW APPLICATIONS DEVISED WITH PEGASUS

Harry Johnson had been persuaded by Bowden to leave the Scientific Civil Service and join the Ferranti computer sales department. He proved a tower of strength. An early application he studied was computer aid to air traffic control. This involved queuing theory. After a long and tortuous negotiation* it resulted in a special-purpose computer related to Pegasus called Apollo. This had the distinction of providing service at Prestwick airport for 21 years.

Harry Johnson

His main area of responsibility was for commercial data processing applications. But for some years this activity was severely frustrated by the absurd arrangements made with the Powers-Samas company. Johnson did, however, have the satisfaction of establishing the applications for which a Pegasus was purchased by Martins Bank, and for the two life insurance companies, South

---

* Described in a document in his Collection in the archive of the Institution o Engineering and Technology of London.

African Mutual and the Trygg Insurance company of Sweden, who purchased Perseus computer systems.

This activity involved becoming familiar with the established punched card data processing practices. This experience of office data processing applications, together with his exceptional grasp of the essentials of any situation, proved invaluable for his contribution to the ultimate descendants of Pegasus, the ICL 1900 series of compatible systems described later in this book.

Stafford Beer and Dr Ken Tocher established their early reputations with many applications in the field of operational research using the Pegasus owned by the United Steel Company of Wales in Sheffield. At University College in London Judith Milledge, the wife of Derek, made her reputation in the field of X-ray crystallography using Pegasus. Because these analyses typically involved error-free runs of 6 to 8 hours, she was greatly dependent on the reliability of the machine. At Loughborough College a suit of programs were developed for the stressing of reinforced concrete slabs in buildings and other structures. A special interest attaches to these, in that although intended and used for production work, they were written entirely in Pegasus autocode.

There follows a listing of other specific applications established on Pegasus, derived from various sources.

A program for the evaluation of flutter coefficients of aircraft (CS 57)

The latent roots program (CS 149)

A binary flutter problem (CS 150)

Normal modes for aircraft frames (CS 178)

A program for the stressing of swept multi-web structures (CS 215)

NEW APPLICATIONS DEVISED WITH PEGASUS

Program for calculating aerodynamic stiffness and damping matrices (CS 220)

The computational procedure when using the Argyris matrix method for structural analysis (CS 72)

Solution of resonant frequencies of a helicopter blade (CS 211)

The critical whirling speeds of a system formed by two consecutive rotors with intershaft bearings (CS 183)

Program for the calculation of whirling speeds (CS 228)

Program for optical ray tracing (CS 240)

Data sheets for meridional ray tracing (CS 160)

Non-linear servo mechanisms (CS 81)

Fourier analysis program (CS 166A)

Solution of simultaneous linear algebraic equations (CS 132)

Factorial analysis program (CS 145)

Linear programming (scope of Simpfix) (CS 186)

Determination of the maxima and minima of a solution of differential equations (CS 201)

Calculation of influence coefficients for a simple beam (engineers theory) CS 184)

A single plane structure stressing program (Livesley method) (CS 194)

A shell plate development program (CS 222)

Program for the stressing of multi-anchor 3-dimensional pipework systems (CS 230)

Digital computer applied to the design of large power transformers *(Proc. I.E.E. vol 105)*

Machine loading – an industrial application of computers, by Berners-Lee *(The Engineer 1957)*

NEW APPLICATIONS DEVISED WITH PEGASUS

Program for the statistical productivity indices (British Steel)

Electrical planning by electronic computer, by Peter Young, *(The New Scientist 1957)*

Production control by electronic computer *(Chemistry and Industry, 1958)*

Survey calculations (MOS Military Survey)

Transformer design (Ferranti, Bruce Peebles)

Example of the application to production control (CS 96)

Sales forecasting demonstration (CS 102)

Sales analysis, stock control (ICI Dyestuffs)

Autocoded program for calculating production schedules for a multi-stage manufacturing process (CS 210)

Autocoded program for sales analysis and forecasting (CS 231)

Program for analysis of commercial data prepared by an accounting machine (CS 199)

Sorting on an electronic digital computer (CS 84)

Example of the application to a medium-sized payroll (CS 97)

Description of a wages program for a large dispersed organization (CS 169)

Application to the Hulton Readership Survey (CS 197)

Road accident records analysis (DSIR)

A bank adopts automatic data processing *(Computer Journal, vol 3)*

Current accounts on a computer *(Data Processing, 1960)*

Pension scheme updating, branch valuations (Scottish Widows)

Train timetabling (British Rail)

Filing business data on magnetic tape *(Data Processing, 1959)*

Descendants of Pegasus

Proposed Computer for British Ordnance Survey

The Ordnance Survey, then a Government service and run by the military, had approached Ferranti regarding the possibility of using a computer to carry out the calculations related to surveys. Initially this work was done in Manchester by Dr John Bennett and Harry Cotton who made themselves familiar with the requirements of the problem and wrote a program for the Manchester Mark 1 Star computer.

When Bennett joined Bill Elliott's London Laboratory and became familiar with the potential for using the packages devised by Elliott and Charles Owen for carrying out the logical processes of a computer he conceived the idea of making a special-purpose computer to meet the requirements of the Ordinance Survey.

The proposal is in Ferranti Computer Laboratory Report No 7*, signed off by Bill Elliott. It is dated March 1955. Being the second computer using packages it was given the identifying code FPC2.

<u>At that date</u> this concept of using packages for a special-purpose computer had attractions:

i Only those features and facilities specifically needed for the Ordinance Survey calculations would be provided, a reduction on

---

* John Bennett gave his own personal copy to me, and I donated it to the Archive of the Institution of Engineering and Technology, London.

those of a general-purpose computer.

ii The total number of packages would be reduced. Thus the Ordnance Survey computer required 350, whereas Pegasus required 440.

iii Power consumption reduced: 7 Kw instead of 11 Kw for Pegasus.

iv Instructions obeyed directly from the magnetic drum, rather than the two-level storage in Pegasus with all its features for transfers between the two.

v The word-length and set of instructions optimized for the specific applications.

vi The packages, being standardized, could be made in quantity and interchanged in case of malfunction. To quote "The advance which this technique represents with electronic equipment may be likened to Henry Ford's introduction of interchangeable parts to the automobile industry, without which mass production would never have been possible."

The Ordinance Survey was heavily committed to using punched cards, the 80-column Powers-Samas type. The Proposal uses a card reader for all input of data, and a card punch for output of results, to be printed on a tabulator. All that is said in the Proposal is "The overall dimensions of the Powers-Samas card feed and punch are not finally known at the time of writing. It is anticipated that they will be about 24 × 24 × 48 ins." In a block diagram a 'converter' is shown between the card reader and the processor itself, and another for the card punch. So these had been provided for in the count of packages, even though no details are mentioned.

With much hindsight, the significance of the silence is that it indicated the lack of awareness at that date within the Ferranti team of the commercial and technical difficulties that were later experienced in working with the punched card companies and their machines.

On the other hand, one of the supplementary sections gives some interesting facts about the usage of punched cards. Thus for input of data from the surveyors in the field about 700,000 cards per year would have to be punched. Using semi-automatic equipment 12,000 key depressions per hour could be attained, or 9,000 per hour with manual equipment. To this would have to be added card usage for output of results.

John Bennett has described elsewhere how, when the Ordnance Survey work had been prepared for the computer at Manchester, a demonstration was planned. A senior officer in full uniform travelled from Portsmouth to Manchester. In the event, the Mark 1 Star computer failed to operate at all that day. The Ordnance Survey decided to stay with their punched card processing system. It is not known whether that episode relates in any way with this Proposal for the FPC2.

Descendants of Pegasus

Three Proposals for Data Processors

These proposals are described in Ferranti London Computer Laboratory reports:

Report No 17, dated 26 July 1955, *System Specification for a Data Processor for the Royal Insurance Company Ltd*

Report No 18, dated 3 October 1955, *System Specification for a Commercial Data Processor*

Report No 19, dated 1 September 1955, *A Small Data Processor*

They are all by Dr John Bennett*, the first being jointly authored with Anthony Baker, who was an actuary seconded by the Royal Insurance Company to explore the use of computers in actuarial work.

Consideration of the dates indicates that the three must have been planned at the same time, and they have many features in common. Strictly speaking, they are not descendants of Pegasus, they are more like cousins; they are related in that that they use the same packages as Pegasus, and their physical appearance was very similar. The differences from Pegasus, lie most particularly in the

---

* John Bennett's personal copies of these Reports were given to me. I have donated them to the Archive of the Institution of Engineering and Technology, London.

word-structure, the set of instructions and the arrangement and use of the stores.

These proposed machines represent the hey-day of the concept that, using the logical facilities implicit in the packages devised by Bill Elliott and Charles Owen, special-purpose computers could be made. It is an extension of the basic concept proposed for the Ordnance Survey, described in the previous chapter.

This approach also represents the hey-day of the emphasis that a computer is an engineering product, that is to say evolved by engineers and logical designers. It is the opposite of that learned later that the facilities, the functions, and the value of a computer derive greatly from, and are dependent upon, the software that is provided. Ferranti pioneered the learning of this lesson with Pegasus, and it entailed much effort.

In all these three proposed machines the word-length is 42 bits, involving the use of delay-line stores with 8% more capacity than those in Pegasus. Words are either full-length, or divided into sections: four sections for the Royal Insurance machine, and two sections for the others. Instructions occupy only one section of a word, for the order codes were much more limited than the extensive set in Pegasus. The particularly useful feature of modifying the address of an order was provided, although less sophisticated than that in Pegasus.

On the Royal Insurance computer there was a working store of 4 blocks each of 32 words on single-word delay-lines, together with a main store comprising 112 8-word delay-lines. Thus all the internal storage was on delay-lines. On the machine of Report No 18 the store provided 1024 words in all on 5 blocks of 32 words on single-word lines plus 54 16-word delay-lines. These details imply that the torsional-mode delay-lines described in Annex No 8 had attained proven reliability. The small machine of Report No 19 had only 16 single-word immediate access store, with a magnetic drum from which instructions were obeyed. On this machine clever means were provided in the addressing of the instructions on the drum to avoid the problems that necessitated 'optimum programming' on some other computers.

The Royal Insurance system was implementing the feature identified by Tony Baker that, for insurance work, the primary value of a computer would be the reduction of paperwork in the office. This involved the extensive use of magnetic tapes as a storage medium, as an integral feature in the processing of records, and as a link to the printer. The features described to ensure error-free use of the tapes are very similar to those when magnetic tape was made available on Pegasus three years later.

A further distinctive feature was that processing could take place using mixed-radix quantities, all implemented by hardware using the logical features in the packages. This specially applied to stirling money quantities, for it was designed before the decimilization of British currency. Thus an amount:

17 pounds, 15 shillings, 11 pence, three farthings

used radices **10**   **20**   **12**   **4**

In all three proposals much emphasis is placed on automatic checking against errors. This included:
- a parity check within each word
- block post-reading when recording magnetic tape
- block pre-reading when reading from magnetic tape
- card pre-reading with punched card input
- card post-reading with punched card output
- odd-parity of decimal digits in punched tape.

Although none of them were implemented in actual machines these three proposals had many innovative features and represent important steps in the evolution of computers for commercial data processing work.

Descendants of Pegasus

Proposal for an Enhanced Pegasus

Proposals for (by J.F. Coales sometime in 1956)
The British Computer Corporation
J.F.C. Nov 19;

Authorised Capital £10,000,000
Issued £5,000,000

Board of Directors.

Chairman :- Sir Alan Saunders (other possibilities Mr Robson of A.R.E
Sir Harold Hartley   Mr Sutherland of Marconi's)
Sir Ben Lockspeiser
Dr M.V. Wilkes
Managing Director - Dr Alexander King ~~of Edinburgh~~ D.S.I.R.
Research Director W.S. Elliott
Commercial Director B.B. Swann
& Salts

1. Recommend a bid be made to Sir Vincent de Ferranti to take over the London Computing Laboratory and Sales organisation together with the whole of the Pegasus business. Since this business is at present worth about £2m (order book standing at £900,000), presumably a takeover bid of about £500,000 should be attractive.

2. Programme
    2.1. The first two-to-three years effort should be mainly directed to the development of a transistorised, miniaturised high-speed machine with a very large store and multiple input facilities capable of on-demand working as required for business purposes.
    2.2. A sales organisation such as exists at Ferranti (about 6 senior engineers and 12 others) should be set up to

107

DESCENDANTS OF PEGASUS

[Handwritten facsimile of proposal pages]

This section presents in the form of reduced facsimile the two initial pages of a Proposal by John F Coales for setting up a British Computer Corporation. Those pages are in Coales' own handwriting. I have donated the original document to the IET Archive in London. The complete Proposal is given in typed format in *Resurrection*, the journal of the Computer Conservation Society, London, issue No 30, Spring 2003, with my introductory notes and subsequent discussion.

The purpose of the Proposal was to present an opportunity to Bill Elliott sufficiently attractive to dissuade him from taking up an offer from IBM to set up a development laboratory in UK.

The Proposal failed, for lack of venture capital at that date, July 1956. However, its relevance to this book lies in its early paragraph 2.1

Programme

The first two or three years effort should be mainly directed to the development of a transistorized, miniaturized high-speed machine with a very large store and multiple input facilities capable of on-demand working as required for business purposes.

It is self-evident that the concepts inherent in that paragraph must have been those in Elliott's mind. And that the great emphasis on Pegasus in the rest of the Proposal implies that this enhanced machine would be a development of Pegasus.

The attraction of the features 'transistorized' and 'very large store' are obvious. Much more interest lies in the phrase 'on-demand working'. This implies the opposite of the very fundamental feature of a computer that the input operations are initiated by orders in the program that are obeyed sequentially.

In practice the need specially arises in a computer serving telecommunications. In this, the timing of signals coming into the computer is determined solely by the remote device, the computer has no control of the situation, but it is essential that it responds.

It is possible that, even at this early stage, Elliott had come up against this requirement in military computer systems dealt with in his London Laboratory, and had the foresight to recognize that the facility would be valuable in commercial computer systems.

The facility only became available a decade later in other computers. In the Ferranti Atlas computer it was provided by a pre-processor. In the Ferranti Orion 2 and FP6000 it was provided by software in the so-called 'executive'. In the Digital Equipment Corporation PDP8 a signal on an interrupt circuit held up the main program and entered a sub-program to process the input data

In the event, a machine meeting this overall specification did not become available until 1963, in the Ferranti-Packard FP6000.

Descendants of Pegasus
The Converters

Bill Elliott's engineers had been planning during 1955 for the extension of Pegasus to provide for the direct operation of punched cards for input and output, plus a line printer. However, Ted Braunholtz recalls that Charles Owen expressed doubts whether the consequent increase in the number of packages might exceed the tolerances he regarded as prudent to ensure error-free working of the augmented system There was also unease that a failure in the extra equipment might adversely affect the error-free operation of the computer itself, which was such an important objective of the design. Bill Elliott accordingly discontinued that work by the start of 1956.

We were being pressed by Imperial Chemical Industries Dyestuffs Division to provide a system they could use for their data processing. This would be integrated into their existing punched card system, which used BTM-type punched cards.

In response to this the concept of a Converter* was devised. This would use a magnetic tape unit identical to the magnetic tape system of Pegasus, and be able to inter-work with a punched card reader and a punch, and a line printer made by Bull. In effect, it provided

---

* The Converter was described in the Ferranti documents CS 147A, May 1957, written by Peter Harrild the engineer chiefly responsible, and CS 144A, November 1958.

an independent, off-line, facility to enable Pegasus to be used in commercial data processing systems and their applications.

The Converter embodied the self-checking concepts and facilities that were an essential component of Pegasus. The magnetic tape system already had highly stringent self-checking. The card reader had two reading stations, the card images after conversion to computer code being held in buffer stores and compared. The card punch likewise had a post-reading stage. The character code used in the Converter to feed the printer was such that any single-bit error would convert a decimal numeral into an alphabetic character, so the error stood out in the printed document.

The Converter incorporated a limited processing capability in the form of a category search facility. This was used where the items in a file on the magnetic tape incorporated a key that comprised classification. An example was given of the stock control application for parts of a car, and all those for gear boxes had the identifier GB. By setting controls on the Converter to that identifying key only those would be printed out from the file on the tape.

The Converter was a substantial machine, embodied in a three-bay cabinet like Pegasus itself. The first model for ICI Dyestuffs was completed in the London Laboratory before mid-1958. Versions of it were made for Shell Oil with Powers-Samas card machines, for British Petroleum like the ICI model, and for the Swedish Flygmotor aero engine company. These subsequent machines were made in the Manchester factory, but because each one was significantly different from the others substantial work was needed by the development engineers, particularly Peter Harrild, Geoffrey Crome and Gordon Harvey. By this time the Ferranti Laboratory had moved to Bracknell in Berkshire. It was forty miles to the west of London, and it did make the close contacts between the sales department and the engineers rather more difficult.

Descendants of Pegasus

Pluto

Pluto was the name given to a Pegasus modified for commercial data processing applications. It was a major contribution by Ferranti to the collaboration with the Powers-Samas company referred to on page 61. It relied on the proven magnetic tape system for the storage of the large files involved with commercial work, and for their processing. It had a card reader for input from Powers-Samas punched cards, and it used a Samastronic line printer for output of results.

It was developed between 1957 and 1959. It used the Pegasus No 23 from the production line, with the modifications and extra equipment being done at the Bracknell laboratory.

Only one system was made. The much vaunted Powers-Samas sales team was unable to sell it, and it was only when the momentum and exclusivity aspects of the collaboration with Powers-Samas had waned that it was left to Harry Johnson of Swann's department to sell it to the London and Manchester Assurance Company. They had the distinction of thus being the first life insurance company in Britain to commit themselves to the use of a computer with magnetic tape for such work.

The computer itself was modified in various ways. Three extra orders was added to the instruction code to facilitate binary-decimal conversion. A group of 16 8-word nickel delay line stores were added, comprising in effect an extension at the start of the main drum store but with quicker access. The magnetic drum was enhanced to provide the increased storage capacity of 7168 words available to the user. This was done by adding more read-write heads with consequent closing up of the recorded tracks on the drum. The servo system of the motor-generator set was enhanced to control its speed more precisely to suit the 8-word delay line stores. All this, together with the logical circuits for the card reader and punch, required a larger cabinet, with four bays.

The reader will recognize that several of these enhancements would be of value to other machines in the future. Therefore the Pluto project was less of a failure than its very limited sales would indicate.

A feature of its design was that this was done by the engineers. This accorded with the fundamental attitude of mind within the Ferranti company. Throughout its history its success had been dependent on the innovative qualities of its engineers, and the imaginative outlook of its management. Pegasus had introduced an alternative to this, in that the needs of programmers had been introduced by Christopher Strachey (supported by Lord Halsbury), and that this variant ethos had been reinforced by Bernard Swann's concept that users should be encouraged and helped to write their own software. One consequence was that this know-how of practical usage accumulated in the company within Swann's group. This is where the user requirements were learnt at first hand, and known.

Descendants of Pegasus

Perseus

Perseus was the largest and most complex machine built with the packages devised by Charles Owen. The computer itself is shown in the photograph on the following page. It also used the ultimate embodiment of nickel delay line storage, in the form of packages holding no fewer than 16 words each of 72 usable bits. The circulation time of the pulses in this store was 4 milliseconds. The store package is shown in the photograph on the subsequent page.*

Furthermore, it comprised a system designed to be optimal for the specific task of processing the data of life insurance offices. It comprised the practical embodiment of the concepts and designs of the proposal made by Tony Baker and John Bennett referred to in the chapter on page 104.

It was also a system optimized for using and processing the enormous files of data involved in a life insurance company, these being held on magnetic tape. Thus the computer itself could be connected to up to 16 magnetic tape units via control units for each group of 4 mechanisms. In addition to an enhanced form of punched tape for input of programs and data, a card reader for any type of punched card was available to expedite its introduction

---

* The formal description of Perseus is in *Computer Journal*, July 1959. It is noteworthy that this is written, not by engineers, but by Peter Hunt, a leading programmer in Bernard Swann's department.

General view of the main processor of Perseus during development

Courtesy ICL Archive

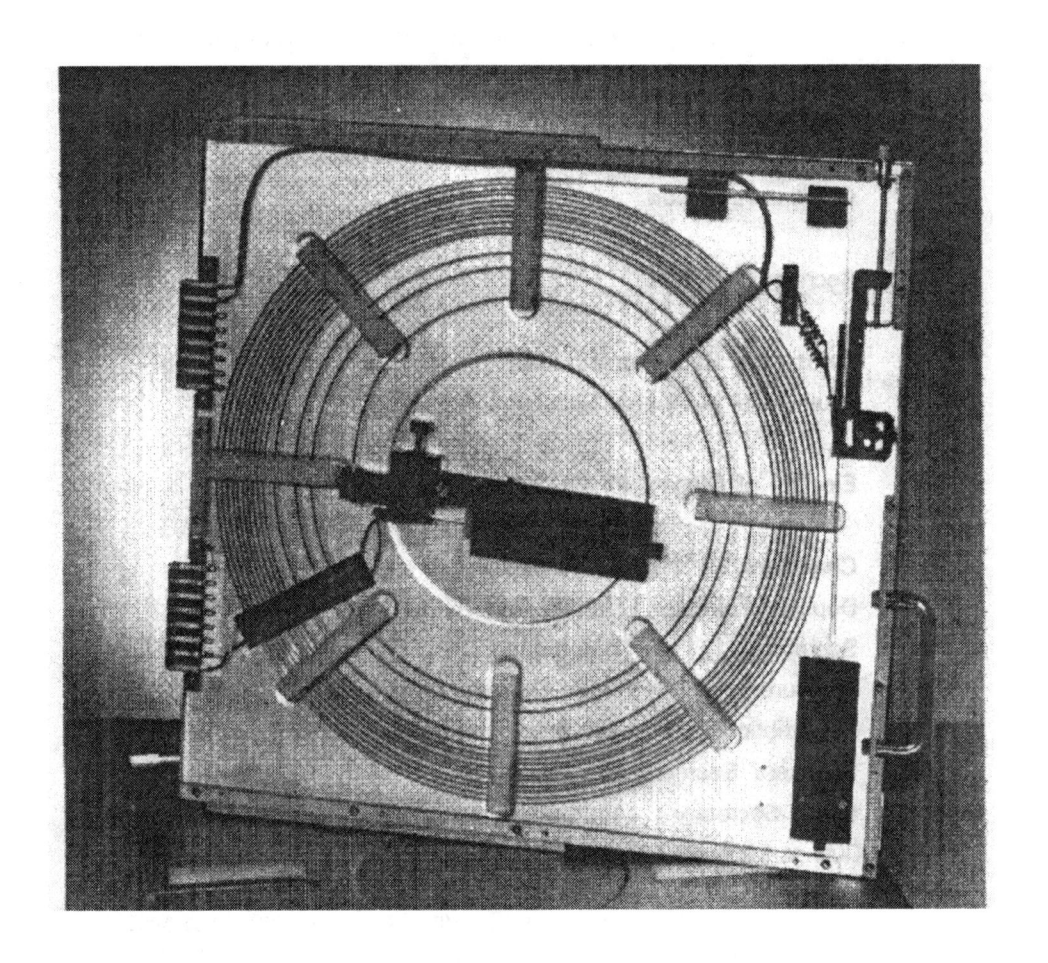

The outstanding delay line store of Perseus. Each unit stored 16 words each of 72 bits, total delay 4 millisec. Steel wire with torsional pulses.

into an office that already had its files on punched cards. The conversion for the code used on the punched cards to that used in the computer was done by program, to ensure adaptability.

Results were first recorded on a magnetic tape, and were subsequently printed out on a tape-driven Samastronic printer. These machines were separate from and independent of the computer.

In all, there were 160 single-word storage packages comprising the immediate-access store, plus 54 16-word storage packages to give the main store for program and intermediate data and results, with an average access time of 2 milliseconds. There was no magnetic drum.

Within the system data was held and processed in either of two forms. Alphanumeric data was normally recorded as 12 6-bit characters within each computer word. This was particularly used for all the names and addresses and so on associated with life insurance policies. Numeric data was dealt with in binary form. Furthermore, especially for the numerical quantities in life insurance work, mixed radix operation was provided (see page 106). This could have been of value for British stirling currency and Imperial measures.

Great emphasis in the design was placed on self-checking. This was summarized by Bernard Swann thus:*

> The need, in commercial work, to check each operation was fully implemented. All arithmetical operations were checked; a parity check was put on each word in the store; punched cards were read twice and compared; and a self-checking paper tape code was used. On the magnetic tape check sums were formed and compared for each block. After writing on tape

---

* In his unpublished *History of the Ferranti Computer Department*.

information was immediately read back and checked automatically. If an error was detected the order which led to it was repeated, if necessary several times, and if the error was still shown to be present the computer stopped.

Two Perseus systems were made. The first was for the Old Mutual Life Insurance Company of South Africa. This company had a special need. With growing material prosperity black people were increasingly taking up life insurance. This was putting a strain on the company to find enough white operators for their existing Powers-Samas punched card facilities, for under the apartheid laws they were not allowed to employ mixed races.

The other was for the Trygg Insurance Company in Sweden. It is not known whether they had any special reason to embark on a computer-based system. Bearing in mind Ferranti's earlier troubled experience of remotely commissioning the new Mark 1 Star computers in Toronto and Rome, it shows great confidence was placed on the development engineers in the Bracknell laboratory.

The design of Perseus was completed in 1958, and a big feature of it was made in a combined Powers-Samas/Ferranti stand* at the Business Efficient Exhibition in November of that year. However, it was too early for the adoption of a computer system of this type by any British company, even the Royal Insurance for whom the original proposal by Baker and Bennett had been prepared.

Bernard Swann again:

---

* I was responsible for this stand. In an attempt to emulate Bill Elliott's impact with the Ellliott 401 computer at the Physical Society Exhibition in 1951, I arranged to have on display a working Pegasus computer with four magnetic tape units. An extant photograph shows one of the tape spools blurred and thus in operation. Also about 200 of our supporting documents that had been done by that date were displayed.

In operation Perseus was very successful but the Ferranti-Powers research work had been concentrating on the idea of making a small, cheap, but powerful tape processing system which did not materialize and the opportunity to promote this powerful Perseus system was lost. It gave in the end a clear demonstration of the effects of divided loyalties. Ferranti would have liked to sell the system and the insurance industry was preparing to accept big expenditure on computers, but the obligation to Powers left the initiative in their hands and they showed no interest in selling Perseus rather than their own computers. All attempts to exploit the complementary interests of the two companies came up against the wall of secrecy which surrounded Powers' selling policy and practices.

Descendants of Pegasus

Pegasus 2

The Pegasus 2 system continued the pioneering qualities of the original Pegasus in a number of respects:

i It was the first European computer enhancement to recognize the immense value of the software that existed for the previous version. All the programs that had been written for Pegasus 1, as we began to refer to it, would run on Pegasus 2 without any change. All the enhancements to the system were additions and extensions, not modifications.

ii It had very comprehensive facilities for using punched cards, so that it could be integrated into any existing punched card system. This adaptation was done by program. We had learnt that a special skill of the punched card companies had been to adapt the coding and layout of the punching on a card to provide for the exceptional cases that arose in any practical application.

iii   It incorporated, in the one system, advances that had previously been made individually in other developments:

- an intermediate store, comprising 16 8-word delay line stores, studies had shown that this doubled the speed of the system for typical data processing applications;

- the larger magnetic drum, providing 7168 words for general use plus 1024 isolated words for basic programs and engineers' test programs;

- a category search facility that permitted selected items to be printed out from a magnetic tape;

- a 'pseudo offline working' facility to permit autonomous conversion of data between any pair of peripheral devices, the central computer being free to do other work, this being equivalent to the Converter of page 112;

- facilities for handling 6-bit coded alphanumeric data;

- orders to convert data in any radix to binary;

- the common interface scheme for connecting a variety of input or output devices;

- an output tape punch operating at 110 characters per second;

- 7-track punched tape, with a parity check-bit on every character.

iv New programs to utilize the enhanced facilities provided by Pegasus 2 were progressively added to the Library or made available in the interchange scheme.

The electronic equipment for each of the supplementary major facilities, such as magnetic tape or punched card machines or a line printer were independent additions to a basic Pegasus 2. This made it simple and more economic to manufacture the systems.

It may have been a coincidence that the evolution of Pegasus 2 coincided with the retirement of Brian Pollard as manager of the Ferranti Computer Department. It was certainly no coincidence that it coincided with the demise of the absurd arrangement with the Powers-Samas company, with all its exclusitivities and its secrecy. It took advantage of the merger of Powers-Samas and British Tabulating Machines in July 1958.

The basic Pegasus 2 system.
The unit on the right is the 110 char/sec tape punch

DESCENDANTS OF PEGASUS

Pegasus 2 data processing system with punched card machines

DESCENDANTS OF PEGASUS

The development appears to have been a spontaneous one in the Laboratory now located in Bracknell. The activity was led by Hugh Devonald supported by a strong electronic engineering and logic design team—Gordon Harvey, Peter Harrild, Geoff Crome, Arthur Jackson, to name just a few. Meeting the needs of programmers and of various users were based on informal contacts established between members of that Laboratory and members of Swann's group.

The first Pegasus 2 was installed in August 1960 in a second Ferranti computer centre, also in the west-end of London, where it was used for program development and for hire to users. The much more open and healthier situation resulted in the sales of eleven Pegasus 2 systems, which became operational at their respective sites during the period October 1960 to October 1962.

More should be explained about the very sophisticated facilities for dealing with punched cards. The objective was to accept and interpret correctly the great variety of punching conventions that occurred in practice, all done under program control.* Data read from a card was first passed to a distribution look-up table, which was used in conjunction with a data buffer store. This permitted the punching in any column to be placed in any position in the buffer store. It also permitted the punching in the card column to be split into two sections, which accommodated all the alphabetic conventions in use.

There was a second look-up table for code conversion. This could be loaded by program to carry out any of the many varieties of conversion used in different systems between the code used for the card punching and the character code used within the computer.

---

* The facilities are described in detail in the document I wrote with much help from colleagues *Ferranti Pegasus 2 Computer System*, December 1960, List DC.44

It could also be set to permit the card punching in any column to be treated as 12 binary digits in the computer.

All these features for handling punched cards were entirely novel. Both with respect to the capability to deal with the vagaries of the different punched card companies and the exceptional punchings that were a feature of individual installations, and also with respect to everything being brought under the control of programs.

Descendants of Pegasus

FP6000

Ferranti-Packard was a wholly-owned subsidiary of the Ferranti company situated in Canada. They designed and manufactured a wide range of electrical equipment. They had significant experience of digital computers, having devised an ingenious on-board system for the Canadian navy. They owned a Pegasus from December 1959.

This work led to their development of a general purpose computer, titled the FP6000. This was made in Canada, using components available in that country. It made use of two technical advances that by then had become available. The first were 'large scale integrated' units. These were about half the size of a matchbox and incorporated a multitude of transistors and related components. Each one could carry out the logical processes of a group of Pegasus packages. (They were before the chip on a silicon wafer that comprises a complete processor.)

The second were magnetic core memory units, typically each held 4096 24-bit words. One type worked at 6 microsec, another more expensive type at 2 microsec.

A substantial number of these units were assembled on a plug-in package. The FP6000 was built of several hundred of these packages.

A small group of their engineers, led by Fred Longstaff, came to Britain to learn of Ferranti computer developments. They found that a group at Wynthenshaw, a suburb of Manchester, had developed a set of transistor-based packages, originally for the guidance system of the Bloodhound guided weapon, under contract to the Bristol Aircraft Company. Maurice Gribble had led this work, and his packages reflected closely the design principles of the original valve-based packages devised by Charles Owen. They proved very reliable and effective. They were nick-named 'Gribblons'.

Longstaff's group worked in the Bracknell Laboratory. Here they were exposed to the work being done on the Ferranti Orion 2 computer, which also used transistor-based packages. In particular, this incorporated a most ingenious software feature whereby several programs could in effect be active simultaneously within the computer. This was controlled by a facility termed the Executive. This allocated control to each program on a priority basis, switching control several times a second. Stringent facilities were provided to prevent any program interfering with the others. One purpose was to permit the use of the processor to be independent of the relatively slow operating speeds of peripheral devices. This technique for overcoming the slow speeds of electro-mechanical peripheral machines, and for permitting several programs to run simultaneously, were key features of the FP6000.

In addition to this, during 1961 and 1962 a working group in Swann's department had been studying the sales requirements for a medium-scale computer system suited for both data processing work and also for technical calculations. Being chaired by Harry Johnson, it produced what was nick-named the Harriac report. This had highlighted the need for it to be possible to attach a wide variety of peripheral machines. The FP6000 was clearly influenced by this, for it was offered with an extensive series of ancillary machines.

DESCENDANTS OF PEGASUS

The order code proposed in the Harriac report, and ultimately provided in the FP6000, was a derivative or enhancement of that of Pegasus. Its objective was to permit the design of both larger and smaller systems that would offer upward or downward compatibility of programs. This was a novel concept. The actual code was devised by Dr Stanley Gill and John Illiffe . It also incorporated the feature devised by Maurice Wilkes of Cambridge University of providing 'extra-code' instructions, whereby a single instruction in a user's program caused a sequence of elementary instructions to be carried out.

Another feature emphasized in the Harriac report was that it was a requirement that addition of peripheral machines, or even the substitution of a different processor of the range, could be carried out with only minimum delay to the user. This was attained by developing the concept of the Ferranti common interface into what became the ICT standard interface.

Ferranti-Packard only managed to sell five FP6000 systems, each having quite substantial auxiliary equipment.* A clue to this poor achievement lies in the fact that in the formal brochure by the company, printed in September 1962, there is absolutely no hint of supporting software, nor is there any mention of software for practical applications being available. Ferranti-Packard were trying to sell clever engineering alone. However, it is known that a further three machines were supplied to various departments of the Ferranti company. The comparatively simple system at West Gorton is shown in the photograph on the following page.

A much more significant consequence was that the FP6000 was used as the basis of the 1900 series of computers of International Computers Limited (ICL). This company had been formed, with

---

* One of these, a very large system, for the Saskatchewan Power Corporation, remained in active use for 20 years.

some government pressure, to integrate the British computer industry, and in late-1963 had offered to buy up the non-military computer activity of Ferranti. During the negotiations, the British Ferranti management had offered to include the design rights of the FP6000. From ICL's point of view it was the jewel in the crown, and possibly was the element that made the deal acceptable. From the Canadian point of view it was devastating, the senior computing staff resigned, and Ferranti-Packard went out of that business.

A medium-scale FP6000 system

Descendants of Pegasus

The ICT 1900 Series

The central processor of the ICL 1904

The early members of the ICT 1900 series of data processing systems were a combination of several elements. Foremost was the FP6000. To this was added the concepts in Harry Johnson's report that has been referred to on page 130. The third constituent was more simple systems that were being developed by the ICT engineers at their Stevenage establishment. A fourth was a large-scale programming effort led by George Felton and managed by Peter Hunt. There were over one hundred programmers. That work was supported by comprehensive documentation.

The initial member of the series was the 1904. As production got under way at the Ferranti West Gorton factory in Manchester, it used British equivalents to the large-scale-integration modules and the ferrite core storage units that were the main components on the packages.

An important feature of the design was that it incorporated what became known as the ICL standard peripheral interface. This was conceptually based on the facility that had been established in Pegasus 2, described in Annex No 9. It was however much more comprehensive so that a wide range of input, output, storage and communication devices could be connected to the processor. The full specification can be found at the relevant section of the website in bitsavers.org

Very advanced software was combined with the hardware to provide
- Multi-programming under automatic control of Executive
- Processor time automatically allocated for maximum productivity
- Simultaneous operation of peripheral devices
- Reservation system to prevent interprogram interference
- Programming compatibility throughout the 1900 series.
- A very extensive repertoire of programs, including compilers for Cobol, Fortran and Algol.

The whole ICT 1900 series has been well written up in the relevant section of the website in bitsavers.org

By 1965 a market for computers had developed, and these machines were well suited to it. ICL were well placed to exploit that market. Accordingly the series comprised a major commercial success.

Epilogue

The theme of this book is that Pegasus in its time pioneered crucial aspects of computers and computing activity. Fifty years later it did it again.

This relates to machine No 25 which, after a series of varied uses and being relegated to storage, was brought back into working condition by a tiny group of grey-haired enthusiasts and put on display in the Science Museum, London. At the time it was the oldest digital computer in working condition in the world.

However, undetected, shreds of inflammable material had passed through the filters of the air cooling system, collected on a terminal strip where the potential differences were 450 volts with currents up to 10 amperes, and caught fire. The fuses in Pegasus soon blew, and the damage was minimal.

Repairs were complicated by the fact that during the intervening years legislation had been introduced banning the use of asbestos (it can cause lung cancer). All traces of this had to be removed and alternatives obtained.

Much more troublesome was that the event triggered an extensive investigation by the museum authorities. Not only were there concerns for the other treasures in the museum, but also it raised arguments whether an exhibit should be only seen and not touched, or whether something like a computer needed to be workable to convey its full impact.

All this took two years to resolve.

EPILOGUE

Apart from the pioneering quality about an early electronic computer being made to work after 50 years, this also pioneered the whole philosophy of the relations between professional curators in a museum and volunteer enthusiasts with the skill and interest to carry out such an outstanding project. It led to a series of understandings and procedures that truly had a seminal quality.*

Three Pegasus pioneers resurrecting the 50-year old machine as a working exhibit in the Science Museum, London.

Courtesy Simon Lavington

---

* The full story is given by Chris Burton, a leading engineer involved, in *The Pegasus Episode and its Aftermath* in Resurrection No 53, Winter 2010/11, the journal of the Computer Conservation Society, London.

Introduction to the Annexes

These annexes* constitute the main contribution by my colleagues. Every one has been written by the engineers involved. Furthermore, except for No 9, they were all published in the professional literature. Thus each was subject to 'peer approval' before publication. One of the conventions of this practice is that only novel work can be described. Anything related to earlier work has to be relegated to a bibliography.

Taken together, they thus comprise a most striking testimony to the pioneering nature of Pegasus.

The significance of the final document is that Ian Merry had worked with Charles Owen for many years, not only in Ferranti but also in the IBM UK Laboratory. Written in 1993 he reflects on that experience. Apart from hearing that Owen had been honoured as an IBM Fellow, it is the only record we have of his work there.

---

* The source documents are:

Annex No 1 *The Elliott Journal,* 1950
Annexes Nos 2, 3 and 4 *Proc. I.E.E.* October 1956
Annex No 5 *Electronic Engineering* August 1957
Annex No 6 *Electronic Engineering* September 1957
Annex No 7 *Electronic Engineering* October 1957
Annex No 8 *Proc. I.E.E.* March 1956
Annex No 9 *Ferranti document EP31* February 1961
Annex No 10 *Computer Resurrection* Autumn 1993

Annex No 1 Elliott's first document on packages

Circuit Standardization in Series-Working, High-Speed Digital Computers*

W. S. ELLIOTT, M.A., A.M.I.E.E.
(Elliott Brothers (London) Ltd.)

STANDARDIZATION of basic circuits in an electronic computer means quicker fault-finding and easier repairing. By using plug-in units of a convenient size faults may be remedied by replacement of units, and the time the machine is out of action both for regular maintenance and for dealing with incidental faults is reduced.

By minimising the variety of circuit elements and so gaining the benefits of quantity production, the initial cost of machines will be brought down. The size of the circuit elements chosen as the replaceable components is important. The lowest level at which a machine can be subdivided is the individual gate or trigger circuit, and the Mark III Calculator engineered by Professor Aiken and his group at Harvard uses single-valve circuits of this size in plug-in colour-coded cans. At the other extreme a machine might be designed with a whole register or accumulator as the replaceable unit.

The illustrations show a number of types of replaceable unit for series-working machines which we have tried experimentally over a number of years. The units tried range from 1-valve to 8-valve circuits. We have found that for our series-working machines the optimum-sized replaceable unit is one of from 4 to 6 valves, and we find it desirable to use a standard physical form and size for all units. The unit size therefore corresponds to the largest individual circuit which we have decided to accommodate, namely the logical elements of the adder/subtractor, which require 5 valves. Other functional circuits, the digit delay for example, are smaller and so the standard physical unit can accommodate two identical digit delay circuits, with common power and separate signal connections. Certain functional circuits are duplicated or triplicated on the standard plate, and in the

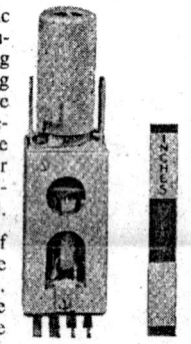

FIG. 1. Plug-in flip-flop circuit (with one 6J6 valve).

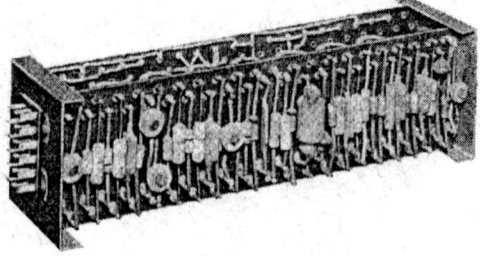

FIG. 3. 7-valve plug-in unit (a subtractor).

FIG. 2. (*Left*). 3-valve plug-in unit using miniature valves. (One stage of a commutator.)

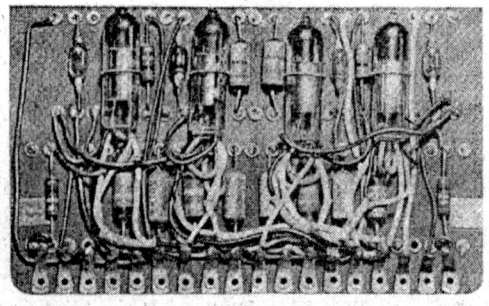

FIG. 4. (*Right*.) 4-valve wired-circuit plate 5" × 3" using sub-miniature valves. There are two separate staticiser circuits on the plate.

* This article is the subject-matter of a paper read by the author at the Conference of the Association for Computing Machinery at Rutgers University, New Brunswick, N.J., in March, 1950.

Annex No 1 Elliott's first document on packages

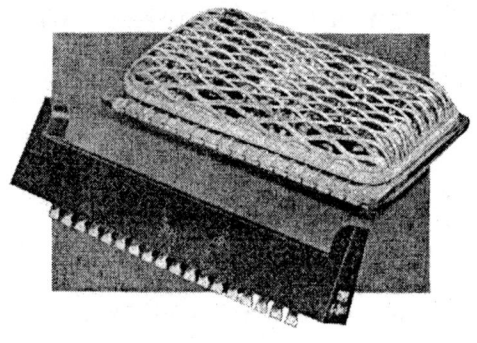

FIG. 5. 4-valve printed circuit on 5" × 3" glass plate with protective covers and 18-way socket.

FIG. 6. 4-valve wired-circuit plate 7½" × 4½" for two staticisers.

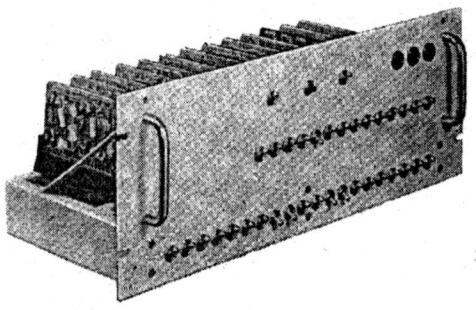

FIG. 7. Order and number generator using 5" × 3" printed circuit plates.

case of the cathode follower there are six to a plate. The complete 4 to 6-valve circuits are replaceable in the machine as units, so the valves are soldered into the circuits. The only sliding contacts are on a standard quantity-produced socket for the one physical component.

The greater the extent of circuit standardization attempted, the greater may be the overall size of the machine, and some increase in machine size may be acceptable in the interest of reduced variety of units. For our series-working machines, for instance, three types of digit-delay circuit were first developed, to 'carry' in the process of addition, for a special multiplier and for regaining pulse shape by 'digit slip.' By slightly increasing the unit size, one single standard circuit was designed for all three applications.

The philosophy of small functional units and standardization has led to the development of a range of about a dozen different types of units which will carry out the logical and control operations in a series-working[†] computer. It is found that this range of units can be put together in different ways to make machines of somewhat diverse types. Extreme speed can be achieved in a machine using the standardized series-working components by providing multiple transfer facilities so that two or more operations take place simultaneously. Series machines which have been described, the EDSAC at Cambridge for example, have one 'input bus' and one 'output bus,' to which any organ of the machine (the store, the input tape, the output printer, etc.) can be connected by gates. In such a machine only one transfer can take place at one time. By providing multiple transfer lines and gates and arranging the programmes to take advantage of the simultaneous transfer facilities, an operating speed can be obtained which compares well with that of a large parallel-working[†] computer.

The detailed development and the engineering for quantity production of such a range of standardized series-working components of optimum size may bring nearer the time when computing machines of diverse types and high maintainability can be produced to order in short development and manufacturing times.

† The term "series-working" is used to describe the system in which the several digits of a number are represented by a series of pulses on one wire or channel, and the term "parallel-working" to describe a system in which the several digits are transmitted along an equal number of channels simultaneously.

137

Annex No 2 Elliot and colleagues describe Pegasus

THE DESIGN PHILOSOPHY OF PEGASUS, A QUANTITY-PRODUCTION COMPUTER

By W. S. ELLIOTT, M.A., F.Inst.P., C. E. OWEN, M.A., Associate Members, C. H. DEVONALD, B.A., and B. G. MAUDSLEY, A.M.I.Mech.E.

(The paper was first received 18th May, and in revised form 5th July, 1956. It was read at the CONVENTION ON DIGITAL-COMPUTER TECHNIQUES *on the 11th April, 1956.)*

SUMMARY

The paper gives an historical account of the development of the packaged method of construction of computers, and the advantages of this method are discussed. The packages used in the computer Pegasus are described from both an electronic and a mechanical point of view. The specification of the machine is given and the arguments which led to this specification are discussed. The detailed logical design procedure leading from the specification to the wiring lists is described. The method of maintenance and some reliability figures are given.

(1) INTRODUCTION

The development of standard plug-in unit circuits ('packages') for digital computers began in this country in 1947, and some of the advantages of the method have been discussed in earlier papers.[1-4] The advantages start in the design stage of a new computer project and follow through production and commissioning to maintenance.

In the design stage, what is known as 'logical' design is separated from engineering design. Once the packages have been designed by electronic engineers and the rules for their interconnection have been laid down, the 'logical designers' (usually, but not necessarily, mathematicians) can begin organizing the packages into various computers to carry out different functional requirements. The electronic and mechanical design work invested in the packages is thus drawn on for more than one computer design, and each computer can be assembled from stock parts without further engineering effort. Design time and cost are therefore much reduced.

In production, whether we consider one design of computer or several designs using the same packages, costs and time are also much reduced. Quantity production lines for the relatively few types of standard package are set up, and are common to different computer designs, thus reducing inspection and planning costs. Standard cabinet work has been designed for Pegasus, and this too can be taken from stock or established production lines to make other computers.

In commissioning a computer, because all the packages have been pretested, when power is first applied to the complete machine it is known that a large part is already fault-free. It remains to detect a few errors which may have been made in the interconnections.

Perhaps an even more important consideration is ease and speed of maintenance. Test programmes will usually indicate the part of the machine in which a fault is occurring. Several monitor sockets are located on the front of each package, and by inspection the faulty package is speedily found and replaced.

The package method has been criticized on the grounds of the cost and questionable reliability of plugs and sockets, and some redundancy of components.

The authors believe that the many advantages far outweigh the cost of plugs and sockets. The present trend is to use copper-etched printed circuits, and these fall naturally into the plug-in unit idea, the plug contacts being part of the printed wiring; there has been no trouble in Pegasus from plugs and sockets. Component redundancy in Pegasus is about 10% of the diodes and a few resistors, the cost of redundant components being about £150.

(2) ELECTRICAL DESIGN OF THE PACKAGES

(2.1) Circuits used for Arithmetic and Switching Operations

(2.1.1) Historical.

A previous data-processing machine[3,5] used 330 kc/s serial-digital circuits; they had originally been designed for 1 Mc/s operation, but 330 kc/s was chosen to suit an anticipation-pulse cathode-ray-tube store. This frequency has been retained to the present time because it suits the magnetostriction delay-line store[6] and the magnetic-drum store.[7] Experience with the data processor led to work (commenced in 1951) on a new set of circuits,[3] particular emphasis being laid on flexibility of use and ability to work without error in high electrical interference fields. These circuits form the basis of those in Pegasus.

(2.1.2) Operations to be carried out.

The following well-known operations are used to build up the logical structure of the computer:

 (*a*) '*And*.' This operation, which may be carried out between two or more input serial trains of pulses, produces an output train in which pulses occur only when pulses are present at the same time on all inputs.

 (*b*) '*Or*.' This operation produces an output train in which pulses occur at all times when a pulse is present on any of a number of inputs.

 (*c*) '*Not*.' 1's are changed into 0's and 0's into 1's; this is achieved by inverting the pulse train.

 (*d*) *Digit Delay*. The passing of a pulse train through a digit delay produces a pulse train similar to the input, but each pulse is one pulse position later in timing and restandardized in shape.

All operations in the computer, including addition, subtraction, and staticizing, are carried out by combinations of these elements. There is no circuit specifically for addition, and there are, in general, no flip-flops such as are often used for staticizing or storing a single digit. A similar philosophy was arrived at independently by the designers of SEAC and DYSEAC,[8] but the detailed working out is considerably different.

(2.1.3) Digit Waveforms.

The timing of digit pulses throughout the machine is controlled by a common 'clock' waveform—a 3 microsec square wave [Fig. 1(*a*)] in which the positive-going portions define digit positions.

The digit pulses, which are routed about the machine and applied to logical circuits, are generally of the form shown in Fig. 1(*b*); as generated, they have their leading edges well in advance of the clock pulse and are of a greater amplitude. This means that considerable distortion of the pulse is tolerable, since only the portion which coincides with positive clock pulse is of consequence. Digit pulse trains are 'clocked' ('and' operation

---

Messrs. Owen, Devonald and Maudsley are with Ferranti, Ltd.
Mr. Elliott was recently with Ferranti, Ltd.

Annex No 2 Elliot and colleagues describe Pegasus

namely a digit delay (half a 12AT7 valve), an inverter (half a 12AT7 valve), and a direct connection. Space does not permit a description of all the circuits, so it is proposed to deal only with the digit delay.

The circuit is shown in Fig. 2, and some typical waveforms are

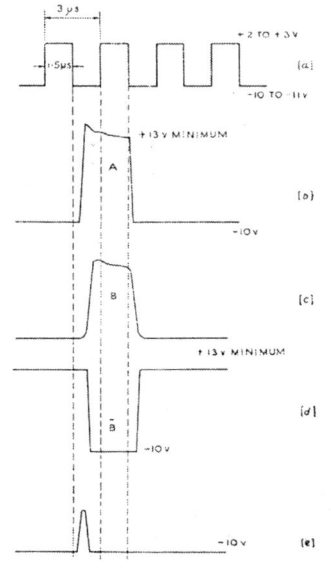

Fig. 1.—Basic waveforms.

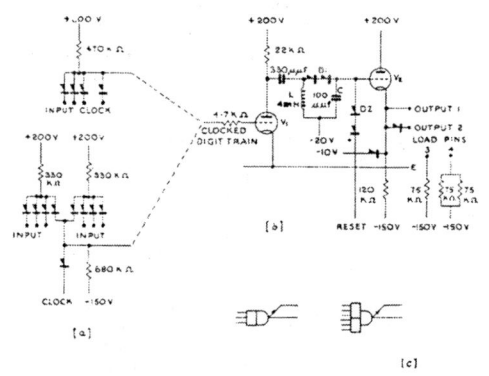

Fig. 2.—Digit-delay circuit.

with clock) only at their entry into a storage system or into a digit-delay circuit.

Inverted pulses are also employed: as an illustration, consider the operation 'A and not B'. Pulses A and B (Fig. 1) are on two lines and are of the same nominal timing, and we wish to form A . $\bar{B}$ (symbolic representation of 'A and not B'). To do this pulse B is inverted (forming $\bar{B}$, or 'not B') and is used to gate pulse A and prevent its passage. The inverted pulse $\bar{B}$ will be a little late on B, which also may have been later than A, as shown in Fig. 1(c); thus when A and $\bar{B}$ are 'anded' together a spike may be produced, as shown in Fig. 1(e). This spike, however, lies between clock pulses and so will be rejected on clocking.

The pulse system used allows several logical operations to be performed in cascade without any loss in nominal timing, so easing the problem of logical design (particularly by permitting afterthoughts). The maximum number of logical operations performed in cascade in Pegasus is five, though up to 12 could be performed in special circumstances.

(2.1.4) **The Logical Circuits.**

Each of the logical packages has more than one circuit unit. A circuit unit is defined as that part of a package which has input and output pins, and no connections to other parts of the package other than supplies. We may make the following generalizations:

(a) Each unit has an 'and' gate at its input.
(b) Each unit has a cathode-follower output (half a 12AT7 valve).
(c) Each unit has an additional output via a germanium diode for making 'or' gate connections.

[Note: There are exceptions to (a) and (c) on one package type.]

There are three possibilities for the part of the circuit unit between the input 'and' gate and the output cathode-follower,

shown in Fig. 3. The input circuit can be of two forms, namely a 3-input 'and' gate and two such gates with their outputs 'or-ed' together. In both cases there is a further gating with a clock pulse. The clocked digits from the gate input circuit are applied to the grid of V_1, the anode voltage of which falls, so building up a current in L. When V_1 is cut off at the end of the digit, this current

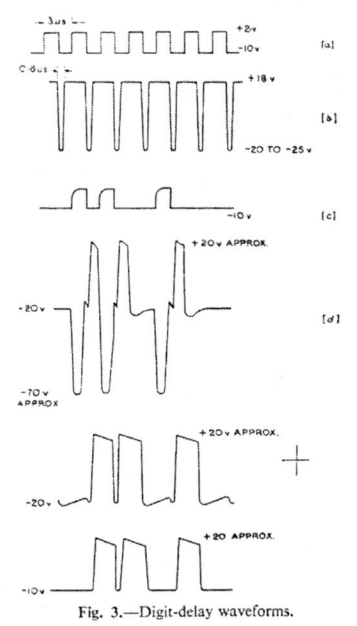

Fig. 3.—Digit-delay waveforms.

Annex No 2 Elliot and colleagues describe Pegasus

flows through diodes D_1 and charges up a storage condenser, C, which is discharged at the end of the next clock pulse by a 'reset' pulse applied through D_2. The reset pulse supply is a common computer supply whose amplitude and phasing relative to the clock pulse is shown in Fig. 3.

It will be noted that the reset pulse is also present at a time, just after V_1 is cut off, when the current in the inductor is about to charge the storage condenser. This merely has the effect of deferring the charging of C until the end of the reset pulse, the current in the meantime continuing to flow through the diodes with little loss in the stored energy of L, since the voltage across L is low at this time.

The output cathode-follower V_2 is caught at -10 volts in the negative direction by a diode; this safeguards the crystal-diode circuits driven by it in the event of failure of the h.t. supply or V_2, and it removes residual ripple on the bottom of the input waveform, and thus reduces the back voltage and hence leakage in diodes of gates driven by the output.

The second output through a diode can be used in conjunction with similar outputs from other circuits and a resistor (pins 3 and 4) to make an 'or' (up to about 16-way).

In general, each output circuit has two available load resistors, disposed between direct and 'or' ouputs according to a set of rules which are applied for each case. The number of units which can be driven by an output can vary between three and 16 according to circumstances; where more have to be driven than the rules allow, use is made of 'booster' cathode-followers available on one of the packages.

(2.2) Some Examples of the Use of the Logical Circuits

Two examples will be given, the first being a simple arrangement—the staticizor—which is used frequently, and the second being a complicated arrangement—the adder/subtracter— which is used infrequently. The symbols used to indicate the circuit units are shown in Figs. 2(c) and 5(b).

(2.2.1) The Staticizor.

The function of a staticizor is to remember the fact that a digit occurred at a particular time, for an indefinite period, the method generally used in Pegasus being shown in Fig. 4. A digit delay

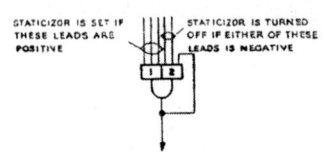

Fig. 4.—The staticizor.

with a twin 'and' gate input has its output connected to one of its inputs. It is turned on by gate 1, which causes a digit to circulate as long as the inputs to gate 2 remain positive. It is normally turned off by an inverted pulse (a '0' following a series of 1's) on one of the gate 2 inputs.

(2.2.2) The Adder/Subtracter.

Fig. 5 shows an adder/subtracter unit with inputs X and Y and an output $X + Y$ for the sum or $X - Y$ for the difference. There are two further input control leads marked 'add' and 'subtract'. If the 'add' lead is held positive while the 'subtract' lead is held negative, the unit acts as an adder. If the 'subtract' lead is held positive and the 'add' lead negative, the unit acts as a subtracter. Carry suppression is controlled by the lead marked 'carry suppression'. Carries are allowed to propagate when this

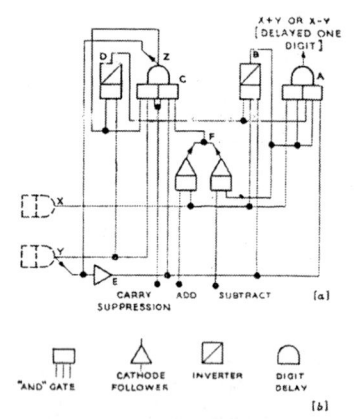

Fig. 5.—The adder/subtracter.

lead is held positive, so that a negative signal on this lead will suppress carry.

Table 1 gives the digits appearing at the outputs of logical elements in the adder/subtracter unit for all combinations of input and carry digits when the unit is operating as an adder.

Table 1

DIGITS AT VARIOUS INTERNAL POINTS OF THE ADDER/SUBTRACTER UNIT WHEN SET TO ADD, FOR ALL COMBINATIONS OF THE INPUT AND CARRY DIGITS

Inputs digits		Present carry digit	Digits at internal points				
X	Y	Z	A (Sum)	B	C (Next carry)	D	E	F
0	0	0	0	1	0	1	0	0
0	0	1	1	1	0	1	1	0
0	1	0	1	1	0	1	0	1
0	1	1	0	1	1	0	1	0
1	0	0	1	1	0	1	0	1
1	0	1	0	0	1	1	1	1
1	1	0	0	0	1	1	1	1
1	1	1	1	0	1	0	1	1

Note.—A and C are at the grids of the digit delay units.

(2.3) Arrangement of Circuits based on Packages

It was required to base the logical circuits on a standard size of package which could also be used for other circuits, e.g. a nickel-line 1-word store.[6] A unit which could accommodate three valves and had a 32-way plug was decided on; the problem then was to arrange the various circuits in such a way as to enable a computer to be designed using a minimum total number of packages without too many types. Five types were arrived at and these are shown in Fig. 6.

As an example of the factors involved, consider package types 1 and 2. The circuit units based on package type 1 can perform all the functions of those on type 2. However, there are many uses for a digit-delay circuit with a single 'and' gate input (package type 2), and since three units of this kind (instead of two for a 2- 'and'-gate input delay) can be based on one package, a saving can be effected. In Pegasus this saving amounts to 32

Annex No 2 Elliot and colleagues describe Pegasus

PHILOSOPHY OF PEGASUS, A QUANTITY-PRODUCTION COMPUTER

Fig. 7.—Standard package.

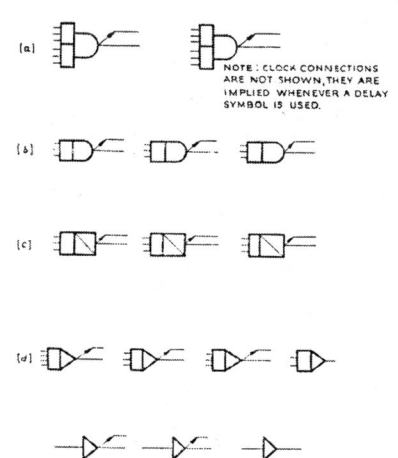

Fig. 6.—Contents of logical packages.
The arrowhead on an output lead denotes the presence of an 'or' crystal connection.

packages, which is considered to be well worth an extra package type.

In addition to the five logical packages, a further 16 types (three of which are peculiar to each computer) are required. The numbers used for the various functions are given below:

	Number
Logical types — Type 1	113
Type 2	64
Type 3	55
Type 4	45
Type 8	37
Nickel-line 1-word store	61
Drum-store packages (8 types)	38
Input/output packages (3 types)	17
Clock and reset waveforms (3 types)	14
Total	444

The magnetic-drum store and the circuit packages used with it are described in another paper,[7] as is the nickel-line store.[6]

(3) THE MECHANICAL DESIGN OF THE PACKAGES

(3.1) General Form

Each standard package consists of three main parts, namely the valve panel, the component panel and the plug.

The valve panel is an aluminium pressing, there being three types—a 3-valve type, a 2-valve type and a blank. The package type number is marked on the panel by two dots according to the standard resistor colour code.

The component panel houses up to 100 components, including small transformers, chokes and coils, the panel and the handle being made in one piece from sheet insulating material. This design provides a minimum resistance to airflow over the valves and gives ample protection to the valves against accidental damage.

The plugs and sockets are used in multiples of eight connections. Most of the packages have four plugs providing 32 con-

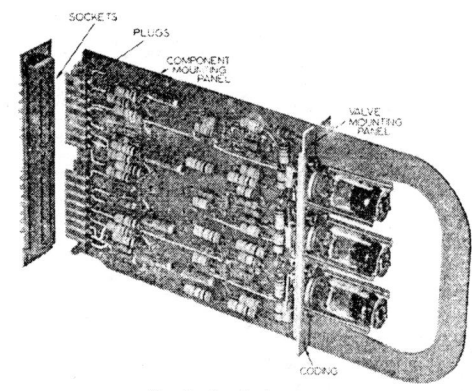

nections, but up to 64 are possible in each package. The plug contacts are made of brass and are heavily silver-plated. The socket uses a proprietary valve-holder contact, which can readily be replaced if damaged.

This combination of plug and socket has a consistently low contact resistance (0·003 ohm at 1 amp); the insertion and withdrawal force is about 4 oz per contact.

(3.2) The Wiring of the Packages

At present packages are wired and soldered by hand. The wiring is point-to-point, and within the limitations of layout for efficient performance, wire lengths are standardized for mass-production on automatic wire-cutting and stripping machines. The symmetry of the eyelet positions makes it possible to use components which are preformed to a standard pitch and would allow for automatic preforming and insertion of components. Experimental packages have been produced by photo-etched wiring and dip soldering.

(4) SPECIFICATION OF THE COMPUTER PEGASUS

(4.1) Summary Specification

A detailed specification would cover the ground of the programming manual[9] and would be out of place here.

Pegasus is a binary serial-digital computer. The word length is 42 binary digits, of which 39 digits are used for a number and its sign (negative numbers are represented by their complements with respect to two), one digit is used for a parity check and the other two are gap digits. The length of an order is 19 binary digits, so that one word may consist of two orders, the remaining digit being a 'stop-go' digit. If the 'stop-go' digit is a '0', the computer will stop before obeying the orders in the word, but will proceed unhindered if the digit is a '1'.

There is a 2-level store, a magnetic drum holding 5 120 words and an immediate-access or computing store of 55 single-word magnetostriction delay lines.

An order is made up of seven N-digits, three X-digits, six F-digits and three M-digits, the N-digits being the most significant and the M-digits the least significant. The N-digits allow 128 addresses in the immediate-access store (of which only 63 are used). The registers in this store are shown in Fig. 8. The X-digits refer to one of the accumulators, the registers corresponding to N-addresses 0–7. Thus the order code is a 2-address

141

Annex No 2 Elliot and colleagues describe Pegasus

ELLIOTT, OWEN, DEVONALD AND MAUDSLEY: THE DESIGN

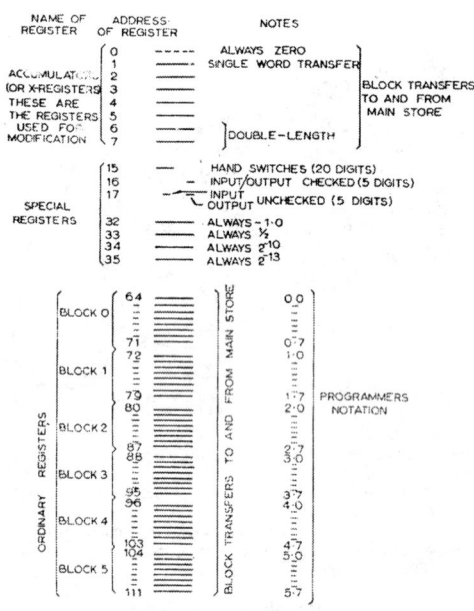

Fig. 8.—Allocation of addresses in store.

code with one address referring to only a limited part of the store. The F-digits indicate the function of the order. A list of functions and their corresponding F values are given in Section 10. The M-digits indicate a modifier for the order: they select one of the accumulators, and the modification process is to add certain parts of the contents of the selected accumulator to the order before it is obeyed, the part chosen depending on the function of the order to be modified. Fig. 9 gives a schematic

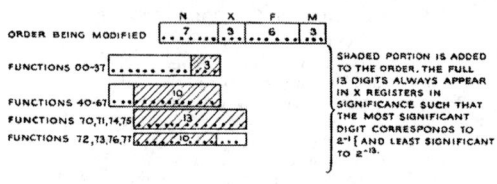

Fig. 9.—Order-modification process.

representation of the modification process. The effect of modifying an order depends on the function of the order and can be to make the effective order length 22 digits. This extension is necessary when specifying an address in the main store.

Transfers of information can take place between the computing store and the main store, and vice versa, either in single words or in blocks of eight words. For single-word transfers, only the register with address 1 in the computing store is involved. For block transfers the address on the drum of the first word of the block must be divisible by eight, and the registers in the computing store that are involved will be one of the discrete blocks indicated in Fig. 8.

Input and output is by means of punched paper tape. An 'external conditioning' order is included in the code to enable a choice of input and output equipment to be made. In the standard machine, two tape readers are used.

All stored information is checked (when read by means of a parity digit, which is such that the total number of 1's in any correctly stored word is odd. The input and output of decimal characters on tape can be checked by a similar process.

(4.2) The Considerations which led to the Specification and the Logical Design

The main features of the design are

(a) The use of a computing store from which all orders and numbers are taken while computing.
(b) The provision of multiple accumulators.
(c) The provision of special orders and facilities for dealing easily with 'red tape'.*

(4.2.1) The Computing Store.

The use of a fast-access store from which all numbers and orders are taken increases the speed of the machine and eliminates the need for optimum programming. It is this computing store which makes it possible to use an inexpensive magnetic drum (with a relatively long access time) as the main store, and yet have a machine which is fast and relatively simple to programme. On the other hand, programmes have more 'red tape' and are not as simple as with single-level storage.

Transfer between levels is in blocks of eight words; this is a simplification and saves time. One block holds a reasonable amount of programme and other blocks hold data. Four blocks in all (32 words) would be just sufficient, and Pegasus was originally designed with this number. The design was subsequently modified to six blocks, which is quite adequate, in conjunction with the seven accumulators. Any further increase in the size of the computing store would be achieved by increasing the size, not the number, of blocks. As it is there is an economic balance between the usefulness and the cost of the computing store.

(4.2.2) The Provision of Several Accumulators.

This is the most novel feature of the logical design of Pegasus. It is generally agreed that the simplest order code from the user's aspect is the 3-address code with orders of the form, $A + B \to C$. An examination of this form of code, however, shows that in many cases two of the addresses are the same, so that the order takes the 2-address form, $A + B \to A$. A further examination shows that in a large proportion of cases the address A is confined to a very few addresses. This leads to the suggestion of a code of the form $N + X \to X$, where X covers only a small part of the store while N covers the whole store. This will have the advantage of yielding a reasonably short order. In Pegasus two such orders are incorporated in one word, leaving sufficient digits to specify a modification register (a Mancunian B-line) in each order.

The extreme case of this code is, of course, the single-address code, where X is confined to one address, the accumulator. However, experience had convinced the programmers collaborating in the design of Pegasus that, with single-address codes, a large number of orders are concerned solely with transfers of numbers from one register to another; the single accumulator is a restriction through which all numbers must pass and in which all operations have to be performed.

In the Manchester University computer the B-lines serve two very valuable but distinct purposes: they allow order modification and rudimentary arithmetic (such as counting) to be done

---
* 'Red tape' is an expression for the non-arithmetic orders in a programme.

Annex No 2 Elliot and colleagues describe Pegasus

without disturbing the accumulator. It was felt that fuller arithmetic and logical facilities on these *B*-lines would have been extremely valuable. The seven accumulators in Pegasus, used for modification and arithmetic, are a development of the *B*-line concept.

(4.2.3) **Special Facilities for Dealing with 'Red Tape'.**

The difficulties associated with the 2-level storage system have been greatly reduced by having an order-modification procedure which depends on the function of the order (Fig. 9). This method of modifying orders, used in conjunction with order 66 of the code (the unit-modify order), enables the counting through blocks of information to be done with relative ease.

The use of the group-4 orders of the code enables counters to be set conveniently and a constant (up to 127) to be placed in an accumulator, the constant being the value of the *N*-digits of the order. Order 67 (the unit-count order) enables the counting of cycles of operations to be dealt with in a simple way. A jump to another part of the programme can be programmed to take place automatically when the required number of cycles has been performed.

Having a large number of jump instructions greatly helps in organizing a programme. In particular, one order enables a jump to be made depending on the condition of an accumulator (being zero, for example), and another order on the complementary condition (being not zero). When only one of these orders is available it is necessary to think ahead to see whether or not the correct condition will be satisfied. Although the eight jump instructions included in the code were felt initially to be enough, it is now suggested by programmers that even more such orders would be helpful.

The logical shift orders, 52 and 53, are also included to simplify 'red tape'. In particular, they are used for packing and unpacking words holding several items of information.

As a result of including these various orders, the order code of Pegasus is quite large. It is worth remarking, however, that by a sensible grouping of the orders in the code the remembering of the code is a very simple task. A sensible arrangement of the code tends to reduce the amount of equipment needed to engineer it. For example, when the equipment for dealing with group 0 of the code has been allocated, groups 1 and 4 require the addition of only three gates.

(4.2.4) **Facilities for Checking Programmes.**

The features mentioned above make the computer easier to programme, and there are other facilities in Pegasus that make it easier to check out and develop new programmes. These include causing the machine to stop obeying orders, either under programme control or when the programme is in error. In particular, the machine stops if an order for writing in the main store is reached and an overflow indicator is set. A further aid when testing new programmes is the automatic punching out of all main-store addresses appearing in block-transfer orders. When this information is examined an indication of the course of a programme is readily obtained. The punching can be inhibited by a switch when a return to full-speed running is needed.

(4.3) **Machine Rhythm**

The logical design of Pegasus is built around a nucleus that deals with the simple arithmetic orders, groups 0, 1 and 4, of the code. This nucleus contains the control section, i.e. the order register and order decoding equipment, and the mill in which these orders are executed. The design of this nucleus could not begin until a basic rhythm for dealing with the extraction from the computing store and the execution of such a pair was determined. When the outline of this nucleus was clear, the equipment for dealing with the remaining orders in the code was designed to fit it.

The following arguments led to the basic rhythm. Since the orders of groups 0, 1 and 4 are similar in many respects, for definiteness, it will be sufficient to consider a particular order, 11 of the code, say. This is an order which takes two numbers from the computing store and replaces one of them by their sum. It would take a prohibitive amount of equipment to extract these numbers, add them together and have the least significant digit of the sum available for replacing in the store in the same digit time as the least significant digits of the two components taken out of the store. In practice, some four digit times at least would be needed for this sequence of operations. Thus, it would be impossible to return the sum to the store in the same word as the operands are extracted without having an entry point to each register which is in a different timing from the normal circulation entry. To produce two such entry points to each register would mean more equipment associated with each register, which was considered an uneconomical use of extra equipment. Instead, it was decided to delay the sum so that it could enter the register in the computing store in the next word time in standard timing. This involves one common delaying circuit instead of one for every register. Such an order therefore takes two word times to execute. It may be argued that this second word time could be made to overlap with the first word time for the next order. Two reasons oppose this: the new contents of the register being changed might be required by the next order; and two different sets of equipment for selecting a storage register would be needed if numbers were to be extracted from one and replaced in another register in the same word time.

Thus, the execution of a pair of orders taken from the computing store requires four word times. The reasons for opposing the overlapping of the execution of two orders also oppose the extraction of an order pair while the previous pair is being dealt with. Five word times are therefore needed for the process of extracting and obeying a pair of simple arithmetic orders. More time may be needed for some of the other orders in the code.

The basic 3-beat rhythm is thus established:

(a) Extract the order pair from the computing store.
(b) Obey the first order of the pair.
(c) Obey the second order.

The duration of beat (a) is one word time; beats (b) and (c) are each two word times long for orders in groups 0, 1, 4 and 6 of the code, but may be longer for other orders.

(4.4) **Times for Typical Operations**

The times for the various arithmetic operations are:

	millisec
Addition and subtraction	0·3
Multiplication	2·0
Division	5·4

These times include an allowance for the time to extract the orders.

Some times for standard subroutines are:

	millisec
Exponential function	29
Sine function	24
Logarithmic function	34

Finally, to give some indication of the time for a typical problem, a set of 50 simultaneous equations (with a single right-hand side) takes about 10¼ min. Of this time, 3 min 8 sec is for input, 7 min 17 sec is for calculation and 18 sec is for output.

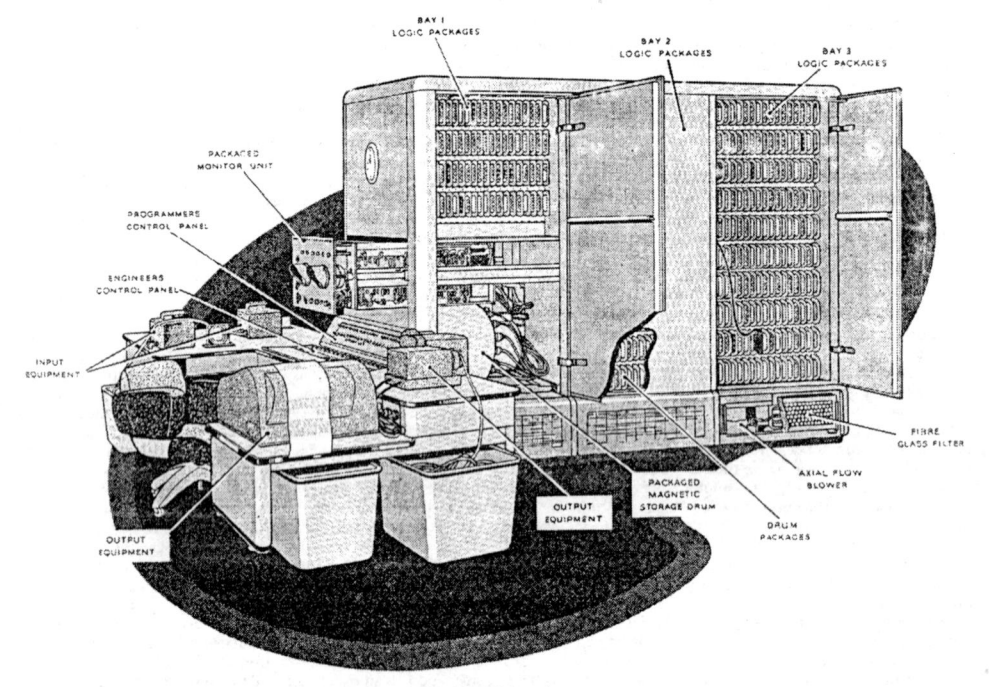

Annex No 2 Elliot and colleagues describe Pegasus

Fig. 10.—Main units.

(5) REALIZING THE SPECIFICATION

(5.1) The Detailed Logical Design

It would take too long to describe fully the detailed logical design. One aspect is worth mentioning, however, namely the avoidance of all 'exceptions' in the results of orders. As an example of an exception consider the overflow indicators, which should be set whenever the final result of an order is outside the permissible range of numbers. In multiplication this can occur only when both the multiplier and the multiplicand are -1, and this is likely to occur very infrequently. Rather than provide equipment to sense this infrequent case, it is easier to put a footnote in the programming manual, where the overflow indicator is described, pointing out the exception. It was felt, however, that such exceptions should be avoided even at the expense of extra equipment or extra complication. For this and other reasons concerned with facilitating machine use, the logic of Pegasus is quite complicated.

The end-product of the detailed logical design is a series of diagrams with symbols corresponding to the circuit units of the packages, as shown, for example, in Fig. 5. The inputs and outputs of the units on these diagrams correspond to the pins of the sockets into which the packages plug. Thus, the wiring lists of connections of these pins can be produced from these logical diagrams. The first step in the production of these lists is to allocate a position in the cabinets to each logical circuit in such a way as to reduce the amount of wire needed. When the layout has been completed, the last stage of producing the wire lists can proceed.

(5.2) General Construction of Machine

The main units are shown in Fig. 10.

(5.2.1) The Package Frame.

This unit is a simple light-alloy frame supporting diecast light-alloy frame racks to which the back socket panels are fixed. The packages slide into grooves in the rack and plug into sockets at the back, a polarizing feature preventing the insertion of a package upside down. If electrical or magnetic screening is necessary between any packages, a special metal plate is inserted in slots in the cast rack and is fixed by a single screw in the back panel. Coded aluminium strips containing coloured plastic studs which identify the position of each package are fixed to the front of each casting.

(5.2.2) Arrangement of the Packages.

There are 200 packages per cabinet, arranged in ten horizontal rows of 20 units per row. The metal valve panels are placed so that the edges almost touch. The component panel of each unit is in register with the unit in the corresponding position in each of the other rows, thereby providing vertical chimneys for cooling the components secured to these panels. Warm air from the main source of heat, the valves, is prevented by the valve panels from reaching the more temperature-sensitive components, such as diodes, secured to the component panel.

(5.2.3) The Back Panel Wiring.

For locating long signal wires between sockets a system of plastic strips is used, which hold the wires at definite positions

Annex No 2 Elliot and colleagues describe Pegasus

given by the instructions on the wiring lists. The exact route of every wire is predetermined, thus making wiring and inspection more reliable and fault finding and maintenance easier.

(5.2.4) **Final Assembly.**

The completely wired frame is assembled in its cabinet, which has already been fitted with the control and auxiliary supply circuit unit, heater transformers, fuses, cooling assembly and cableforms. The work of connecting the cableforms, heaters and earths can be done by relatively unskilled labour working to clearly written instructions and diagrams.

(5.2.5) **The Cooling System.**

Each cabinet has its own cooling system as an integral part of the construction; there is therefore no difficulty in cooling cabinets added to existing computers. Two axial-flow turbo blowers are mounted in the base beneath an airtight pressure chamber, each providing 300 ft^3/min of air at a total pressure head of 1 in (water gauge). The maximum temperature rise is 10°C.

(5.2.6) **The Power Supply.**

A separate cubicle houses metal rectifiers, shunt stabilizing valves and control circuits. The power is obtained from the mains through a motor-alternator set, the output of which is stabilized to 2%, the main purpose of this set being to act as a buffer against switching surges and other mains voltage variations. The valve heaters in the computer are energized from the stabilized alternator output, which is expected to extend the valve life.

(6) MAINTENANCE

(6.1) **General**

All digital computers so far have a fault rate which cannot be ignored. When the best has been done in the choice of components, circuits and mechanical construction, attention must be paid to the following points to get the best out of a machine:

(a) Rapid fault location.
(b) Getting the machine working again as soon as possible after locating a fault.
(c) Preventive maintenance.

(6.2) **Fault Location**

There are parity-checking circuits on both the main and the high-speed stores. Errors of a single digit in the stores stop the machine. The fault can then be quickly located by examination of the monitors.

For other faults the general method is to run a test programme (assuming the fault is not in the main control) which will indicate the area of the fault. Detailed examination can then be carried out with the monitors.

All outputs of circuit units are readily accessible at monitoring sockets on the front of each package, and in addition about 80 points can be directly selected by switches from the monitoring position: these include all store lines and a number of key waveforms. Fault-finding is normally a matter of tracing 0's and 1's through the machine with reference to logical diagrams rather than electronic circuit diagrams.

A variety of triggers can be selected for the monitor time-bases, these including

(a) Trigger at any word position within a drum revolution (128 different times selectable by switches).
(b) Trigger at any word time of any selected order.

These triggers and some other monitoring facilities are produced by 19 standard packages and are found to be well worth the extra equipment.

(6.3) **Fault Repair**

Once a faulty package has been located, the machine can be got working again immediately by replacement of the package with a spare; repair of the faulty package can be done at leisure with the aid of a package tester. With this equipment a package can quickly be given a series of standard tests; each is selected by switches, and the performance is measured either by observation of meters or a built-in oscillograph.

During commissioning not one case was found of the first machine doing other than what one would expect from the logical diagram (except for a very few cases of incorrect wiring).

(6.4) **Preventive Maintenance**

The machine h.t. supplies are reduced while the test programmes are being run. This marginal testing shows up incipient faults such as deterioration in valves, crystal diodes or resistors. The machine is at present kept in good running order down to 10% margins (the supplies are normally controlled to about 1% of nominal), although correct running at about 20% reduction has been observed.

(7) CONCLUSIONS

The first machine has been computing regularly for only a few months and has been on regular preventive maintenance (about 1 hour per day) for a few weeks. Error-free runs of over 30 hours are common, and at the time of writing there has been no error for 55¾ hours' running. The majority of package replacements are done during routine maintenance.

The packaged method of construction of computers has proved to have great advantages in design, construction and operation.

(8) ACKNOWLEDGMENTS

The authors would like to acknowledge the contributions that Mr. C. Strachey and Dr. D. B. Gillies, of the National Research Development Corporation, and Dr. J. M. Bennett and Mr. T. G. H. Braunholtz, of Ferranti, Ltd., made to the logical design of Pegasus: particular thanks are due to Mr. C. Strachey for originating the order code.

They also thank Ferranti, Ltd., and the National Research Development Corporation for permission to publish the paper.

(9) REFERENCES

(1) ELLIOTT, W. S.: 'Circuit Standardization in Series Working, High-Speed Digital Computers', *Elliott Journal*, **1**, No. 2, Sept., 1951, p. 49, and *Proceedings of the Association for Computing Machinery* (Rutgers Conference, March, 1950).

(2) JOHNSTON, D. L.: 'Standardized Printed Circuit Units for Digital Computers', *Proceedings of the Association for Computing Machinery* (Pittsburgh Conference, May, 1952), p. 135.

(3) ELLIOTT, W. S., CARPENTER, H. G., and OWEN, C. E.: 'Development of Computer Components and Systems', *ibid.* (Toronto Conference, September, 1952).

(4) ELLIOTT, W. S., CARPENTER, H. G., and JOHNSON, A. ST.: 'The Elliott–N.R.D.C. Computer 401—A Demonstration of Computer Engineering by Packaged Unit Construction', Symposium on Automatic Digital Computation (H.M. Stationery Office, London, 1953), p. 65.

(5) ELLIOTT, W. S., ROBBINS, R. C., and EVANS, D. S.: 'Remote Position Control and Indication by Digital Means', *Proceedings I.E.E.*, Paper No. 1897, November, 1955 (103 B, Supplement No. 3).

Annex No 2 Elliot and colleagues describe Pegasus

(6) FAIRCLOUGH, J. W.: 'A Sonic Delay-Line Storage Unit for a Digital Computer', *ibid.*, Paper No. 2041, March, 1956 (**103** B, Supplement No. 3).
(7) MERRY, I. W., and MAUDSLEY, B. G.: 'The Magnetic Drum Store of the Computer Pegasus' (see next page).
(8) ELBOURNE, R. D., and WITT, R. P.: 'Dynamic Circuit Techniques used in SEAC and DYSEAC', *Transactions of the Institute of Radio Engineers*, 1953, EC-2, No. 1.
(9) Pegasus Programming Manual (Ferranti Ltd., London).
(10) Pegasus Maintenance Manuals (Ferranti Ltd., London).

(10) APPENDIX

The Pegasus Order Code

00   $x' = n$
01   $x' = x + n$
02   $x' = -n$
03   $x' = x - n$
04   $x' = n - x$
05   $x' = x \& n$
06   $x' = x \neq n$
07   Not allocated

10   $n' = x$
11   $n' = n + x$
12   $n' = -x$
13   $n' = n - x$
14   $n' = x - n$
15   $n' = n \& x$
16   $n' = n \neq x$
17   Not allocated

20   $(pq)' = n \cdot x$
21   $(pq)' = n \cdot x + 2^{-39}$
22   $(pq)' = p + 2^{-38}q + nx$

23   $(nq)' = n + 2^{-38}q$ (justify)   { this order assumes that any overflow is due to operations in 7. Clears overflow unless n' overflows

24   $q' + 2^{-38}\left(\dfrac{p'}{n}\right) = \dfrac{x + 2^{-38}q}{n}$ { $0 \leq p'/n < 1$ (unrounded division); $-\tfrac{1}{2} \leq p'/n < \tfrac{1}{2}$ (rounded division)
25

26   $q' + 2^{-38}\left(\dfrac{p'}{n}\right) = \dfrac{x}{n}$; $-\tfrac{1}{2} \leq p'/n < \tfrac{1}{2}$ (rounded single-length division)
27   Not allocated

30
31
32
33
34   Not allocated
35
36
37

40   $x' = c$
41   $x' = x + c$
42   $x' = -c$
43   $x' = x - c$ } $c = N2^{-38}$
44   $x' = c - x$
45   $x' = x \& c$
46   $x' = x \neq c$
47   Not allocated

50   $x' = 2^N x$ } single-length arithmetical shifts
51   $x' = 2^{-N}x$ (rounded)   Note: $x' = x$ if $N = 0$
52   Shift x up N places   } single-length logical shifts
53   Shift x down N places
54   $(pq)' = 2^N(pq)$ } double-length arithmetical shifts   Note: $p' = p$ and $q' = q$ if $N = 0$
55   $(pq)' = 2^{-N}(pq)$ (unrounded)

56   (Normalize) $(pq)' = 2^\mu(pq)$; $x' = x - 2^{-38}\mu$ { either (1) $\tfrac{1}{4} \leq (pq)' < \tfrac{1}{2}$ and $-1 \leq \mu \leq N - 1$; or (2) $-\tfrac{1}{2} \leq (pq)' < \tfrac{1}{4}$ and $-1 \leq \mu \leq N - 1$; or (3) $-\tfrac{1}{4} \leq (pq)' < \tfrac{1}{4}$ and $\mu = N - 1$

57   Not allocated

60   Jump to N if $x = 0$
61   Jump to N if $x \neq 0$
62   Jump to N if $x \geq 0$
63   Jump to N if $x < 0$
64   Jump to N if overflow staticizor clear; clear overflow staticizor.
65   Jump to N if overflow staticizor set; clear overflow staticizor.
66   (Unit-modify) $x'_m = x_m + 1$. Jump to N if $x'_m \neq 0 \pmod 8$
67   (Unit-count) $x'_c = x_c - 1$. Jump to N if $x'_c \neq 0$

70   Single word read to accumulator 1. $1' = s$
71   Single word write from accumulator 1. $s' = 1$
72   Block read from main store $u' = b$
73   Block write into main store $b' = u$
74   External conditioning
75   } Not allocated
76
77   Stop

The notation used here is as follows:

N is the first address (the register address) in an order.
X is the accumulator specified in an order.
n is the word in N before obeying the order.
x is the word in X before obeying the order.
p and q are the words in 6 and 7 before obeying the order.
$(pq) = p + 2^{-38}q$, with $q \geq 0$. This is a double-length number.
x', n', p' and q' are the corresponding values after obeying the order.
B is a block in the main store (the drum).
U is a block in the computing store.
P is the position number of a word within a block.
OVR is the overflow indicator.
x_m is the modifier in X, i.e. an integer represented by the digits 1 to 13 of x.
x_c is the counter in X, i.e. an integer represented by the digits 14 to 38 of x.

Annex No 3 Fairclough on basic delay-line store

A SONIC DELAY-LINE STORAGE UNIT FOR A DIGITAL COMPUTER

By J. W. FAIRCLOUGH, B.Sc.Tech., Student.

(The paper was first received 7th October, 1955, and in revised form 19th January, 1956. It was published in March, 1956, and was read at the CONVENTION ON DIGITAL-COMPUTER TECHNIQUES, *12th April, 1956.)*

SUMMARY

The paper describes a sonic delay-line storage unit for 42 3 microsec digits for use in the easy-access or computing store of the FPC 1 computer and other computers and data-handling equipments.

The utilization of the magnetostrictive effect to initiate sonic pulses in a length of pure nickel is explained. Details of the transducers and their operation, together with the various losses and limitations which occur in the initiation, propagation and reception of the sonic pulses, are given.

The effect of temperature change is also discussed.

The paper gives details of the associated circuit with the necessary setting-up procedure.

(1) INTRODUCTION

The functions required of a digital computing machine store are four in number:

(a) It must be capable of storing incident digit patterns for an indefinitely long time.

(b) It must be capable of emitting such data when called upon to do so.

(c) It must be possible to erase stored information and to substitute new.

(d) It should be inexpensive.

In addition, the speed at which data can be inserted or recalled, i.e. the access time, must be considered. In the FPC 1 computer[1] a high-speed, or rapid-access, store in which all the arithmetical operations are carried out, is combined with a large-capacity drum store. The present paper describes a simple unit which stores 42 binary digits of 3 microsec digit time. This unit fulfils the above conditions and is of rapid access. A number of units are used together in the FPC 1 computer to form the rapid-access or computing store of the machine. The units are of the same physical plug-in package form as the logical circuits for the FPC 1[2] and they use the same basic waveforms as the logical circuits. They can therefore be used as 'building bricks' along with the logical circuits to achieve any desired computing system at their digit rate.

(2) PRINCIPLES OF A SONIC DELAY-LINE STORE

(2.1) Basic Store

A sonic delay-line store consists, basically, of a sonic conductor C together with circuits and transducers. A transmitter A transforms an incoming signal into a sonic pulse, receiver B detects the transmitted sound pulse and transforms it back into electrical form and a gate G is used either for recycling the output from B to A (or not recycling when erasure is desired) or for permitting the insertion of information from an external source. Thus stored information is constantly circulating and is available for immediate use. One example of such a store is the mercury delay-line, in which a tube of mercury is the sonic conductor and quartz crystals are the transducers. The present store uses the magnetostrictive effect for launching a pulse in a sonic conductor.

Mr. Fairclough is with Ferranti Ltd.

(2.2) Delay Time and Storage Capacity

It is clear that the delay introduced depends on the length of the path and the speed of sound in the material used. The velocity of longitudinal waves is given approximately by $\sqrt{(E)/\rho}$, where E is Young's modulus and ρ is the density. The capacity depends on the delay time and digit separation. For example, if nt is the delay, n digits separated by time t can be stored in the system. Hence in order to store 42 3 microsec digits an overall delay of 126 microsec is required.

(2.3) Need for 'Strobing'

If we consider a sonic line which is incorrectly adjusted such that its overall delay time differs by a small time Δt from an integral number of digit widths (variation of temperature has this effect, see Section 3.8), in every circulation the output will be displaced in time by Δt. This obviously would have disastrous consequences: e.g. after $t/\Delta t$ circulations, the stored information would be out of phase by one digit period. Hence it is necessary to 'strobe' (i.e. sample at a fixed repetition period) the output to give a delay which is an integral number of digits long and independent of small incorrect adjustment.

(3) USE OF THE MAGNETOSTRICTIVE EFFECT FOR A SONIC DELAY-LINE STORE

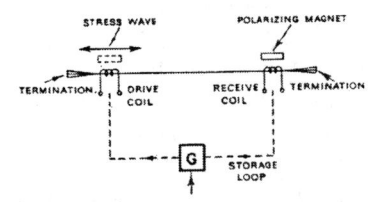

(3.1) Basic Magnetostrictive Store

In its simplest practical form, the sonic conductor is a length of magnetostrictive material threaded through a coil at each end, as shown in Fig. 1. If a current pulse is applied to one coil,

Fig. 1.—Magnetostrictive store.

that portion of the line affected by the resulting flux pulse undergoes a change of dimensions. This results in a longitudinal sonic pulse, or stress wave, being propagated down the line with the speed of sound in the material used. By virtue of an inverse magnetostrictive effect the stress wave, in passing through the other coil, causes a change of flux and hence a voltage to be induced in the coil.

(3.2) Need for Polarization

The stress wave causes changes of flux in the magnetic domains of the material, the direction of the change depending on whether the material possesses positive or negative magnetostriction. To make these changes of flux additive, the domains must be aligned

[491]

Annex No 3 Fairclough on basic delay-line store

by means of a static magnetic field, and to do this a small permanent magnet is most suitable, although an adjustable d.c. magnetizing current through the coil could be used. The polarity and magnitude of the output is dependent upon the direction and magnitude of the polarizing field such that positive, negative and zero outputs can be obtained.

The magnitude of the output is a function of the magnitude of the polarizing field. With a longitudinal field the output rises to a maximum as the field is increased, and then diminishes as saturation is reached. The location of the magnet is so chosen that the output is maximum; the magnetostrictive material is then biased to the optimum part of the magnetostrictive characteristic. A 25% increase in output signal is obtained with the polarizing magnet at the input in the case of the unit to be described.

(3.3) Terminations

It is necessary to terminate the delay line with some form of damping in order to prevent reflections from the free ends of the line. Some of the most suitable materials for this are thick grease, rubber, adhesive tapes or p.v.c. For the FPC 1 unit, p.v.c. in the form of Welvic paste has been found most suitable. This is a smooth-flowing viscous liquid which when heated to 150° C forms a soft rubbery solid. The termination is formed by repeated dipping, draining and heating to form a roughly conical shape. This provides a gradual change of mechanical impedance.

(3.4) Output Pulse-Shape

With reference to Fig. 2, consider a line with 'transmit' and 'receive' coils of effective lengths l_1 and l_2 where $l_2 > l_1$. Consider now a step function of current applied to the drive coil. The resulting current flow is shown in Fig. 2(a). If we consider the flux to change by a small amount $\delta\Phi_1$, then, by the magnetostrictive effect, a disturbance over the length l_1 results. Hence a stress wave of length l_1 is propagated. In time τ this will travel a distance $v\tau$, where v is the velocity of sound in the magnetostrictive material, and if the flux continues to change for a similar time τ, the resulting stress wave will be of length $v\tau + l_1$. It is obvious that the stress distribution is a function of $d\Phi_1/dt$ and will be of length $v\tau + l_1$. The distribution of the stress along the line is shown in Fig. 2(b). As the stress wave passes through the receive coil, the flux (Φ_2) produced by it (approximately proportional to stress), integrated over the coil length (l_2) is as shown in Fig. 2(c). The resulting output, proportional to $d\Phi_2/dt$, is shown in Fig. 2(d). In practice l_2 is chosen such that an output as shown in Fig. 2(e) is obtained. If we consider a square pulse of current to be applied to the drive coil, the resulting current flow is as shown in Fig. 2(f), and output voltage as in Fig. 2(g). By a reduction of the width of the input pulse, the two parts of the output can be combined as shown in Fig. 2(h). This is the output waveform used in the unit.

The digit spacing is such that consecutive '1's are combined as illustrated in Figs. 2(i) and 2(j), with a saving in bandwidth for a given resolution. Fig. 3 is a reproduction of the output waveform for the pattern 01101, reversed in polarity from Fig. 2(j) to show as positive-going the parts to be strobed.

An important factor which has been neglected in the above explanation is the finite time which it takes for the flux to penetrate the line material. This has the effect of modifying the length of the stress distribution by a further amount, corresponding to the time of penetration. A reduction in the resolution of the system results. Hence it is desirable to reduce this time to a minimum by making the eddy currents as small as possible. This can be done by using thin strip, thin-wall tube, etc., under the coil.

Further factors, such as attenuation and dispersion, have also been neglected and these are dealt with in Section 3.7.

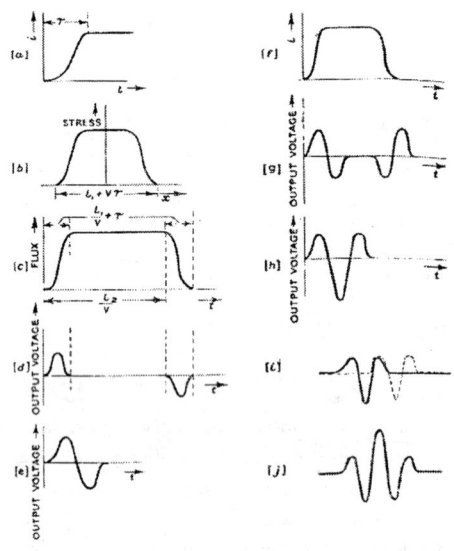

Fig. 2.—Output pulse-shape.

(a) Input current through drive coil resulting from applied step function.
(b) Distribution of stress along line at one instant of time.
(c) Variation of flux integrated over coil length l_2 as stress wave (b) passes through.
(d) Voltage induced in output coil due to (c).
(e) Output voltage obtained by reducing l_2.
(f) Input current through drive coil resulting from applied square-wave.
(g) Output voltage due to (f).
(h) Output voltage obtained by reducing pulse-width.
(i)
(j) } Illustrating combination of two consecutive digits.

Fig. 3.—Signal output resulting from digit pattern 011010.

(3.5) Coils

It is apparent that the lengths of the coils are determined by factors contained in Section 3.4 if we bear in mind that dispersion and flux-penetration time account for some loss in resolution. The time τ in Fig. 2(a) is defined by the 'transmit' coil inductance and its associated self- and stray-capacitance. Hence the inductance is so chosen that τ together with the coil length provides the necessary resolution. The maximum possible inductance of the 'receive' coil is determined by the frequency to which it is required to respond.

The object of the 'transmit' coil assembly is to convert the induced magnetic energy into mechanical energy. Hence it is necessary to ensure that as much as possible of the flux produced passes through the magnetostrictive material. To ensure this, the coil must be wound as close as possible to the line material. The same argument can be applied to the receive coil, only the object here is to convert the mechanical energy which has been propagated back into electrical energy. This demands that the magnetic flux links the whole winding, and again a closely-wound coil is desirable.

The coils used were wound with 1 500 turns of 48 s.w.g. wire on small moulded formers giving a winding diameter of 0·085 in

Annex No 3 Fairclough on basic delay-line store

and a coil width of 0·125 in. The 'transmit' and 'receive' coils were similar.

(3.6) Suitable Line Materials

The material in the transducer should exhibit high magnetostriction, and high change of permeability with stress (inverse magnetostriction, known as the Villari effect). The best commonly available material with these properties is annealed nickel. Initial experiments were carried out using various diameters of pure nickel tube of 0·0025 in wall thickness. Electrically this was quite satisfactory, but bending to the desired shape was difficult. Also, in order to improve the resolution of the system, to accommodate 3 microsec digits satisfactorily, it was necessary to slit the tube for about 0·75 in along its length under the coils, to minimize the eddy currents. This presented difficulties, to eliminate which a bundle of six 0·02 in × 0·005 in pure nickel strips were used and found satisfactory. Improved electrical performance was also obtained because of improved transducer efficiency, there being a larger bulk of material inside the coil and hence more energy transferred. Only the part of the nickel under the coil is annealed, since hard-drawn nickel has better transmission characteristics than annealed nickel.

(3.7) Losses and Limitations

The losses in a magnetostrictive delay line are such that amplification of the output is necessary in order to obtain a signal of usable magnitude. These losses are largely due to the inadequacy of the electro-mechanical coupling at the input and output. Further losses are outlined below:

(a) All wire materials cause attenuation of the sonic waves, which increases with frequency. Thus the wave is progressively robbed of its h.f. components as it travels along the wire, resulting in a reduction of the available bandwidth and hence a restriction of the digit spacing which can be accommodated, i.e. loss of resolution.

(b) Also, in order to accommodate a length of material in a practical system, some bending into spiral or helical form is necessary. This causes dispersion and further restrictions in digit spacing.

(c) Further dispersion and attenuation is caused by the sonic conductor supports. Expanded polythene tube has been found to be the most suitable material for minimum support attenuation and dispersion, since the sonic conductor becomes supported on a random selection of membranes formed by thin bubbles in the polythene.

Hence, for a given material and digit separation the maximum length of line is limited by the total amount of distortion which can be tolerated. This limit, however, is well above the length of the line in the present unit at the digit period of 3 microsec.

(3.8) Temperature Stability

It has been stated earlier that the delay time is a function of the elastic constants and length of line (Section 2.2). The delay time is therefore temperature dependent. The variation is largely due to the change of Young's modulus, the effect due to linear expansion being negligible by comparison. For nickel the thermal coefficient of the delay time is 0·14 microsec/millisec/deg C. This is negligible in the case of the FPC 1 and a variation of ±20° C results in a change of delay time of ±0·35 microsec; this is well within the capabilities of the type of strobe circuit used).

(4) DETAILED DESCRIPTION OF THE UNIT

(4.1) General

The rapid-access store in FPC 1 consists of 56 single-word lines of 42-digit capacity, and four of 35-digit capacity. Since a single-digit delay is inherent in the signal-shaping circuit, delays of 41 and 34 digits are required in the line (see Section 4.2.3), which corresponds to 23·5 in and 19·5 in of nickel respectively. With reference to the block schematic (Fig. 4), the associated line

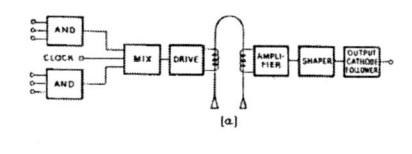

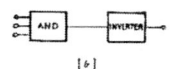

Fig. 4.—Block schematic.

circuit provides means for writing, storing and continuous reading of information, together with facilities for erasing by means of an inverter and associated input gate. The circuit utilizes three 12AT7-type double-triode valves, two and a half of which are used in the line circuit. The spare half-valve is the inverter.

The basic waveforms are as described in a paper[2] on the logical circuits with which the sonic stores are used, and are as shown in Fig. 5 of that paper.

(4.2) Circuit (Fig. 5)

(4.2.1) Drive Circuit, V_2.

The input facilities provided [as shown in the block schematic (Fig. 4)] are two triple-input 'AND' gates, the outputs of which are mixed together to produce 1·5 microsec-wide clocked-up digits at 3 microsec digit spacing, at the grid of the driving valve. This forms the gate for circulation control (as discussed in Section 2.1), and line selection in decoding operations. A clocked-up digit switches a current of 13 mA through the drive valve, and this current is stabilized by the use of a 'long tail' cathode resistor. The damping of the coil (l_1) to prevent ringing consists of a parallel 47-kilohm resistor. A 150-ohm resistor in series with the drive coil (on the h.t. side) is provided to monitor the drive current, the h.t. supply being +300 volts.

(4.2.2) Amplifier, V_3V_4.

The amplifier consists of two stages of triode amplification with a small degree of overall negative feedback. This provides some stability against valve ageing and at the same time is useful as a gain control to take into account the small variation in line performance. The pick-up coil (l_2) which drives the amplifier is the same as its associated drive coil. The useful output voltage from this is approximately 1 volt when damped by a parallel 22-kilohm resistor. As a further guard against ageing, the second stage has a long tail which stabilizes the no-signal current at 8·5 mA, and the h.t. supply for this stage is also +300 volts. The output signal from the second stage must be positive and a magnitude of 30 volts is required.

The polarity of the output is determined by the direction of the polarizing field, and the input and output coil connections (the reversal of any of the latter reversing the output polarity). The direction of each, on assembly, is so chosen that the output is positive. The feedback control is used to give the required +30 volts: in this condition the feedback is approximately 12 dB, and only slight variations from this figure are required to take into account line differences.

(4.2.3) Shaper and Output Circuits, V_5, V_6.

The shaping and output circuits consist of a digit delay circuit,[2] which produces standard digits as used throughout the computer. The input grid of the digit delay circuit is biased at −15 volts. Positive-going signals from the amplifier reach about 1 volt positive, at which point they are limited by a diode and series

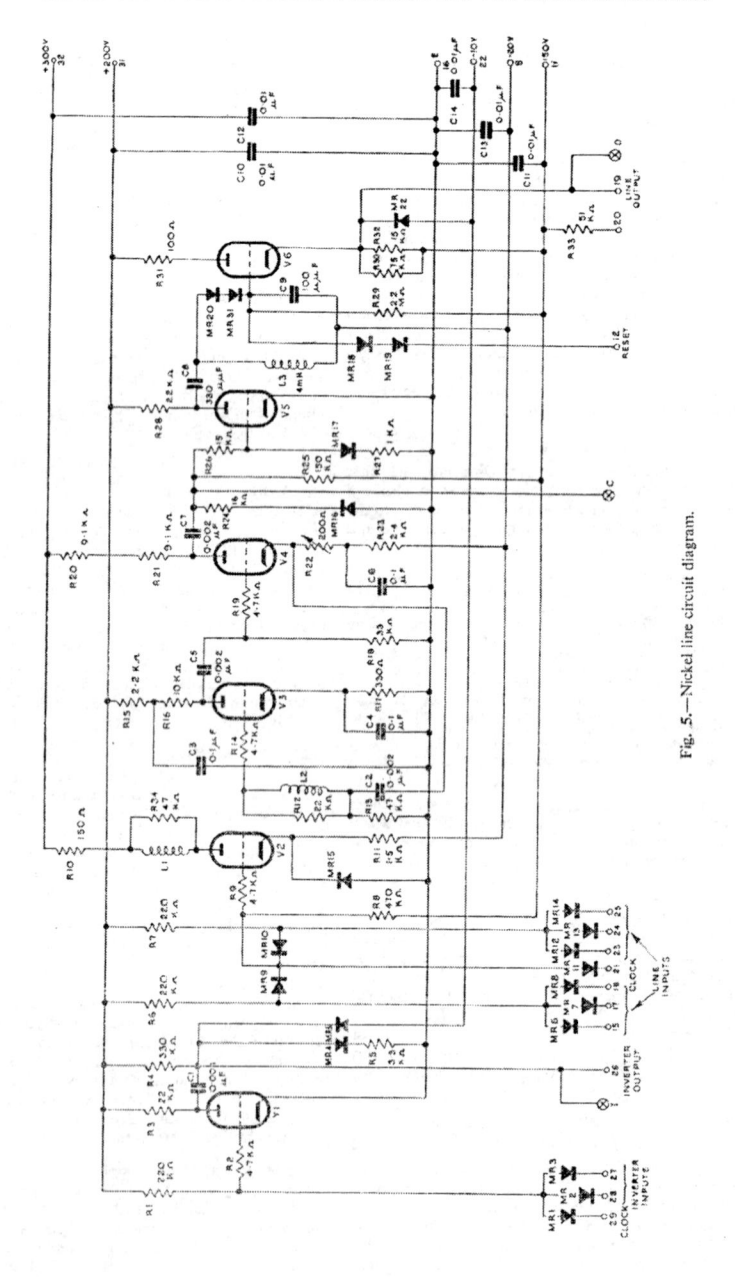

Annex No 3 Fairclough on basic delay-line store

Fig. 5.—Nickel line circuit diagram.

Annex No 3 Fairclough on basic delay-line store

resistor between grid and earth. The result is that the positive peaks of the signal simulate clocked-up digits (i.e. the width of the signal at earth level is approximately 1·5 microsec). Any 'noise' present (in the form of slight reflections in the line or pick-up) is at −15 volts and well beyond cut-off of the valve.

(4.2.4) **Inverter, V_1.**

The inverter is an a.c.-coupled circuit preceded by a triple-input 'AND' gate. By means of the gate, inverter input digits are 'AND'ed with clock to produce clocked-up digits at the grid. The 'clocking' is necessary to provide a signal out of the inverter which can be condenser-coupled and d.c. restored, a d.c. coupling which could drive the circulation gate being undesignable without an extra valve. The resulting inverted anode-swing is diode-limited from −10 volts to a few volts positive. The two inputs to the 'AND' gate are used as part of the decoding and line-selection arrangements in the computer.

(4.3) Mechanical

The nickel line is mounted on a sub-assembly which forms a plug-in unit, mounted on the wiring side of a standard package as shown in Fig. 6. The two lengths (35 and 42 digits) are accommodated on the same assembly, and the circuit plate for each is similar. A screwdriver adjustment of the position of the 'transmit' coil relative to the line is available at the bottom left-hand corner of the valve platform.

(4.4) Strobing

As mentioned in Section 2.3, strobing of the output signal is necessary, and is effected by the 'clocking' of the line output signal at the input gate, the line output signal being lengthened to the end of the next clock pulse (defined by 'reset') in the output shaping circuits. The effect of varying the length of the line by the input-coil adjustment is shown in Fig. 7, where it is seen that considerable tolerance on the coil position produces digits suitable for feeding to the input 'AND' gate. There is a range of adjustment (about 2 turns) over which the width of the output pulses hardly varies, owing to the fact that the front edge of the pulse is determined either by the back edge of 'reset' or the back edge of the signal at the grid of V_5—whichever is the later. Further adjustment in the direction of lengthening the line reduces the width of the output pulse. The line will store correctly with the output pulse narrowed down to clock width. However such a reduction in width reduces the allowable delay due to logical operations in external circuits driven from the line unit. In fact the outputs from the lines in FPC I are not involved in any complicated logical operations before further clocking, and so the allowable adjustment range is considerably greater than two turns.

(4.5) Setting-up Procedure

Two adjustments have to be made: (a) amplifier gain, and (b) overall delay time.

Adjustment (a) is effected by feeding any convenient digit

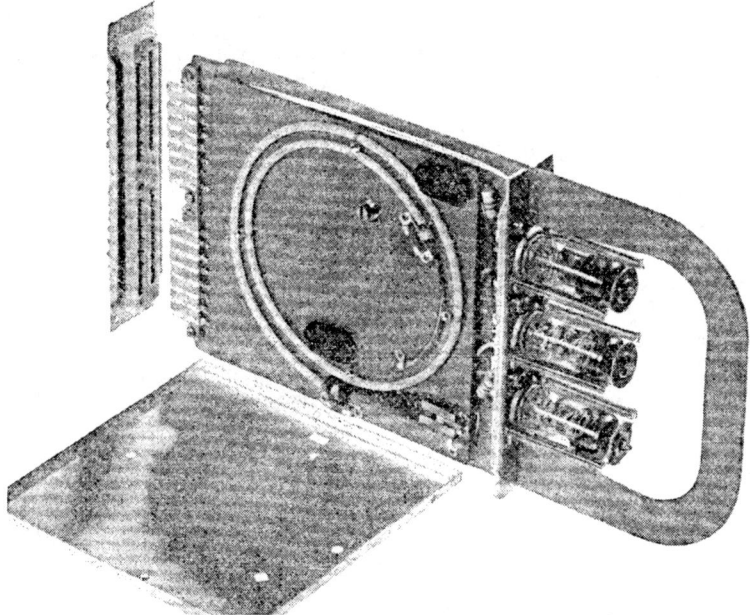

Fig. 6.—A package with a nickel delay-line forming a single-word register.
The recirculating amplifier and the control circuits are also carried on this package.

pattern into the line and adjusting the feedback control (as already explained) to give a +30-volt (magnitude) signal at monitor point C (Fig. 5).

Adjustment (b) is carried out by viewing both the input and corresponding output digits on a cathode-ray tube, the input being a single digit which repeats after a known interval. If this digit interval is 42 (assuming that a 42-digit line is being adjusted), the output digit, when the line is properly set up, corresponds in time with the input digit. Hence they give a coincident picture

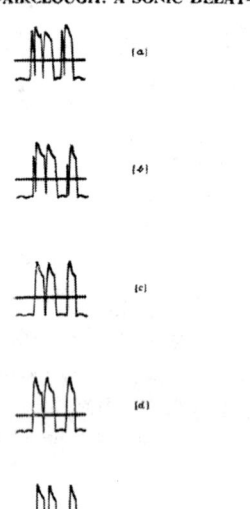

Annex No 3 Fairclough on basic delay-line store

Fig. 7.—Waveforms.

The effect of varying the length of the line through the range of adjustment provided. 4 turns (equivalent to 0·34 microsec) of the adjusting screw between each picture. Digit pattern 011010. (c), (d) and (e) are suitable outputs.

on the cathode-ray-tube screen. By adjustment of the position of the 'transmit' coil with respect to the line, this condition can be obtained. The procedure is similar for the 35-digit line, where a repetition frequency of 35 digits is used. However, a digit which repeats every 42 or 35 digits may not be readily available, but the procedure is substantially the same for any digit period. Say, for example, a digit which repeats every 10 is available, and a 42 line is being adjusted; when comparing the input and output there should be a difference between the two pictures of two digit periods, the output lagging the input.

Fig. 7 shows the effect of varying the length of a line, through the optimum setting, by four screw-turns at a time. This gives the procedure for adjusting to the correct length. Outputs (c), (d) and (e) are suitable (see Section 4.4).

(5) ACKNOWLEDGMENTS

Earlier work on nickel delay-line units was described by Robbins and Millership[4] and further work has been done by G. G. Scarrott. Thanks are due to the latter for suggestions on line construction. Thanks are also due to C. E. Owen for suggestions on the circuit designs in the unit described, and to Ferranti Ltd., for permission to publish the paper.

(6) REFERENCES

(1) Paper on the FPC 1 Digital Computer to be communicated.
(2) OWEN, C. E.: 'A Set of Standard Logical Circuit Packages for Series Digital Computers.' (Not yet published.)
(3) DE BARR, A. E., ROBBINS, R. C., and MILLERSHIP, R.: 'Magnetostriction, Storage Systems for a High Speed Digital Computer', *British Journal of Applied Physics*, 1951, **2**, p. 304.
(4) ROBBINS, R. C., and MILLERSHIP, R.: 'Applications of Magnetostriction Delay Lines' (H.M. Stationery Office, 1953), p. 199.
(5) PINKERTON, J. M. N.: 'Automatic Frequency Control', *Electronic Engineering*, 1951, **23**, p. 142.
(6) ARENBERG, D. L.: 'Ultrasonic Delay Lines,' I.R.E. Convention Record of 1954, Part 6, p. 63.
(7) BRADBURD, E. M.: 'Magnetostrictive Delay Line', *Electrical Communication*, 1951, **28**, p. 46.
(8) CZERLINSKY, E.: 'The Propagation of Supersonic Waves in Wires', *Akustische Beihefte*, 1942, **7**, No. 1, p. 12.
(9) HUNTINGDON, H. B., EMSLIE, A. G., HUGHES, V. W., and OTHERS: 'Ultrasonic Delay Lines', *Journal of the Franklin Institute*, 1948, **245**, p. 1 and p. 101.
(10) MEES, R. W., DARR, J. H., and GRIMSLEY, J. D.: 'Metal Ultrasonic Delay Lines', *Journal of Research of the National Bureau of Standards*, 1953, **51**, p. 209.
(11) BOZORTH, R. M.: 'Ferromagnetism' (D. Van Nostrand, 1951).
(12) KOLSKY, H.: 'Stress Waves in Solids' (Oxford University Press).
(13) HUETER, T. F., and BOLT, R. H.: 'Sonics' (Wiley, 1955).
(14) FAGEN, M. D.: 'Bibliography on Ultrasonic Delay Lines' (Bell System Technical Monograph No. 2317).

Annex No 4 Merry & Maudsley on the magnetic drum

THE MAGNETIC-DRUM STORE OF THE COMPUTER PEGASUS

By I. W. MERRY, B.Sc.(Eng.), Graduate, and B. G. MAUDSLEY, A.M.I.Mech.E.

(The paper was first received 23rd May, and in revised form 29th June, 1956.)

SUMMARY

The paper describes the mechanical detail, logical arrangement and electronic design of a fully-packaged drum storage system. The mechanical design of the drum has been based on current extreme-precision machine-tool practice, for reliability. Methods of track selection are electronic on both writing and reading, taking the form of electronic cross-bar switches. On the reading side, the switch is formed by an array of balanced germanium-diode gates which are interposed directly after the magnetic heads, prior to amplification. The system reliability proved to be very satisfactory in the light of the first 1 500 hours' operating experience.

(1) INTRODUCTION

The main characteristics of a digital information-storage system which determine its suitability as the main store of a computer are capacity, mean access time and cost. Subsidiary considerations include non-volatility of storage, insusceptibility to interference and freedom from temperature or humidity dependency. No storage method in use at present can be said to be satisfactory from all aspects, but in the majority of digital computers a magnetic-drum store[1] is employed, since this offers the most satisfactory compromise between the various criteria; it is, in fact, the cheapest storage medium per stored binary digit with the exception of magnetic tape, where the mean access time is several orders greater.

Since information recorded on a magnetic drum is not available instantaneously, but can be read only at intervals of one revolution, one of the aims of the computer-logic designer is to organize the operations involving the main store so as to retard computation as little as possible. In the computer Pegasus[2] this is achieved by transferring information from the drum to the computing store in blocks of eight 42-digit words. The computing store consists mainly of 48 single-word immediate-access registers, so that operations not involving the main store commence virtually instantaneously.

Paralysis of the reading amplifiers after writing and the time taken in switching from one track to another introduce delays in the system. These are reduced in the store to be described to 504 and 252 microsec respectively. Fully electronic switching is required for this speed of operation, and by switching before amplification in diode gates, a saving in the number of reading amplifiers is achieved.

(2) SPECIFICATION OF THE MAIN STORE

A total storage of 5 120 words each of 42 binary digits is provided, with a mean access time of approximately 8 millisec and a digit period of 3 microsec; 1 024 of these words form an isolated store to contain initial orders, assembly subroutines and engineer's test programmes.

For convenience in address decoding, the store is subdivided into 40 information tracks, each of 128 words; each information track thus consists of 16 blocks of eight words. The tracks are numbered from 0 to 39; tracks 32–39 contain the isolated store, on which it is not possible to write directly by programme, so that the contents are protected against accidental erasure or modification; information is read from these tracks in the normal way, as for tracks 0–31.

(3) THE STORAGE DRUM

(3.1) Mechanical Assembly

The drum is a packaged unit of robust construction (Fig. 1). The actual rotating drum is 10 in in diameter and 6¼ in long, machined from an aluminium-alloy forging, and is housed in a machined cast-aluminium body. After final assembly, the working surface is diamond-turned at the working speed to be concentric to within 0·00005 in.

The drum and the rotor of the driving motor are mounted on a rigid nickel-molybdenum-steel shaft running in three matched pairs of preloaded angular-contact ball-races to specification ABEC7. The mounting of the drum in the computer is such that a replacement could if necessary be fitted in a matter of minutes.

(3.2) The Driving Motor

The drum is driven by a 3-phase squirrel-cage 4-pole induction motor of high rotor resistance, which is air cooled by an internal blower mounted on the drum shaft. To permit of rotational speeds in excess of 3 000 r.p.m. a special supply of non-standard frequency is required, and for convenience 150 c/s is selected. A small alternator coupled to the main motor-alternator set of the computer is the source of this supply, and under full excitation the drum motor develops a maximum power of approximately ⅓ h.p. Under these conditions the drum runs up to full speed in less than 35 sec. Speed control of the drum is obtained by altering the alternator output voltage through control of the excitation. This is described more fully in Section 7.

(3.3) Magnetic Coating

The drum is coated with a suspension of magnetic iron oxide—Fe_2O_3—of medium coercivity in an epoxy resin. No great difficulty is found in applying this coating, which is sprayed on to the drum with a conventional paint spray. Subsequent curing of the coating is accelerated by infra-red heating, but the curing method is not critical. After this operation, the coating is lightly buffed with a lint-free duster, and is then ready for use. The coating could be diamond-turned, but this is unnecessary since the thickness is sufficiently uniform.

(3.4) Head Construction and Mounting

Common single-gap writing and reading heads are used and are made from standard low-frequency sintered-ferrite blanks (Fig. 2) 60-mil thick, ground to a track width of 30 mils. The head winding has 34 turns divided equally between the two halves of the head.

Groups of 10 heads are mounted in pre-assembled blocks with head-centre spacings of 120 mils (Fig. 3). A total of 100 heads are mounted on the drum and tracks 30-mil wide are interlaced

Annex No 4 Merry & Maudsley on the magnetic drum

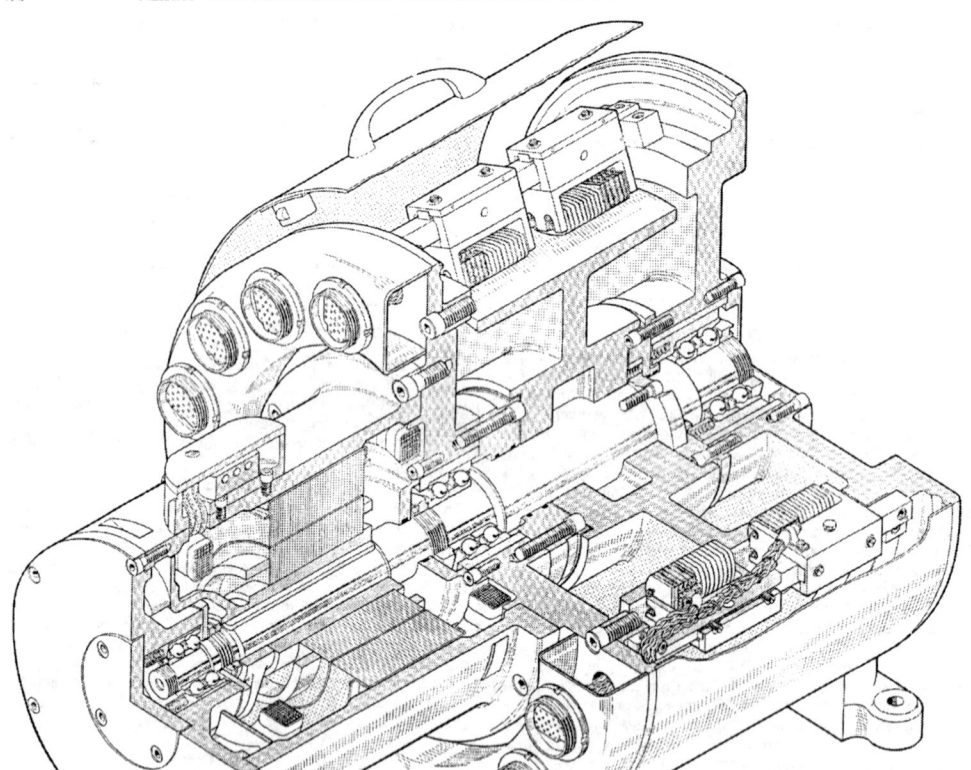

Fig. 1.—Mechanical assembly of the storage drum.

at 60-mil centres. The mounting fixtures (Fig. 4) each carry a pair of blocks of heads.

The head gap is formed by a beryllium–copper shim 1 mil thick, and in any block the accuracy of gap alignment is within 0·2 mil. Much greater variations occur in the depth of the gaps, and this has an undesirable effect on head sensitivity (see Section 6).

(3.5) **Arrangement of Tracks on the Drum**

(3.5.1) Diplexing for 6 microsec Operations.

A packing density of 80 digits per inch was chosen for the drum; with a drum diameter of 10 in and a rotational speed of approximately 4 000 r.p.m., this represents a digit rate of approximately 6 microsec, whereas the computer digit period is 3 microsec. No great increase in packing density, drum diameter

or speed were desired, and with an actual speed of 3 720 r.p.m., words from the computer proper are written on to pairs of tracks on the drum, alternate odd or even digits being routed either to an odd or an even track.

On reading, the pairs of signals are gated with odd and even digit pulses respectively before recombination.

An ambiguity in the use of the term 'track' arises from this diplexing operation; for programme purposes a track is a complete entity storing whole words, but the engineering usage refers to the location of signals recorded by a single head.

(3.5.2) Timing-Signal Tracks.

(3.5.2.1) *Clock Tracks.*

In the computer Pegasus, the basic timing waveform from which all other waveforms are derived is a square wave of

Annex No 4 Merry & Maudsley on the magnetic drum

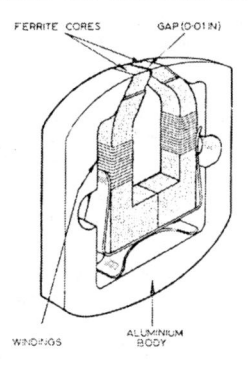

Fig. 2.—Single unmounted head.

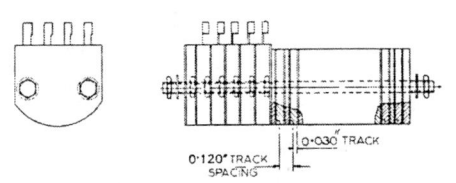

Fig. 3.—Block of ten heads.

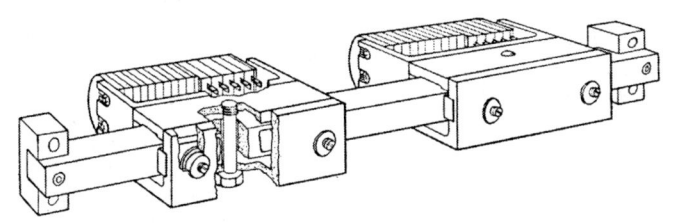

Fig. 4.—Slide assembly containing two blocks of heads.

track head is used only for reading the semi-permanent isolated store. However, the isolated store must itself be written in, and occasionally amended; for this purpose the second working clock track is provided, read by a head in a block remote from that used by the isolated store.

(3.5.2.2) *Address Tracks.*

The relative angular position of the drum at any instant is read from an address track. As with the information tracks, the address track is in reality a pair of tracks on the drum, in order to accommodate both odd and even digits in the address. Furthermore, two separate address track pairs are needed, for the same reason as for the two clock tracks; each of the pairs of address tracks on the drum is associated solely with one of the two clock tracks, and is read by heads in the same block as its associated clock track.

From the programmer's point of view the address track is divided into 128 single-word divisions exactly like an information track. Written permanently in every word in digit periods 0–12 is a different 7-digit binary number representing the address of that word, from 0 to 127. Addresses within the eight word blocks beginning at word 0, 8, 16, etc., are in natural sequence; the order of the blocks, however, is simply permutated so that successively numbered blocks are separated by two blocks. When the block containing tracks 0–7 is called block 0, that containing tracks 8–15 is called block 1, and that containing tracks 16–23 is called block 2, etc., the block order around the address track becomes 0, 11, 6, 1, 12, 7, 2, 13, 8, 3, 14, 9, 4, 15, 10, 5.

The purpose of this block address permutation is to allow successively numbered blocks to be written or read back

3 microsec period and unity mark/space ratio known as the 'clock' pulse.[2]

There is no asynchronous buffer between the magnetic-drum store and the rest of the computer, so that signals read from the drum must be in exact synchronism with the clock pulse. This is most simply arranged by deriving the clock pulse from a square wave actually recorded on the drum, closing on itself in exactly 42 × 128 cycles.

As a precaution against accident, and also because two distinct clock tracks are required, the output waveforms of which must be in phase, a master clock track is first written on the drum, from which further identically phased clock tracks may be copied; the master clock track is not used for any other purpose, and no connection is made from it to the computer circuits, except temporarily when the operating clock tracks are being written.

Two operating clock tracks are required, since it is not possible to write on a head which lies close to the head reading the clock track, for the crosstalk disturbs the clock phasing. Normally, the block of heads adjacent to the block containing the clock

sequentially with a small amount of intervening computation or logical operation in the rest of the computer. In this way a small but worth-while degree of optimum programming is obtained automatically at no extra cost or complexity.

An odd-parity check digit is written in digit period 39 in conformity with the principle of making all words throughout the computer of odd parity except where this is impossible.

To ensure that words in the magnetic drum are correctly phased, digit by digit, with words in the rest of the computer, a '1' is written in every word in the address track in digit period 0. This '1' is called the 'locking digit', and no other digit time contains a '1' in every word. The commutator of the computer will circulate a single digit in a stable mode only if a gating digit supplied from the address track is present every word time in digit time 0. When the computer is switched on, the commutator jumps cyclically from one unstable condition to the next until it reaches the condition where the address-track locking digit occurs at the instant when the commutator circulating digit is at position '0'. A stable condition is then reached.

Annex No 4 Merry & Maudsley on the magnetic drum

The address track also contains a number of 1's varying from word to word which, when gated out of the address track and fed through a suitable amplifier to a small loudspeaker, act as a source of an approximately 500 c/s signal which can be arranged to indicate that the computer has ceased operation either as the result of a 'stop' order, or through some fault condition.[2]

(4) THE WRITING WAVEFORM

The writing waveform employs the phase-modulation[1] principle, where a '1' is represented by a cycle of trapezoidal waveform balanced about the zero axis, in a definite phase with respect to a timing waveform, and a '0' is represented by a similar signal of opposite phase. A sequence of alternate 1's and 0's is represented by a waveform roughly similar to that for a sequence of 1's, but of twice the period.

(4.1) Generation of Phase Modulation from Computer Logic

Since the digit period within the main store circuits is 6 microsec, two computer digit periods are available for the generation of each cycle of writing waveform.

Considering for simplicity a 10-digit number [Fig. 5(a)],

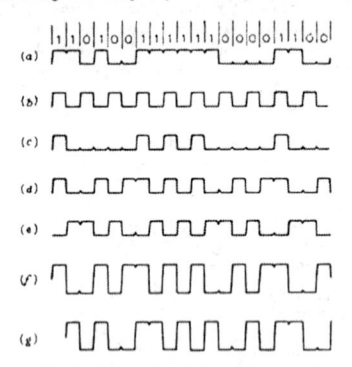

Fig. 5.—Generation of the writing waveform.
(a) Number.
(b) Even gate-waveform.
(c) Gated even digits.
(d) and (e) Push-pull signals to writing power amplifiers.
(f) Even 'write' waveforms.
(g) Odd 'write' waveforms.

alternate, odd or even, digits are routed by suitable gates [Fig. 5(b)] into two distinct channels, and are thereafter treated separately but similarly. Restricting discussion to the even digits [Fig. 5(c)], two waveforms are generated by the computer logic from the even digit pattern, namely

(a) That containing the original even digits and also the 1's in the odd digit periods which follow a '0' in the even periods [Fig. 5(d)].
(b) The complement of (a) [Fig. 5(e)].

These two waveforms are then applied to opposite sides of a push-pull amplifier which produces the writing waveform in its output transformer [Fig. 5(f)].

In a similar manner, the odd-digit pattern produces the waveform shown in Fig. 5(g).

(5) TRACK SELECTION

(5.1) Track Decoding

In both writing and reading operations, an information track is selected by its track number which must be in the range 0–39.

The track number is specified by suitable partial decoding of the six most significant address digits to give a 'one out of eight' and a 'one out of five' selected row and column of an 8 × 5 switch matrix; the remaining 24 decoding possibilities do not represent addresses and must not be called for.

The selected row-switching voltage is an output on a particular lead at −10 volts, the other seven row-switching outputs are at +13 volts. For column switching the converse is true, the selected-column output being at +13 volts.

In the following Sections, the descriptions of the various circuits refer to the odd or the even digit channel separately unless the contrary is stated.

(5.2) The 'Write'/'Read' Switch

The circuits in which track selection occurs are contained in five special packaged units known as 'write'/'read' switches, each with an associated package on which is mounted a small push-pull power amplifier for generating the writing currents. These ten packages form, in effect, two separate electronic crossbar switches in an 8 × 5 array, one for writing selection and the other for reading selection. The common elements in the two switches are the head transformers, which have three windings: a high-impedance primary connected to the writing circuits; a low-impedance secondary connected to one of the heads; and a high-impedance tertiary connected to a balanced diode gate leading to the reading amplifier circuits.

(5.2.1) Writing Selection.

The pairs of anodes of the five power amplifiers are connected to pairs of busbars in their respective 'write'/'read' switches (Fig. 6). Each half-primary winding is connected to its busbar through two germanium diodes in series. The eight centre-taps are brought out on contacts, and connected in common across the five switch packages in the computer back-wiring[2] to give eight row-selection connections.

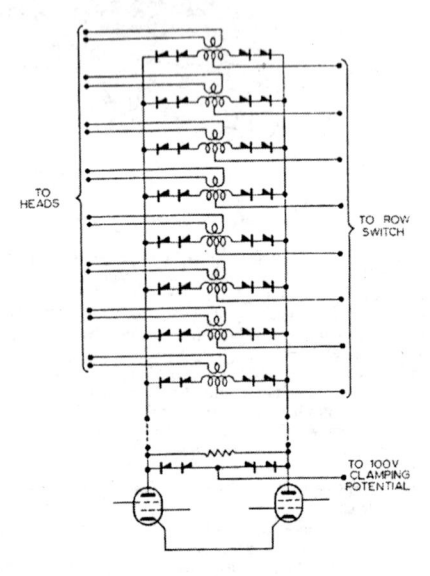

Fig. 6.—'Write' busbar details.

Annex No 4 Merry & Maudsley on the magnetic drum

Similarly, the address track is written throughout with odd parity. A counter circuit, shared between the drum-store and the address-track circuits is arranged to check that all words read from the drum retain this odd parity. The address track is checked continuously except during 'read' orders, when the words transferred are checked. Any single error in reading will cause the words read to have even parity; this is arranged to stop machine operations and to light a warning lamp on the control console.

A check on the timing margin of the strobing circuits is possible by altering the phase of the clock signal from which the strobe waveform is derived. Any marginally strobed pulses will then cause failure.

(9) CONCLUSION

Over a period of approximately 1 000 hours' operation the magnetic-store circuits have worked satisfactorily with only three circuit failures, none of which has occurred in the 'write'/'read' switch package. Low-level switching using germanium point-contact diodes has been shown to be very satisfactory.

Although variations in the phase of signal output occur from head to head, these have been found insufficient to cause trouble and do not necessitate individual adjustments on the various channels although the heads are mounted in blocks of ten.

(10) ACKNOWLEDGMENTS

Acknowledgments are due to Mr. W. Boneham of Boneham and Turner, Ltd., for assistance in mechanical design of the drum, to Mr. N. Katz of Epsylon, Ltd., for the special heads, to Messrs. H. Marchant, B. A. Nolan and J. Woodgate for their assistance in the design of the storage system, to Mr. W. S. Elliott for his help and encouragement, and to Ferranti, Ltd., for permission to publish the paper.

(11) REFERENCES

(1) WILLIAMS, F. C., KILBURN, T., and THOMAS, G. E.: 'Universal High-Speed Digital Computers: A Magnetic Store', *Proceedings I.E.E.*, Paper No. 1191 M, October, 1951 (99, Part II, p. 94).

(2) ELLIOTT, W. S., OWEN, C. E., DEVONALD, C. H., and MAUDSLEY, B. G.: 'The Design Philosophy of Pegasus, a Quantity-Production Computer' (see page 188).

(3) WESTMIJZE, W. K.: 'Studies on Magnetic Recording', Philips Research Report No. 8, 1953, pp. 148, 161, 245 and 343 (Thesis, University of Leyden, March, 1953).

Annex No 5 Braunholtz describes Pegasus

The Design of the Pegasus Computer

(Part 1)

By T. G. H. Braunholtz*

It is three and a half years since the structure and Order Code of Pegasus were decided on. This article records some of the background of opinion from which the design was thought out. Only topics which can be discussed simply have been included, and the article is intended to be comprehensible to readers with only a slight knowledge of computers.

In Part 2 of this article the more detailed engineering aspects will be dealt with, with particular emphasis on the implications of building the machine from standard plug-in packages.

THE Ferranti Pegasus Computer is a medium-sized general-purpose digital computer, designed by Ferranti Ltd in collaboration with the National Research and Development Corporation. To give a general picture of the scale of the machine: the store consists of a drum of 5 000 words and an immediate access store of 55 words, the multiplication time is 2msec, the basic operation time is 0·3msec, and the digit repetition rate is 330kc/s. It is perhaps worth remarking that, as a guide to the overall speed of a computer, none of the figures given is any use by itself. Speed can only be judged by considering the whole structure of a computer.

It is clear by now that a second stage in the development of digital computers is underway, marked by a serious endeavour to make them less difficult to use. Since the Pegasus goes some way in this direction and contains a number of novel features, an account of the ideas behind the design may be of interest.

A typical arrangement of the Pegasus computer

This article is limited to the less technical and detailed aspects of computer design, and does not attempt to discuss points which can be of interest to programmer's only.

After a few remarks on the cost and reliability of computers, there follows a discussion of the principal subject of this article, the design of a digital computer from the programmer's point of view. This is divided into two sections, of which the first is more general, and the second is concerned with the order code.

MINIMIZATION OF COST

A considerable part of the cost of the more expensive computers is due to such features as very fast multipliers and shifts, and very large immediate-access stores. These have been dispensed with in Pegasus, but the design is such as to minimize the loss in convenience and speed arising from their exclusion.

Reliability, of course, takes precedence over cost. However, the cause of unreliability lies generally in a few weaknesses in the machine design, and though a great deal may be spent in investigating and eliminating these weaknesses, their correction is not generally very expensive in equipment. Thus, with well developed techniques, cost and reliability are not in serious conflict with one another.

Ease of use in a computer is, too, as much a matter of careful analysis of the problems of programming in relation to the design of the computer, as of the size and cost of the machine.

RELIABILITY

An unreliable machine involves the user in much more trouble than simple doubt as to the accuracy of the solutions obtained. A programmer using an unreliable machine wishes to ensure checked results even when occasional errors in computation are occurring. To do this he divides his programme into sections each of which is checked separately and can be repeated if the check fails. His programme consequently becomes far longer and more difficult to code; its speed drops and its complexity rises. A programmer can easily involve himself in more thought and effort in executing his safety measures than in the whole of the rest of his problem.

With a really reliable machine, checking can be simple. The question naturally asked by electronic engineers when computers were first built was how reliability was to be achieved. That problem has long since been largely solved. It is more pertinent today to ask why reliability is sometimes not achieved, and two principal reasons can be found.

Firstly, some of the computers which have been in use for several years have been prototype models incorporating new electronic techniques for experimental purposes. Naturally these were not often completely reliable in their first embodiment, and it may have been impossible to carry out the needed modifications within the framework of the existing computer.

In view of this, it has been the policy in designing Pegasus to use only existing and well-tried engineering techniques.

Secondly, there is a great temptation to solve difficult design problems by lowering the safety margins. But in computers the consequences of errors are so serious that wherever there is doubt as to the performance of a component, the most pessimistic view should be taken. It is tempting to reduce safety margins because engineering problems would be greatly eased by doing so, but the temptation has to be resisted.

---

* *Ferranti Ltd.*

Annex No 5 Braunholtz describes Pegasus

Programmer's Analysis of Machine Design

In this section design from the programmer's point of view is discussed in some detail. The broad aims in design were to achieve

(a) Ease of programming.
(b) Ample capacity for handling general engineering and scientific problems.
(c) High speed of computation.

MAIN STORE CAPACITY

Opinions as to a desirable size of main store are bound to be at variance with one another, but it seems wise at present to err on the side of too much storage rather than too little. While it is true that almost any amount of storage seems to be profitably used if it is available, it is our experience that 1 000 words would be inconveniently small, that 2 000 words might possibly be sufficient, and that 4 000 words should be ample, especially if magnetic tape is used in addition. The main store of Pegasus is a magnetic drum with a capacity of 5 120 words of 40 digits each. The drum consists of 40 tracks containing 128 words each. Since the speed of rotation is 3 750 rev/min the maximum access-time is 16msec.

OPTIMUM PROGRAMMING

It is possible in machines with a magnetic drum main store, or any other form of storage with a long access-time, to arrange that orders are obeyed directly from that store. If, however, the drum revolution time is long in comparison with the basic order time, the orders should be placed so that it is only rarely that a drum revolution is wasted through waiting for an order or a number. The accomplishment of this is known as optimum programming. An alternative is to have sufficient immediate-access storage (or, at any rate, quick access storage) to be able to carry out all operations in the fast store. The size of fast store required, both for ease of coding, and for speed of computation, can be made surprisingly small if access to the main store is made easy.

Optimum programming, on the other hand, gives rise to many difficulties. It has been stated half seriously that for a reasonable expenditure of effort by the programmer on optimum programming, the average time spent in obeying orders is proportional to the square root of the revolution time of the drum (the unit of time being the basic operation time of the machine). With optimum programming, the achievement of high speeds requires a great deal of thought and ingenuity, which, though presenting an attractive challenge to the programmer, does not lead to good use of the computer. A highly developed use of sub-routines is exceedingly difficult with optimum programming, and moreover it is found that when more than about half the available storage is occupied by a programme and its data, the difficulties in optimum programming become very great. These last two remarks apply particularly to forms of storage with a maximum access-time greater than 32 word-times. With 32 word-times or less, efficient sub-routines can be constructed, and an efficient use of the storage can and has been achieved.

For these reasons optimum programming was rejected as unsatisfactory for Pegasus.

THE COMPUTING STORE

By providing an immediate-access computing store in which all operations are carried out, it has been possible to avoid optimum programming in Pegasus. This computing store contains 55 words of 39 digits each. There is immediate access to each word.

Each word contains either one number or two orders. All orders are obeyed from the computing store and all arithmetic operations are carried out on numbers held in the computing store.

Transfer between the main store and the computing store is either by eight-word blocks or a single word at a time.

The reader will probably feel surprised that 55 words should be sufficient for general programming purposes. He will convince himself most easily by trying programming for himself, but some examination of the problem may be helpful.

USE OF COMPUTING STORE

For general usefulness, a more important factor than the absolute size of the computing store is the number of blocks into which it is divided for purposes of transfer to and from the main store. We have found that six blocks, each of eight words, in addition to the seven accumulators, is ample. Transfer between the computing store and main store is normally in eight-word blocks (single-word transfers being used for storage of rarely used counters when counter space is short). Generally, three blocks will be used for data and results, one for counters and other variables, and two for programme. Often this allocation is not kept to, and in simple programmes several blocks may well be left unused.

The change-over from one block of programme to the next, which might be expected to be a serious difficulty, may be accomplished very simply. Two orders are picked up at once (i.e. in one word), so that if the first is a block-transfer and the second a jump order, then the sequence of operations will be as follows: the new block of programme will be brought down over the old (which is therefore obliterated) by the first order; then the second order, which is a jump, sends control to any position in the new block that is desired. This allows each block to be coded quite independently of the others.

SPEED AND INNER LOOPS

Generally 80 per cent or more of the time in a computation is spent in one or two inner loops. Consequently the speed of the inner loops determines the speed of the programme. One would like these inner loops to be held entirely in the fast store, and be run through perhaps eight times (a likely number since each block of data contains eight words), until further transfers of data become necessary. In fact this can almost always be done, and in this case one may expect half to one-third of the time to be spent on block transfers. The time spent in the rest of the programme will be small, and will probably consist mostly of block transfers, and we conclude that the high operating speed of the machine will at any rate not be smothered by block-transfer time.

THE SIZE OF THE COMPUTING STORE

The effect of variations in the size of the computing store may now be considered.

It is an interesting fact that there is little advantage to be gained by increasing the size of the fast store if the size of blocks is kept constant. However, if the size of blocks were increased to, say, 12 or 16 words and there were still six blocks a general improvement in the machine's performance would result, but the size of the computing store would be nearly doubled, which would be very expensive.

If the size of blocks were decreased to four words, not only would the machine be considerably slowed down, but programming would become more difficult because of the small number of orders held in each block.

It might be that the machine would be faster and easier

Annex No 5 Braunholtz describes Pegasus

to use if the number of blocks were increased from 6 to 8. However, so have more than 8 would only add to programming difficulties without a compensating gain, until the computing store were made large enough to carry out a computation almost without reference to the main store. This point is naturally enough rather ill defined, but is perhaps in the region of 500 to 1 000 words.

PROBLEMS OF TWO-LEVEL STORAGE

Two levels of storage are necessary if one is to get both a fast machine and an ample store at a reasonable price. The double store does complicate programming but the complication has been reduced to a minimum by special facilities in the order-code.

THE ORDER-CODE

Given a small computing store of the sort described, it is clearly very important that the order-code should allow concise coding. Quite on its own merits, however, it is felt that a very full, carefully organized order-code is essential to a computer. The coding and testing of a programme is a very lengthy process, and great increases in effectiveness may be gained by simplification of coding.

THE PROBLEM OF CODING

In applying a computer to a problem, the first stage is to decide on the mathematical method to be used. The next stage is to prepare a 'flow-diagram' (describing the operations to be carried out, broken down into small units). The third stage is the translation of the flow diagram to coded sheets. The following discussion is limited to the problems that arise during that stage. In fact, however, each stage affects the other stages, and, since alterations are always made as the structure of the problem broadens out and clarifies, each stage reacts on the previous stages, so that the problem is so interconnected that it cannot accurately be considered as broken into separate stages.

There is little agreement as to what constitutes a useful coding facility, and what a coding difficulty. It seems that programmers tend not to be aware of the amount of effort they are diverting from their main problems to the coding of awkward points. For, when coding, the full powers of a programmer are called forth to weigh, compare, co-ordinate and to mould his programme into an elegant and unified whole.

If this is not done, then alterations, which will certainly be made as the work develops, will each add to the illogicality of a rapidly complicating programme. The final results will be errors in programming, and unreasonable interrelations and particularities in the programme which make it slow, difficult to use, and difficult to adapt.

An effect of coding difficulties more serious than the obvious waste of time involved is that the programmer's attention is diverted from the more fundamental features of his problem to tricky points of coding. As a result the fundamental features may not get the attention they deserve.

Since the greater part of a programme is concerned with organization, particular attention should be paid to easing its coding.

CODING DIFFICULTIES

A coding difficulty is defined as a point in coding which takes much of the programmer's attention, and which might reasonably be avoided by an alteration or addition to the code. An experienced programmer will naturally develop his ability to overcome coding difficulties with little effort. It is therefore particularly important to avoid coding difficulties in a machine to be used much by part time or inexperienced programmers.

Coding difficulties arise from (among other things)

(a) *Exceptions;* that is, such details of the actions of orders as have no reason obvious to the programmer for their existence, which are not automatically remembered, and which are not common to a whole series of orders.

(b) *Confusion,* as when two orders are very similar and apt to be confused.

(c) *Lack of independence,* arising when one order affects others in ways that are not naturally in the programmer's mind.

(d) *Complexity,* as in subtle codes, the possibilities of which delight many a mathematician, and in which remarkably concise sequences are often possible by sufficient thought.

(e) *Ambiguity,* as when an operation can be carried out by two sequences of orders about as good as one another: it is inhuman to waste effort in selecting the best. To do so is not as over-meticulous as might appear, since the programmer will feel that the decision reached will have further application whenever in the future a similar situation arises. The trouble is that the number of such situations is very great in certain codes.

(f) *Awkwardness,* for example, when floating-point operations are lengthy to code. (Many troubles of awkwardness can be avoided by a well organized system of sub-routines.)

A few particular conditions which it is felt a code should satisfy are listed below:

A code should be easy to remember, both to aid the actual coding, and to facilitate reading and checking the coded sheets; so that it may be easy to remember, the orders should be arranged according to some simple rules. Particularly, if there are many jump orders (as there should be) these must be arranged logically. Again, the code should be 'consistent'—there should not be gaps in the series of arithmetical or jump instructions.

A code should avoid unsigned numbers; the gain of one digit is small compared with the confusion created.

A code should allow simple working with both integers and fractions; allow simple programming of such operations as floating-point and double length arithmetic, and include many jumps in pairs with contrary sense. Jumps and switches in organization can then be arranged without much doubt as to the best coding.

The orders and their details should be as simple as possible.

It is perhaps not often realized how little extra equipment a full order-code needs beyond the requirements of a bare minimum code. The total equipment in a machine is certainly not increased by as much as 10 per cent.

PROVISION OF MULTIPLE ACCUMULATORS

This is one of the unconventional features of the design of Pegasus; it is based on a detailed examination of various possible order-codes.

An obvious starting point is the three-address code, with orders of the type $A+B \to C$. An examination of the use of this code shows that very often two of the addresses are the same, i.e. the order takes the two-address form $A+B \to A$. A further examination shows that in a high proportion of these cases the address A which occurs both as a source and destination is confined to a very few numbers. This leads to the suggestion that a restricted two-address code of the type $X+N \to X$, where X ranges over only a few addresses while N can be anywhere in the

Annex No 5 Braunholtz describes Pegasus

computing store, may be a very economical type of code.

An alternative starting point is the common single-address code. It is found generally that one-third or more of the orders are used simply to shunt numbers to or from or via the accumulator. This is because in coding one often carries out a few operations building up one number, and then transfers attention to other numbers, meanwhile holding the first number in store for further use. Hence the large amount of shunting. It seems reasonable, therefore, to provide several accumulators, in which the partially processed numbers may be left. One is thus led by simple arguments from two opposite extremes to the type of order code adopted in Pegasus.

Modifying registers are considered indispensable, and by giving the accumulators the additional function of modification, facilities for arithmetic operation on the modifying registers are automatically provided.

The orders in the multiple-accumulator code are moreover very concise, so that it is possible to get two orders comfortably into a word of reasonable length.

The arrangement

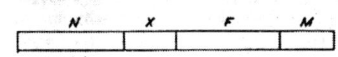

| N | X | F | M |

of the instruction is the most convenient from the engineering point of view. (Usually N is the register address, X the accumulator address, F the function and M the modifier address).

WORD AND ORDER LENGTH

For a general-purpose computer the most satisfactory number of digits in a word lies between 35 and 40. 35 digits seems to be a minimum for comfort, any excess over 40 superfluous.

In order to economize in storage space it is very desirable to have two orders per word, and the form of order in Pegasus has been chosen partly with this in mind. Each order contains 19 digits, and the two orders together with the 'stop-go' digit give a word length of 39 digits. (The 'stop-go' digit, when it is '0', causes the machines to stop before obeying the order-pair in the same word.)

PARITY CHECKS

A parity check digit is a digit associated with a number or character, and chosen so as to make the total number of ones in the number odd (or even). If the total number of ones is made odd it is called an odd parity check, and if the total number of ones is made even it is called an even parity check. The parity digit of a number, once formed, is carried about with it and is used for checking that the number is stored and transferred correctly.

The parity digit check is not a complete test for the correctness of a number, because a change of an even number of digits would not be detected. But used to its best advantage, it will detect perhaps 99 out of 100, or even 999 out of 1 000—we do not know what proportion of the storage and transmission faults which occur, before they have caused computational errors in data output from the machine. Storage and transmission faults might constitute 10 per cent or 20 per cent of the total number of faults which occur in the computer, and so by eliminating the storage from the part of the machine to be investigated when the computer is known to have a fault, and by saving the time which would be spent in tracing storage errors, an important reduction in the time spent hunting faults could result.

In Pegasus, all words on the drum and nearly all nickel lines of the computing store have a parity check digit, and also a parity digit can be formed during input or output of a character, and it is up to the programmer to make proper use of it.

Whenever a number is read from the drum its parity is checked. A failure stops the machine. The parity check is odd, and the number of bits in a word, including the parity bit, is even, so that the three most important types of faults will be detected:

(a) A single digit error, due perhaps to bad recording on the drum.

(b) The number and parity digit all zero, probably due to an electrical or electronic failure.

(c) The number and parity digit all ones, probably due to an electrical or electronic failure.

Notice that had the parity check been even, then all zeros would not be detected; and also, if the parity check is odd, the total number of digits including the parity digit must be even if all ones are to be detected.

The parity digit on the drum is particularly important because the only alternative check on storage is regular testing by programme, which is lengthy, and not easily made comprehensive.

Some Details of the Order-Code

BINARY-POINT CONVENTION

Consider, from first principles, the question of how the digits stored in the computer are to be interpreted. It is in fact up to the programmer to decide, and the computer only comes in because if the digits are interpreted in a particular way the orders of the machine carry out simple arithmetic operations. But several other interpretations are regularly used. One, for instance, is as orders for the use of the machine's operational circuits. Another interpretation is as orders in an 'interpretive scheme'—in which the orders are decoded and obeyed by sub-routines constructed by the programmer. A third way is as numbers. In this case the numerical value to be attached to the individual digits, that is, the position of the 'binary-point', has to be chosen. It is clear on reflection that the only operation in which the position of the binary point affects the interpretation of the action of the machine are multiplication and division. However in describing the order-code some convention is needed, and the following has been adopted as being the most natural, and the most frequent in practical use:

Numbers (in digits D_0 to D_{38} of a word) are considered to lie in the range $-1 \leqslant x < +1$ except where otherwise stated.

The digit positions of a word are numbered as below:

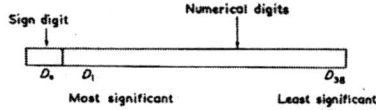

Sign digit	Numerical digits
D_0 D_1	D_{38}
Most significant	Least significant

On this convention, therefore, the D_1 position represents 2^{-1}.

FRACTIONS AND INTEGERS

An alternative is to interpret numbers as integers. In this case the D_{38} position represents unity. In Pegasus it is as easy to work with integers as with fractions, since multiplication is arranged so that for both, the binary point remains in its natural position; division is independent of the position of the binary point provided the quotient is interpreted as a fraction.

OVERFLOW

The value of this overflow facility is that it gives a

Annex No 5 Braunholtz describes Pegasus

simple test, which can be applied at the end of any stage of a calculation, as to whether any number has run out of scale during that stage.

When an attempt is made to transfer to the main store a number which has overflowed, the machine will stop. This facility should prove useful in locating errors of mathematical reasoning behind the programme, since these are otherwise extremely hard to find.

DOUBLE-LENGTH NUMBERS

Double-length numbers occupy two words of storage. The more-significant word is interpreted normally. The less-significant word is given a zero sign-digit D_0 so that it represents a positive number, as it should. The numerical digits then carry on in decreasing significance from where the more-significant word left off; that is, when the double-length number is interpreted as a fraction, D_1 of the less-significant word represents 2^{-39} instead of 2^{-1}.

Writing p, q for the standard interpretation of registers P, Q (accumulators 6, 7) and writing the double-length fraction formed from them $(p\ q)$ with the q the less significant, one has

$$(p\ q) = p + 2^{-38} q.$$

This is the standard interpretation of double-length numbers. The alternative interpretation as an integer is similar:

$$(p\ q)_{\text{integer}} = 2^{38} p_{\text{integer}} + q_{\text{integer}}$$

Pegasus permits simple working with double-length numbers principally through the following facilities:

(a) Accumulating double-length products.
(b) Double-length shift and normalize in registers 6 and 7.
(c) The 'justify' order.

(a) It is often required to add together a series of products, as in matrix algebra. Although the result may only be required to single-length accuracy, nevertheless, in order to prevent loss of accuracy due to rounding errors, it is often desired to accumulate the double-length products.

(b) Shift and normalize applied to accumulator 7 is skipped in shifting, as shown:

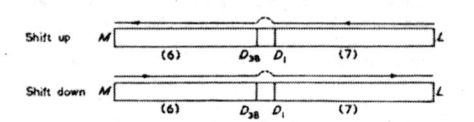

Shift up M | (6) | D_{38} D_1 | (7) | L
Shift down M | (6) | D_{38} D_1 | (7) | L

(c) In double-length addition, for example, when the two less-significant halves are operated on, overflow may occur into D_0 of accumulator 7. This '1' should really be added in the least significant digit position of accumulator 6.

The 'Justify' order does this, and restores D_0 of accumulator 7 to zero.

The total effect of all these facilities is to make the handling of double-length numbers very simple; in particular, the problem of carry from the less-significant to the more-significant half of double-length numbers is solved with very little equipment and without introducing new programming difficulties.

COUNTING

The methods of modifying and counting on Pegasus are two of the novel features of the machine. The methods adopted have been developed especially to simplify the organizing sections of programmes, and will be found extremely convenient to use.

The counting needed to decide when to write-up or bring down blocks of the main store, and when to end cycling around the loops of a programme, makes a special use of accumulators in the following way, The accumulator contains two numbers, one occupying D_1 to D_{13}, the other D_{14} to D_{38}. Both numbers are thought of as integers.

The number in D_1 to D_{13} is called the modifier. It is used to keep track of where the machine has got to in the main store when running through data and to decide when to transfer information between the computing store and main store.

The number in D_{14} to D_{38} is called the counter. It is used to count the number of times the machine has cycled round a loop, and so to determine when to stop cycling.

There are two orders which make it simple to carry out these operations. These are described later.

COUNTER-ORDERS

These orders are used particularly in setting and altering counters.

Each ordinary arithmetic order has an analogous counter order; both sets of orders can thereby be more easily remembered.

In a counter-order, the integer formed by the N-digit of the order is one of the operands; the counter in the accumulator specified is the other operand, and the result of the operation is placed in the same accumulator. Thus if N contains the integer 13, then 13 can be added, subtracted etc. from the counter specified in the X-digits.

MODIFICATION

If it were not for the fact that in long mathematical problems the same series of operations have to be repeated very many times, then digital computers would be of little value for such work, a fact which has often been pointed out. But this repetition does occur, with slight regular alterations carried out by the sequences of orders on themselves each time round the cycle. In most early computers the alterations—which generally consist of adding or subtracting small integers from the addresses of orders—were carried out on the orders themselves, but in the Manchester University computer the idea of modification was introduced. The contents of certain registers, the B-lines, could be added to an order before it was obeyed without altering the orders in their store position, so that by altering the B-line the appropriate modification of the sequence of orders was carried out.

This system has three major advantages.

First, the alteration of a B-line is very much simpler than the alteration of an order, particularly since orders are often over-written on the Manchester machine (both it and Pegasus have two-level storage).

Second, one modifier can often be used to modify several orders in a sequence.

Third, the counter can also be used to test for the end of the loop.

In Pegasus modification has been carried a stage further; different orders are modified differently according to their needs. In particular, the difficulties of organization associated with two-level storage have been greatly reduced by special modification arrangements.

There are four types of modification:

(a) *With arithmetical orders*, in which one is interested in modifying an address within a block of eight, modification adds to N the part of the modifier less than 8.

(b) *With shift, normalize, and counter orders*, modification adds to N the whole modifier (this is not often used).

Annex No 5 Braunholtz describes Pegasus

(c) *With block transfers*, one is not interested in the part of the counter less than eight, since this refers to a position within a block. It is the rest of the counter which is important, so the modification adds the block number part of the modifier to N.

(d) *With single-word transfers*, in which the whole counter may be used to specify the word, and in which the N and X digits of the order are used to specify the word, the whole modifier is added to the N and X digits.

'UNIT MODIFY'

The unit modify order adds one to the modifier in X and jumps to N if the three least-significant digits of the modifier are not all zero. This order makes it simple to carry out a routine process on consecutive numbers running through several blocks of the main store, since it moves on the modifier by unity each time, and also determines when transfer of data to or from the main store is required.

'UNIT COUNT'

The unit count order subtracts one from the counter in X, and jumps to N if the counter is not zero. It is used to count the number of times the machine carries out a routine process. An illustration of the use of these two counting orders is given:

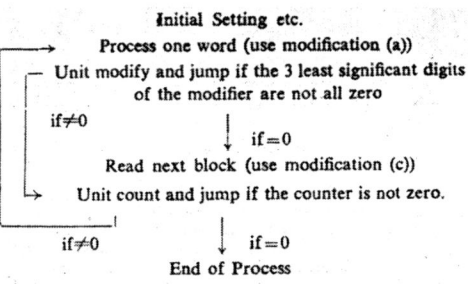

Initial Setting etc.
Process one word (use modification (a))
Unit modify and jump if the 3 least significant digits of the modifier are not all zero
if≠0 → if=0
Read next block (use modification (c))
Unit count and jump if the counter is not zero.
if≠0 → if=0
End of Process

Note. The jump after unit modify will occur eight times between runs through the block read order. Hence the modifier will have eight added to it between one order and the next, so that the block number in the modified transfer-order will increase by one each time round.

Acknowledgments

The author would like to acknowledge his debt to Mr. C. Strachey, to whom the form taken by the Pegasus computer is largely due.

Acknowledgment is made to Ferranti Ltd for permission to publish this article.

(*To be continued*)

Annex No 6 Emery describes Pegasus

The Design of the Ferranti Pegasus Computer

(Part 2)

By G. Emery*, M.A.

PART 1 of this discussion dealt with the considerations affecting the system design of a medium-sized general-purpose computer: Part 2 is concerned with the more detailed engineering aspects of the problem, and in particular with the implications of building the machine from standard plug-in packages.

Packaged construction leads to a number of economies, which become even more marked if the majority of the packages used are of a relatively small number of types. Economies arise

(a) In design because, the packages once having been developed, the machine can be designed almost entirely from a logical standpoint without the need for further laboratory work.

(b) In manufacture, particularly if quantity production is envisaged and the number of package types is small.

(c) In commissioning because, with pre-tested packages, the number of possible faults is greatly reduced.

(d) In maintenance, because for a relatively small number of package types a correspondingly small quantity of spare equipment need be held.

(e) In operation, as the time during which a fault makes the computer inoperative is reduced to the time taken to locate the fault, the faulty package then being replaced and removed elsewhere for repair.

Two disadvantages have been alleged against packaged construction; the first is that it leads to a number of redundant components; the second is that it increases the number of plug-and-socket connectors through which signals must pass, with a possible decrease in reliability. With the package types adopted, it is mainly the cheaper components —resistors and crystal diodes—that become redundant, their cost being far outweighed by economies in manufacture. The plugs and sockets have proved to be entirely reliable. The sockets are of the type used in standard octal valve bases, mounted in line; the plug pins are simply plated metal strips folded around a plastic moulding.

Package Types

Inevitably there must be several package types associated with special functions within the machine, of which only one or two will be needed in any installation. The majority of the machine, however, will be concerned with arithmetical and logical operations on digit-pulse trains, and can be made up from a relatively small number of package types. The basic operations required are the logical AND and OR operations and the NOT operation (inversion) and delays of one digit-time and one word-time. There is also a requirement for cathode-followers when the loading on a particular signal is heavy. The AND and OR operations can be conveniently performed by crystal gates; the other operations require some form of valve circuit. Thus the basic packaged elements can be envisaged as valve circuits fed from crystal gates or combinations of crystal gates. A convenient package size will accommodate up to three miniature-valve bases and a thirty-two-pin plug, allowing from two to six identical, or closely similar, elements per package.

Typical crystal AND and OR gates are shown in Fig. 1. It was decided to predesign all AND gates by building them on the packages and choosing a value of bleed resistor suitable to the succeeding valve circuit. OR gates are made up for the most part from 'mix' crystals provided as alternative outputs for the packaged elements; a choice

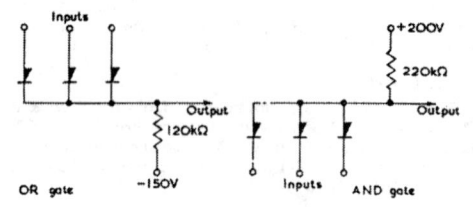

Fig. 1. Typical AND and OR gates

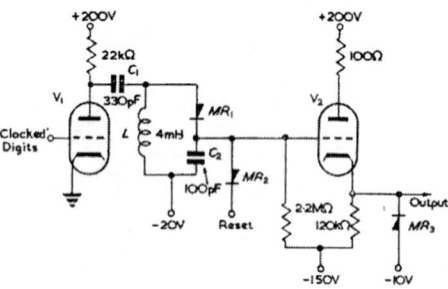

Fig. 2. Basic delay circuit

of bleed resistors, connected to the negative line, is provided on each package, the ends of the resistors being brought to pins on the package plugs. These resistors are also available as extra loads for the package output valves, which are cathode-followers, to enable the logical designer to adjust each functional element to suit the external load imposed on it.

The packages are designed for a pulse frequency of $\frac{1}{2}$Mc/s. The digit pulses are positive-going, and consecutive pulses are separated by gaps of about 0.6μsec. They are generated in the first instance in the digit-delay circuit by the use of two auxiliary waveforms, 'clock' and 'reset'. 'Clock' is a $\frac{1}{2}$Mc/s square wave of unity mark-to-space ratio; 'reset' is a negative-going $\frac{1}{2}$Mc/s pulse of width 0.6μsec. The basic digit-delay circuit is shown in Fig. 2. It accepts a 'clocked-up' digit pulse (i.e. a pulse that has undergone an AND operation with 'clock' to standardize its timing); this causes a current to be built up in the inductor, which is diverted to capacitor C_2 when the input level falls. The output is now positive until the end of the next digit-time when C_2 is discharged by 'reset' and the output falls again. Owing to the degenerative effect

* Ferranti Ltd.

Annex No 6 Emery describes Pegasus

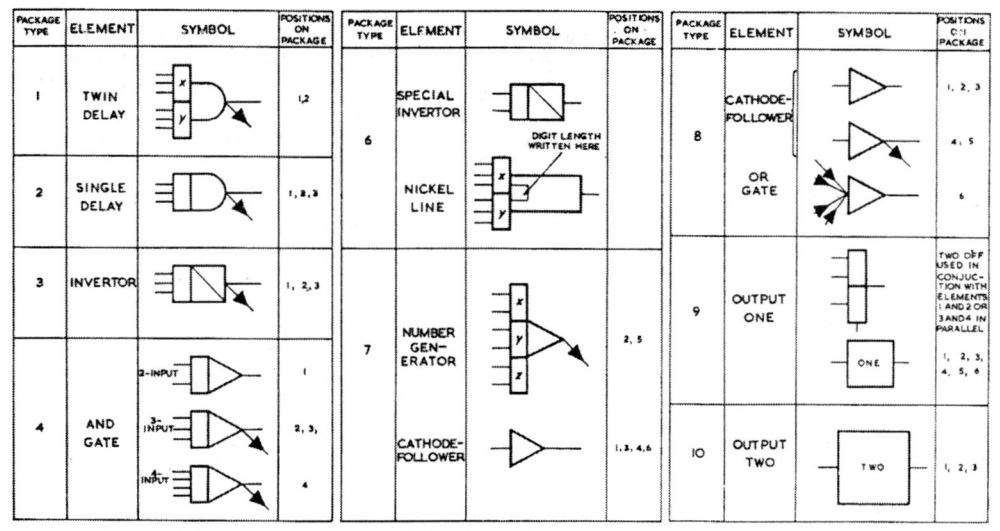

PACKAGE TYPE	ELEMENT	SYMBOL	POSITIONS ON PACKAGE	PACKAGE TYPE	ELEMENT	SYMBOL	POSITIONS ON PACKAGE	PACKAGE TYPE	ELEMENT	SYMBOL	POSITIONS ON PACKAGE
1	TWIN DELAY		1,2	6	SPECIAL INVERTOR	DIGIT LENGTH WRITTEN HERE		8	CATHODE-FOLLOWER		1, 2, 3
2	SINGLE DELAY		1,2,3		NICKEL LINE				OR GATE		4, 5
3	INVERTOR		1, 2, 3	7	NUMBER GEN-ERATOR		2, 5	9	OUTPUT ONE	ONE	TWO OFF USED IN CONJUC-TION WITH ELEMENTS 1 AND 2 OR 3 AND 4 IN PARALLEL 1, 2, 3, 4, 5, 6
4	AND GATE	2-INPUT / 3-INPUT / 4-INPUT	1 / 2, 3 / 4		CATHODE-FOLLOWER		1, 3, 4, 6	10	OUTPUT TWO	TWO	1, 2, 3

Fig. 3. Packaged logical elements

of cathode-followers, which must be inserted between gating operations, it is necessary to re-form digit pulses in this way at intervals in their travel. Because pulses are 'clocked-up' before entering delays, only the part of a waveform 'overlapped' by 'clock' has any real signifi-cance; consequently inter-digit spikes produced by logical operations between digit-pulse trains with slightly different timing can have no effect on the operation of the machine.

Digit-delay packages are of two types: in one the delay is fed from an AND gate, in the other from the mixed out-puts of twin AND gates. This so-called 'twin' delay has the facility that it can be used as a staticizer, a function for which flip-flops have more generally been used. This is done by feeding the output of the element back to one of the input gates; a pulse injected through the other gate will then circulate until the feedback gate is closed.

The other packaged logical elements are invertors—a simple triode inverting amplifier direct-coupled to a cathode-follower and preceded by an AND gate—AND gates feeding cathode-followers, OR gates feeding cathode-followers, and cathode-followers alone. There is also a dynamicizer element consisting of three two-input AND gates with their mixed outputs feeding a cathode-follower; this is intended for generating serial numbers from hand-key settings or tape-reader outputs. Finally there is a delay-line package, which is used primarily for immediate-access storage. The line material is nickel, which has a dispersion characteristic and thermal coefficient of delay sufficiently low for the lengths used, and in which a sonic pulse can conveniently be induced by magnetostriction. The pulses received at the remote end of the line are amplified and then reshaped in a circuit identical with those on the digit-delay packages, to give a standard digit-pulse output over a temperature range of some 20°C. The amplifier at the transmitting end of the line is fed from twin AND gates, one gate being used for filling the line, and the other for recirculation. The line and its associated coils are mounted on a panel that can be easily removed from the package and replaced if necessary.

Fig. 3 shows how the packages are made up from the basic elements. It will be seen that most elements have the alternative of direct and mix-crystal outputs. Types 9 and 10 are intended for controlling output equipment; the type 9 package also carries twin AND gates, which are use-ful when the element is to be used for setting and resetting relays. Some examples of the use of the packaged elements are shown in Fig. 4. The parity counter is essentially a staticizer that is cut on and off alternately by the pulses in the input signal; it is set at the beginning of the cycle, and its output at the end of the cycle is positive for an even-parity signal. Parity counts are used as checks at several places in the computer. The adder-subtractor shown is the most convenient with the package types adopted; a delay is used at the output point to give a standardized 'sum' signal.

The packages are built on plates of a plastic laminate, 12in long and 6in wide, with a cut-out arranged to form a carrying handle. Within the cut-out is an aluminium platform, which is mounted at right-angles to the main plate and will accommodate up to three miniature valve bases and up to eight monitor-probe sockets. When the packages are mounted in the cabinet these platforms form a division that separates the cooling-air stream over the valves from that over the rest of the package.

The Drum Store

The main backing store in Pegasus is a drum of diameter 10in rotating at 3 720rev/min. To record digits at the standard 3μsec rate would imply a cell length of about ·006in, which might not have given the desired reliability; consequently digits are recorded at 6μsec, a pair of tracks being used at a time to record alternate digits. The method of recording is the so-called phase-modulation system, in which a binary 'one' is represented by magnetic saturation for 3μsec in the negative direction followed by magnetic saturation for 3μsec in the positive direction, a binary 'nought' being represented by the inverse of this. The logical circuit shown in Fig. 5 generates suitable phase-modulated signals and provides double-ended outputs for feeding the push-pull write amplifiers. Gating waveforms

Annex No 6 Emery describes Pegasus

T_3 and T_4 select odd and even digits respectively from the original signal. The read signal derived from the drum is strobed to eliminate timing variations (the 'reset' waveform is used for this) and gated again with T_3 and T_4 to reconstitute the original information.

The drum is provided with one hundred write/read heads, fitted in ten stacks of ten. Eighty heads are used for storage purposes, giving a maximum storage capacity of forty track pairs, of which eight pairs are used for a permanent record that can be read from but not, in normal circumstances, overwritten. Four heads are used for two address-track pairs, and three heads are used for clock tracks, which provide synchronism between the drum and the rest of the computer. The address and clock tracks are duplicated to allow the permanent record to be written without the necessity for reading and writing with two heads on the same stack. The third clock track is necessary to enable the other two to be written in exact synchronism. The remainder of the heads are treated as spares.

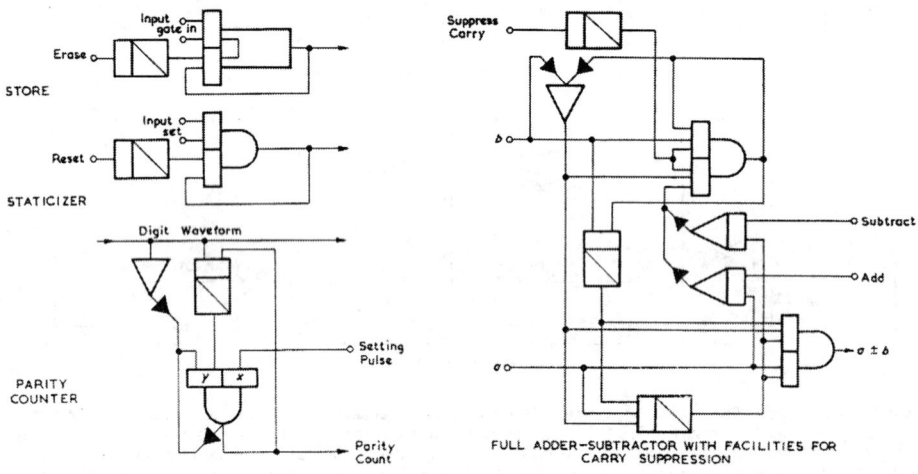

The drum clock track provides a sinusoidal signal which is amplified and shaped to give the 'clock' and 'reset' signals that control the digit-pulse frequency throughout the computer. It is additionally necessary to keep the drum-clock frequency constant within narrow limits to ensure that signals in the fixed-delay nickel lines are not spoiled. The drum-clock frequency is therefore compared with the output of a crystal oscillator, the error being used to control the field current of the generator supplying the drum motor. For testing without a drum, 'clock' and 'reset' can be generated direct from the output of the oscillator.

Each track pair carries 5 376 digits (128 words or 16 blocks); thus the total storage capacity is 5 120 words. A word or block is selected from a track by address-track coincidence. The tracks themselves are switched electronically on the special packages designed for reading and writing. For this purpose the heads are assumed to be arranged as matrices of eight rows and five columns; there are two identical matrices, one for the odd digits and one for the even digits. A column generally corresponds to eight heads in the same stack; these are connected to eight transformers on a special switch package, which are switched to the read amplifier by suitable low-level selection signals. The switch package also carries a buffer amplifier, which presents to the read amplifier a signal substantially the same as would be obtained direct from the head; thus the same read amplifier circuit can be used for the information tracks as for the address tracks, where there is no switching. Column selection for writing is carried out at a low level by gating operations at the inputs to the write amplifiers. (There are only four write amplifiers for odd digits and four for even digits, as the permanent record occupies one complete column.) Each head transformer carries a third winding connected so that the eight transformers on one switch package provide a choice of anode loads for one write amplifier; row selection within a column for writing is then achieved by applying the h.t. for the write amplifier to a centre-tap on the winding of the appropriate transformer.

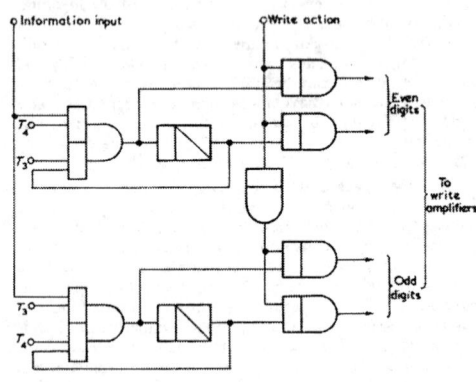

To ensure that words on the drum have a fixed timing relative to words in the immediate-access store, the commutator, which provides p-pulses at word frequency for use

Annex No 6 Emery describes Pegasus

throughout the computer, is locked to a signal on the address track. The commutator is shown in Fig. 6. Essentially it consists of three loops cycling with periods of 7, 3 and 2 digit-times respectively, giving a combined cycle time of 42 digit-times, or one word-time. The arrangement is such, however, that the overall cycle time is 42 digit-times only if the signals from the pair of address tracks, H_8 and H_9, are both positive at the beginning of a new cycle, when the outputs of all delays in the loop are negative. As long as this condition is not fulfilled, the cycle time of the commutator will be 43 digit-times. The address-track signal is such that H_8 and H_9 are positive together in one particular place relative to every word on the drum, so that the commutator will eventually become locked after a settling-down

duct after multiplication or the quotient and remainder after division. As the order structure allows only two addresses to be specified, the less significant half of a double-length dividend must be placed in the multiplier-divider by a previous order. The two accumulators of the multiplier-divider cycle independently, and digits are shunted from one into the other during the course of an operation. During multiplication, the product is formed initially in the more significant of the two accumulators by means of three adders, three digits of the multiplier being sampled each word-time. It is possible to form the product three digits at a time because only 39 of the 42 digits in a word are arithmetically significant, leaving three gap digits into which the growing product can expand. Facilities are

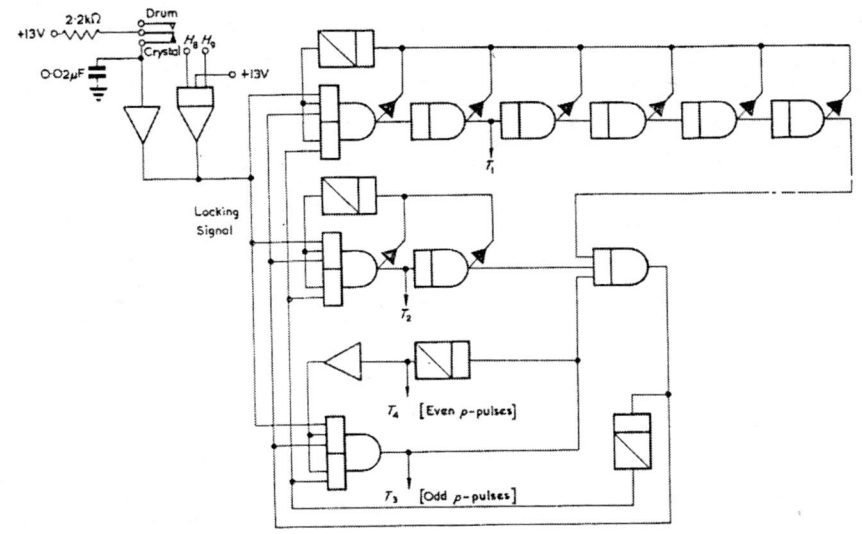

Fig. 6. Commutator

period of a few drum revolutions. The effect of the address-track signal is over-ridden when the computer is switched to operate on crystal-oscillator clock.

Arithmetical Circuits

As explained in Part 1 of this article, Pegasus is provided with multiple accumulators. To economize on equipment, it was decided not to associate a separate arithmetical circuit with each accumulator, but to carry out all simple arithmetical operations in a central 'Mill'. The delay necessarily involved in reshaping pulses during their passage through the Mill is padded out to one word-time to preserve standard timing in store; consequently orders must take at least two word-times to be obeyed. The separate Mill does give some saving in computing time, however, by enabling the source of either operand, i.e., any register in the immediate-access store, to be used for replacement after a simple arithmetical operation. The Mill is also used as a shifting register, and contains facilities for testing 'jump' conditions and for carrying out the arithmetic associated with the 'unit count' and 'unit modify' jump orders. Operands used in shift and jump orders are always taken from an accumulator.

Two of the accumulators are used as the basis of the multiplier-divider, and will contain the double-length pro-

available for forming a double-length product or a rounded single-length product, or for accumulating double-length products.

Division is by a standard non-restorative process, the dividend being gradually reduced in numerical size by adding or subtracting the divisor (according to the sign of the residue) in successively lower significance, the quotient being built up in the other accumulator by corresponding half subtractions or additions. As the least significant digit of the quotient so far formed is a 'one' at every stage in this process, the operation must be carried one step beyond the end of the dividend to obtain the correct values of quotient and residue. For unrounded division (residue having the same sign as the divisor) the extra quotient digit is removed by a single half subtraction, a corresponding operation being carried out on the residue; for rounded division (minimal residue) the sign of the residue is sensed one step further still to determine the last operation. In either type of division the last two operations are carried out with the same significance, leaving a quotient and residue of standard length.

An interesting feature of the process is the method used to ensure that the final unrounded quotient and residue are correct when the residue has been reduced to zero at some intermediate stage. This condition is sensed; but

167

Annex No 6 Emery describes Pegasus

the process is not terminated. Instead, an addition is forced on the quotient (and a subtraction on the residue) regardless of the sign of the divisor; the net effect of subsequent operations is then to restore the original values of quotient and residue while shifting them into standard timing. This special procedure is necessary, of course, only for unrounded division, though, for simplicity, it is allowed to operate for rounded division too.

The multiplier-divider circuit is used also for double-length shifting (including normalization for floating-point working, which is a double-length operation) and for justification. It comprises 54 packages, which is less than one eighth of the total package content of the machine.

Control

Following normal practice, the order pairs are routed in sequence (in the absence of 'jumps') into an order register, from which they are decoded. The first order is modified on entry; the second order when the operation prescribed by the first order is nearly completed, the first order then being deleted to allow the second order to be extended by modification. The adder used for modification is also used to step on the order address, so that order pairs are selected in the sequence in which they are stored, and for counting shifts, which are performed at the rate of one place per word-time. Orders are decoded by setting their digits up separately on staticizers of the type already referred to. The staticized outputs and their inverses are then combined to provide suitable gating waveforms. It should be noted that the logical arrangement of the function code, while providing a useful mnemonic for the programmer, sometimes enables the outputs of the function-decoding staticizers to be used directly as action waveforms in cases where several different functions require parts of the machine to be associated in the same way. Two sets of address decoding are used, one for the N-digits, which may specify any immediate-access address, the other for the X-digits, which specify one of the accumulators. The N-decoding is always used for replacement, leaving the X-decoding circuit free for setting up the modifier address for the next order. (It will be remembered that modifiers in current use are held in accumulators.)

Control can exist in one of three states: the C-state, during which the new order pair is entering the order register; the A-state, during which the first order is being obeyed; and the B-state, during which the second order is being obeyed. The C-state persists for one word-time, and the other two states for at least two word-times each. A beat counter provides signals to define the three states and to control the operations that are peculiar to each one. When computation is stopped, whether intentionally or due to a component failure or a programming error, the operation of the beat counter is suspended, so as to keep the order to be obeyed next circulating in the order register but unable to exercise control over the machine. The stop order and the optional stop (stop-go digit) operate in this way, also parity failure or the decoding of a function to which no significance has been assigned. Overflow does not of itself cause a stop; but the machine is stopped if there is a subsequent attempt to transfer information to the drum. Overflow can occur in the Mill or multiplier-divider after an addition, subtraction or left shift, or after a division operation in which the dividend numerically exceeds the divisor. Overflow can be cleared by either of the two jump orders that are conditional on the overflow setting, or by a 'justify' order.

Input and Output

Input and output are by five-hole paper tape, an interpreter unit being provided to give a print-out of the output tape. The input and output units are treated in orders as an address in the computing store, the two being distinguished by the function in the order according as it prescribes the address as a source or destination. Two addresses are however allotted to input and output. One of these implies a straightforward conversion from tape holes to digit pulses, and is generally used for reading in warning characters for routine interpretation; the character is read, for convenience, into the modifier position of an accumulator. When the other address is specified, the machine carries out an automatic conversion, replacing the most significant digit with a digit depending on the parity of the character. As all the odd-parity characters on tape are numerical or other characters used in programmes, a single-digit error in the reading mechanism, followed by the conversion, will cause to appear in the machine a character that is completely out of context. The input routine is arranged to test the significance of what is read in, and to enter a loop stop (a jump order transferring control to itself) if an error of this kind has occurred.

A great deal of time can be saved if alternative tape readers are available, one for reading in a master programme and the other for reading subroutines. It is a convenience, too, to have alternative tape punches. An external conditioning order allows a choice of up to nine pieces of tape equipment to be switched by relays operating under programme control.

The optional facility is provided in Pegasus for punching out addresses in drum block-transfer orders. A warning character is punched, followed by the ten digits of the block address in the form of two tape characters. The facility is particularly useful during programme development, and is achieved at the expense of very little extra equipment.

The Monitor

Monitoring facilities are required not only by the maintenance engineer but also by the programmer, especially during the development of a programme. Accordingly two c.r.t. displays are provided. One of these is referred to as the Programmer's Display, and will show either the current order pair or its address. The form of presentation is one in which binary 'ones' are shown as vertical lines, and binary 'noughts' as dots. The order pair is shown on a twin-line trace. The other display is referred to as the Engineer's Display, although many of the facilities associated with it are used by programmers too. All store lines are switchable to this display, as are several other crucial places in the machine, but it is possible to monitor the output of every packaged element in the machine on this display, as all packages carry monitor sockets, and probes connected to the monitor switch are provided in each computing bay. The left-hand display will give a presentation of the 'lines-and-dots' type used on the other display, or it will show 'clocked' digits or the raw digit-pulse waveform, the 'clocked' presentation enabling the engineer to determine whether any 'spikes' produced by the logic are occurring in significant positions relative to clock. A range of time-bases is provided, from the 'half word' length as used for the right-hand tube up to 30msec.

The time-bases are triggered as determined by the programmer in coincidence with a particular order address or drum address set up on hand-keys, or on a particular operational beat. Provision is made for triggering repetitively (which is generally required when an order is being run from the hand-keys for test purposes) or for triggering from an internal waveform derived from a probe in one of the computing bays.

Annex No 6 Emery describes Pegasus

Physical Layout

The computer comprises a three-bay computing cabinet with control desk attached, a two-bay power supply cabinet, and a motor-alternator set. The first bay of the computing cabinet, which abuts against the control desk, contains the drum and monitor unit and four rows of packages; the other two bays contain ten rows of packages each. The packages are mounted vertically between cast aluminium-alloy racks in rows of up to twenty. The sockets that mate with the package plugs are mounted in panels which divide the bays laterally into two parts, interconnexions between packages in the same bay being made by wiring between the socket pins in the back portion of the cabinet. Special plugs and sockets identical with those used for the packages are used for bay-to-bay interconnexions.

The lower portion of the cabinet, between the packages and the floor, contains heater transformers and cooling fans; the upper portion, above the packages, contains the inter-bay power wiring and protective circuitry. When refrigeration is fitted, which is necessary for the comfort of the operator if the computer is installed in a confined space, cooling batteries are mounted over the air intakes under a false floor at the front of the cabinet.

Acknowledgments

The author acknowledges his debt to all those who were responsible for the design of Pegasus. He would also like to thank Ferranti Limited for permission to publish this article.

REFERENCES

1. ELLIOTT, W. S., CARPENTER, H. G., OWEN, C. E. Development of Computer Components and Systems. Proceedings of the Association for Computing Machinery. (Toronto Conference, Sept. 1952).
2. FAIRCLOUGH, J. W. A Sonic Delay Line Storage Unit for a Digital Computer. Pro. Instn Elect. Engrs. 103B, 491 Supplement No. 3. (1956).
3. MERRY, I. W., MAUDSLEY, B. G. The Magnetic Drum Store of the Computer Pegasus. Proc. Instn Elect. Engrs. 103B, 197 Supplement No. 2. (1956).
4. ELLIOTT, W. S., OWEN, C. E., DEVONALD, C. H., MAUDSLEY, B. G., The Design Philosophy of Pegasus, a Quantity-Production Computer. Proc. Instn Elect. Engrs. 103B, 188 Supplement No. 2. (1956).

The Magnetic Tape Store for Pegasus

By T. G. H. Braunholtz and D. Hogg, Ferranti Ltd.

The design of the magnetic tape store attached to Pegasus[1] was started two years ago, and the first model has now been in operation for about six months. A general description of the tape store is given first, followed by a brief description of some of the principal anticipated applications. This is followed by more detailed description and discussion, first of the engineering design and then of system design.

THE general arrangement of the tape store is quite standard and is shown in Fig. 1.

Information to be transferred from the computing store of Pegasus[1] is first of all deposited in a buffer store, eight words at a time, by means of a special order. This order is called the 'interchange order' and interchanges the contents of any block in the computing store with any block in the buffer store. From the buffer store the information is written on tape by the tape control, and Pegasus can, in the meantime, continue with computation.

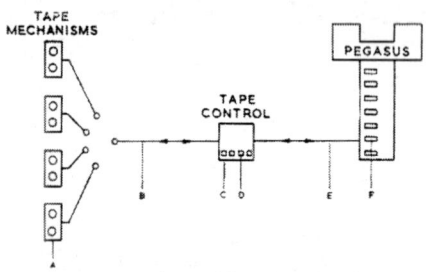

Fig. 1. Schematic diagram of Pegasus with magnetic tape

A Four tape mechanisms can be attached. A switch on each mechanism selects 16 or 32 word working
B Each tape order can select any one of the mechanisms
C Each tape order is carried out by the tape control, autonomously, only one tape order at a time can be carried out by the tape control
D Four blocks of eight words in the buffer store
E Interchange the contents of any block in the buffer store with any block in the computing store
F Computing store of 55 words

The buffer store contains four blocks of eight words, making 32 words in all. When reading and writing on tape the buffer can either be used in one 32-word section or two 16-word sections.

Four tape mechanisms may be connected to a tape control, and two tape controls with four mechanisms each could be connected to Pegasus.

A tape control can carry out four orders. The specification of an order is contained in one word, which states:

(1) Which tape order is to be carried out (search, read, write, rewind).
(2) Which mechanism is to be used.
(3) The address of the section of tape referred to.
(4) Which half of the buffer is to be used.

To set the tape control into action this word is sent to register 20 where it is stored for use by the tape control. The act of sending a word to register 20 starts the tape control.

The four control orders are:

SEARCH: the tape in the selected mechanism is moved (forward or backward) into position for reading or writing on the specified section.
READ: read the specified section from the selected mechanism into the buffer store. The tape control will search for the correct section before carrying out the read order.
WRITE: write on to the specified section of the selected mechanism from the buffer store. Again, the tape control will search for the correct section before carrying out the write order.
REWIND: set the selected mechanism into Rewind. This will take a few milliseconds, after which the tape control becomes free to carry out other tape orders while the mechanism is rewinding.

If an error in carrying out a tape order is detected by the checking circuits an indicator is set. The setting of this may be sensed by the programme through register 21, which will be all ones if an error was detected and will be zero otherwise. The order may then be repeated. Whenever an error is detected a buzzer on the tape control sounds, in addition to register 21 being set.

The interchange order, the tape control word sent to register 20, and the register 21 staticizor are the only controls over the tape store the computer requires.

The reader will have gathered that tapes are addressed for 16 or 32-word sections. Each tape, of course, is either all 16-word sections or all 32-word sections, and the tape control carries out a 16 or 32-word transfer depending on a switch setting on the selected mechanism, which must be set by the operator to correspond to the tape in the mechanism.

There is a special feature for checking that writing has been carried out correctly: each mechanism has two heads, and writing is carried out by the forward head and is checked by reading back with the trailing head as part of the write order. The two heads are at present mounted one inch apart.

The following is the specification for the tape store:

(1) Tape is $\frac{1}{2}$in wide, and can be supplied in lengths of multiples of 600ft (up to 3 600ft) with the tape tested and addressed.

(2) The tape speed is 75in/sec.

(3) The time to stop or start between rest and full speed is less than 7msec for either stopping or starting.

(4) Writing (and reading) speed: 9 250 characters per second.

(5) Transfer times per section:
   32 words: 53msec
   16 words: 41msec
   assuming that the tape is in position for the quickest possible transfer.

170

Annex No 7 Braunholtz & Hogg on magnetic tape system

(6) Rewind time for a 3 600ft tape: 6min (average speed of 120in/sec).

(7) *Property (3 600ft tape)*   16-word section   32-word section

	16-word section	32-word section
Number of sections per tape	13 000 or more	10 000 or more
Number of words per tape	208 000 or more	320 000 or more
Length of section	2·84in	3·75in
Length of address	0·23in	0·23in
Length of stop-start space	0·7in	0·7in
Length of head spacing gap	1·0in	1·0in
Length of information	0·91in	1·82in

(8) Search time per section:

    32 word: 53msec.
    16 words: 41msec.

This is the time it takes to run over one section at full speed and is also the time per section for continuous reading or writing. It is actually the same time as in (5) above, which is the time from rest to completion of the order.

The Application of the Tape Store

The designer of a computer for scientific and commercial use, and for use by organizations with very different amounts of money available, is faced with a difficult choice in deciding how expensive a tape system he should plan. The principal variables at his disposal are the size of sections of information on tape (which may be variable) and the degree of autonomy to be given to the tape control.

In scientific and engineering computation Pegasus will use magnetic tape for two principal purposes. First there are the problems using more data than can be stored on the drum. Second it will be found very valuable to reserve one mechanism for a tape containing the library of subroutines, and also perhaps individual's private routines and intermediate results; all this saving a great deal of programme assembly and paper tape input time, and allowing more efficient use of machine time.

These uses of the tape store account for some aspects of the design chosen. Both will involve dividing the tape up into parts for storing different sets of data, and so on, as distinct from using a tape as one long file. If the tape is not supplied marked into sections in some way, but is a continuous medium for recording, there is a problem in overwriting one portion of the tape while leaving adjacent portions unaffected; for instance variations in tape speed cause difficulty. Therefore it was thought desirable to mark out sections, either with or without addresses. If addresses are not recorded on tape the programmer will either have to keep count of where he is on each tape in use, or, when he wishes to go to a particular section, he will have to run back to the beginning of the tape and start counting from the beginning. This situation, together with some considerations on tape life and quality, determined the use of addressed tapes.

The applications of magnetic tape to commercial problems also divides into categories, which will be taken as sorting, file processing and programme aid.

The programme aid category covers the second use mentioned for scientific applications.

Sorting usually involves four tape mechanisms, A, B, C, D. The basic cycle as it affects magnetic tape is as follows.

Either mechanism A or B is selected, more or less randomly, and the next section forward on the tape is read into the computer. One section of information is then written on the next section forward on tape C, D being unused, and the cycle is repeated. If two tape transfers can be carried out simultaneously (i.e. if there are two tape controls connected to the computer) then the write on to C takes place concurrently with the read from A or B. But more quick access storage is then required in the computer for information in transit between A or B and C, in order that it may be examined by the computer, while the tape orders are in progress, to determine which of A or B is to be used next. In either case the transfer time to and from tape is probably the limiting factor on the speed of the sorting operation. On the usual methods for estimating cost, sorting on the computer comes out more expensive than using a punched card sorter, but nevertheless its greater real speed and completely automatic functioning make it an important activity of commercial computers.

File processing involves running a master file (for instance of insurance policies, or stock control information in a factory or warehouse) through a mechanism, and probably writing out an amended copy of it, while taking in or putting out a number of other smaller files of information from the computer. The proportion of items in the master file which are affected will vary between one in one and one in twenty or less. The number of input and output channels required varies a great deal, and may be either punched cards or paper tape, or magnetic tape for subsequent printing or conversion to cards. If the amount of information to the output channels is small and there are many of them it may be preferable to put them all on one tape first and separate them after the main file has been processed, when more tape mechanisms will be free. If there are any alterations to the master file a completely new copy of the main file will usually be produced, for reason of security of information, which means that all the unaffected records will be copied too. Main files will often occupy a number of tape spools, and for very large files hundreds, and in this case rewinding the tape and changing the spool becomes a major time consuming operation. This time can be saved by using two mechanisms alternately for the successive tapes of a file, and thus rewinding and loading one mechanism while the other is in use.

Tape Mechanisms

It is considered that ½in tape is a useful minimum width for computer use since 8 channels may readily be accommodated. A separate address track is used, and since a clock track is necessary for identification of '1's and '0's on the information tracks ½in tape can accommodate 6 information channels. ¼in tape would accommodate only 2 information tracks assuming 4 tracks in all. It is not true to say, however, that ½in tape carries 3 times the information of ¼in tape since the start-stop gap between blocks on tape is proportionally greater on ¼in tape than on ½in tape for a given size of information block. Given then that ½in tape be used, as specified, a minimum length of tape of 2 400ft is necessary for a large number of commercial applications. Moreover a high tape speed is necessary on a tape system for use with a computer so as to obtain the highest frequency of signal from tape, consistent with a packing density of digits on tape which does not introduce unduly stringent limitations on tape guiding, skew of tape across recording heads, etc., and unreliability due to digits being small compared with blemishes in the tape surface. Finally a rapid start-stop time is necessary so as to reduce to a minimum the tape wasted between blocks of information on tape. For both programming and engineering reasons fixed block lengths are used on Pegasus and in the case of 16-word blocks these occupy 0·91in of tape.

In view of the time that would have been involved in developing a suitable tape unit it was decided to purchase tape units made by ElectroData Division of Burroughs Corporation of Pasadena, California. These tape units were chosen as being considered the best available. As supplied the units have a tape speed of 75in/sec ±1 per cent and a start-stop time of 7msec. Standard 10½in NARTB spools are used which in fact accommodate up to 3 600ft of the thin polyester base tape.

Reference to the photograph, Fig. 2, will give a general idea of the unit. The tape passes over two contra-rotating capstans from which it is drawn into two tape vacuum columns. With the unit at rest the tape in each column takes up a position between two rows of holes. Each row of holes communicates with a pressure chamber which operate magnetic blowout microswitches. The tape is moved into the forward or reverse direction by selecting a solenoid which presses the tape against the appropriate capstan by means of a pinch roller. As the tape moves into one vacuum column it passes the bottom row of holes. This operates the microswitch which directly switches the tape spooling motor armature current so that the tape spool takes up the surplus tape from the column. Similarly as tape is drawn from the other column so it passes the top row of holes in that column. This operates the microswitch so that the other tape spooling motor delivers tape to the vacuum column. In this manner loops of tape are held ready to permit the rapid start-stop time required as well as to ensure a continous drive of tape as required. A high-speed rewind operation is provided in which neither pinch roller is actuated. The bottom spooling motor drives continuously at its maximum speed with the tape in the left-hand column running over the pulley wheel at the top. The right-hand column maintains the flow of tape from the top spool as required, by the normal servo action. N.B., the left-hand column with the bottom spooling motor and the right-hand column with the top spooling motor form two independent servo systems.

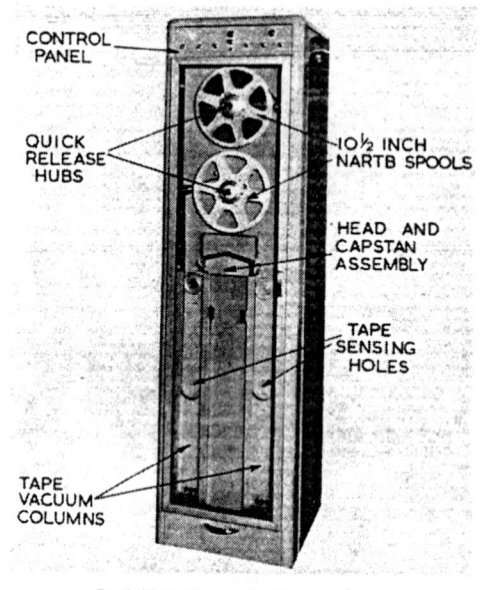

A further interesting feature of the tape unit is that single-edge guiding of the tape is used. This results in reduced modulation of tape signals as compared with the more common double flange guiding.

On each tape unit the tape chamber itself, i.e., that part of the unit containing the tape spools, capstans, tape vacuum columns, etc., is connected in a closed circuit air conditioning system which maintains the air at a temperature between 65° and 85°F. and 40 to 60 per cent relative humidity. This is necessary to ensure reliable operation of the tape irrespective of conditions in the computer room. Excessive temperature rise may lead to static electricity causing the tape to stick in the vacuum columns, and moist conditions lead to oxide sticking upon the heads and tape guides. The pressure in the tape chamber is slightly greater than atmospheric, preventing the entry of dust, and an electrostatic filter is built into the air conditioning system to maintain a high order of cleanliness in the tape chamber. The air conditioning equipment is mounted on the rear door of each unit. Each tape unit is on wheels and immediate access may be had to all working parts.

Magnetic Tape

When work was started on this tape store the only tapes available from European suppliers were standard audio quality. Such tapes all contain, depending upon the makes, greater or less quantities of impurities in the oxide, blemishes in the base and splices per given length. All these factors prevent the correct recording of digits on tape and so lead to unsatisfactory and unreliable operation of a tape store. It is therefore necessary to arrange that no recording takes place on bad regions of the tape. This is done by setting aside one track of the available eight as a block marker track (in fact addresses are used on Pegasus, as explained previously) in which the block markers or addresses are so positioned as to avoid the bad regions of tape. Having decided to do this it is better to choose a tape for its mechanical properties, specifically, mechanical strength and bonding of oxide to base, than for comparative freedom from blemishes. If bonding is poor the recording heads will get dirty quickly and loose oxide will accumulate in the tape unit and cause reading errors. It will have been gathered that the magnetic properties of the tape are comparatively unimportant. It so happens that the tape finally chosen is not only guaranteed splice free in lengths of 3 600ft, mechanically strong since it has a polyester base, but is also among the best from the point of view of purity of oxide and absence of blemishes. Blemish free tape is still not available in Europe.

Tapes are checked and addressed on a special piece of equipment—not on the computer. In this way it is possible to check and address a tape in two passes, by using a series of heads as follows. The first head records throughout all tracks at approximately double the working frequency, the second head is a reading head and checks for drop-outs, i.e., loss of signal amplitude. The third head erases 7 tracks and writes addresses at the correct spacing (for 16 or 32-word operation) on the address track. The fourth head checks that every address is correctly written. Evidently the distance between the second and third head is dependent upon the required block length on tape. Basically the principle of operation is that no address is written until a portion of error-free tape of the required length has passed the second head. It is found that

Annex No 7 Braunholtz & Hogg on magnetic tape system

about 93 to 95 per cent of the tape used is acceptable to the tape addresser. Each address is approximately 0·23in in length.

Layout of Information on Tape

In addition to a general requirement for a very high order of reliability of the tape store it was considered essential to be certain that every tape write order had been carried out successfully before proceeding with the next tape order. If a single read-write head were used this would involve reversing over the block of information and then reading it off in the forward direction and checking that it was correctly written. This would result in every write order taking about three times as long as a read order. The alternative scheme, which was adopted, is to mount read and write heads side by side, as close together as possible. There is a distance of 1in ±1/64in between the lines of the gaps of the two heads. A simplification in switching is also then ensured since one head only is ever connected to the reading circuits and the other to the writing circuits.

A tape write order causes the selected tape unit to search for the specified address. When this is found in the forward

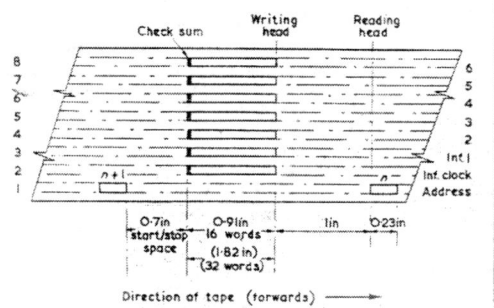

Fig. 3. Layout of information on magnetic tape

direction of tape as read by the reading head the writing head starts to write the block of information on the tape. There is, therefore, a gap of 1in between the address on tape and the block of information to which it refers. At 75in/sec tape speed this represents an increase of 13·3msec per transfer but this is felt to be more than justified for the reasons given above. The tape continues forward and the block is read immediately it reaches the reading head. A check is then made on the written information. It is generally true to say that once a block of information has been written on tape and read successfully then it will always subsequently be read correctly. The general arrangement of the heads and layout of information on tape is shown in Fig. 3.

It is necessary to specify the head spacing to 1in ±1/64in so that tapes written on one unit may be over-written on any other unit. In point of fact the writing head does not start writing immediately the required address is found but switches to a d.c. erase condition for a period of time sufficient to ensure that any digits of a block written on a tape unit whose head spacing is less, within the limits specified, than that on the unit currently used are erased. In this way interchangeability of tapes from unit to unit is readily ensured.

Information is written on the tape at the rate of one 6-bit character every 108μsec, i.e., at a frequency of 9·225kc/s. A clock pulse is written in the clock channel with every character. The clock track is not a parity track.

At a tape speed of 75in/sec a packing density of 9 225/75 = 123 bits/in is obtained. Thus each digit on tape has a cell length of about 0·008in. It would appear from our experience that packing densities of 250 to 300 bits/in are quite feasible.

Reading and Writing Heads

Reading and writing heads are identical and interchangeable. Each head has 8 tracks 0·045in in width separated from the adjacent tracks by 0·015in. The individual heads are made from mumetal laminations in a simple ring form. There are 200 turns of 46 s.w.g. wire per limb. The gap width is ·0005in and the inductance of each track is approximately 3·0mH. A direct current of 15mA will completely saturate all medium coercivity tapes. The method of recording is the return system[2]. It is felt that the recording techniques are sufficiently well established to warrant no further description in this article. The read signal from the reading head is approximately 15mV peak-to-peak. Such a large signal from a low impedance head means that head amplifiers on each tape unit are unnecessary provided

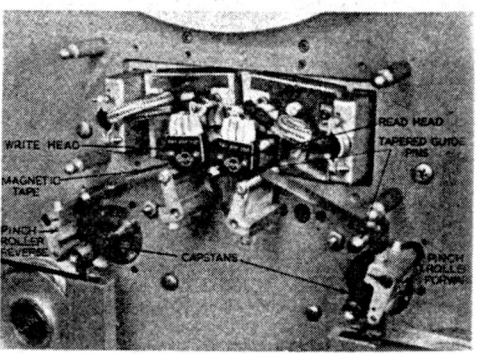

Fig. 4. Head and capstan assembly

earth return loops are avoided and adequate screening provided.

Each head is mounted on an individual head mounting plate and may be adjusted so that the tracks on the head register with the channels on a specially prepared master tape, so that the head face is parallel to the tape and so that the line of the head gaps is perpendicular to the direction of movement of the tape. In addition each head may be moved up and down in a vertical direction so that the amount of wrap-around may be adjusted. The use of pressure pads is not, in our view, practicable in a high speed tape unit. Our experience is that the wrap-around should be the least possible consistent with reliable operation. Excessive wrap-around leads to oxide sticking to the heads. With the adjustments described it is possible to adjust, and to lock into position, the two heads on each tape unit to exactly the same relative position with respect to the tape by means of a double beam oscilloscope and the specially prepared master tape referred to above. It is evidently necessary for interchangeability of tapes that all heads should be in the same relative position, as well as that the heads on each unit should be 1in ±1/64in apart, as described previously. It will be appreciated that with fine screw adjustments of the heads and a tape recorded at 20kc/s, which means at 75in/sec that one cycle corresponds to about 0·0038in, head adjustment is both easy and precise. The photograph, Fig. 4, shows the disposition of the heads, tape and tape guides.

Annex No 7 Braunholtz & Hogg on magnetic tape system

Control Desk, Reading and Writing Circuits

There is one set only of reading and writing circuits for all four tape units. These circuits are built on Pegasus packages and are mounted in the control desk attached to the side of the cabinet of equipment which controls all tape operations. Relay switching is employed to connect the heads of the selected unit to the reading and writing circuits. The drive signal to the tape units is selected electronically and since the relays operate in about half the time taken for the tape to get up to full speed the heads on the selected tape unit are connected to the reading and writing circuits before signals are reached. In this way relay switching is not a limiting factor on speed of changeover between tape units.

Separate 25-way cables are used for reading and writing head leads. The read cable carries only 8 pairs of leads to the 8 amplifiers. The write lead carries, in addition to writing currents, all control signals to and from the tape unit, i.e., drive forward, and reverse, rewind and rewind hold, 16 or 32-word operation, etc. Associated with each tape unit there is mounted on the control desk a 'write inhibit' switch so that a master file may be safely placed on a given tape unit with the 'write inhibit' switch on in the certain knowledge that no errors in programming or faults in the equipment can cause erasure of important records.

Length of Sections on Tape and Size of the Buffer Store

Variable length sections on tape were excluded by the decision to use addressed sections. It is desirable to use long sections on tape both in order to pack more information on a tape and to obtain higher effective tape speeds. On the other hand the buffer store to hold the long sections is expensive, since in Pegasus it is made of single-word nickel delay lines. A section length of 16 words is desirable on the ground that it contains 92 alpha-numeric (6-bit) characters, and therefore one 80 column punched card comfortably. (A card to tape, tape to card, and tape to printer convertor unit has been designed and built as part of the Pegasus System, and will be described in a later article.) Also, for uses in which the tape speed is adequate, 16-word sections have an advantage in being often simpler to handle by programme than 32-word sections, since twice the number of such sections can be kept in the quick access store at one time as of 32-word sections. But with 16-word tape only 40 per cent of the tape length is actually used to hold information. Therefore an alternative longer section was introduced. A length of 32 words was chosen, with about 60 per cent tape utilization. A longer section of, say, 64 words would be too large to be contained in the computing store, and would have to be transferred to the Pegasus drum in two halves, wasting about 20msec, which would cancel out the gain in effective tape speed.

The buffer store can be used to hold either one 32-word section or two 16-word sections. When it is used for 16-word sections it is possible to use one half of the buffer for transferring to or from tape and the other half for eight-word transfers to and from the computing store of Pegasus.

Reading and Writing Backwards

In some large commercial problems it would be useful to be able to read and write on tape in both directions. But it would be very expensive to do this, and appeared to be one of the least worthwhile of possible refinements.

Inter-Section Gap

The distance required along the tape for stopping from full speed and reaching full speed again (called the stop-start space), with safety tolerances added, is 0·7in. The problem arises whether or not to make this gap much shorter and expect the computer either to be ready for the next section when it arrives, while running the tape at full speed between sections, or to waste time in stepping back to the beginning of the section. But 6½msec gap time must be allowed in any case, for 32-word transfers, for testing the error register, clearing the buffer store and initiating the next order and during this time the tape moves nearly 0·5in. Thus with a 0·5in stop/start space the question of inter-gap wastage no longer arises, and with 0·7in is not a significant problem. If there were two buffer stores used alternately, however, the possibility of saving the stop-start space would arise again.

Method of Control

The division of the buffer store into blocks of eight words for transfer to and from the computing store is obvious, since transfers between the drum and computing store are in blocks of eight words. The interchange order exchanges the contents of a block of the buffer store with a block of the computing store; an alternative arrangement would be to have two orders, one transferring a block from the computing store to the buffer and the other transferring a block from the buffer to the computing store; the choice was one of convenience of design.

The method of specifying a tape order and initiating it is based on the assumption that each order would contain the address of the section to be read. The alternative would be to have tape orders of the form 'Read the next section forward' and 'Step back one section', and have only the search order specify an address. This method has been adopted on the Ferranti Perseus computer, but requires a little more equipment. With the Pegasus system the information required to specify a tape order will not fit into one computer order, so one Pegasus word is used, and given this control word the form of initiation of a tape order is as simple to use as any.

A method of repeating orders that have been incorrectly carried out alternative to that adopted in Pegasus would be to have, say, up to three repetitions carried out by the tape control automatically. But the Pegasus system leaves complete freedom to the programmer to take what action he wishes. The order to be repeated is still held in the tape control so that the programme does not have to try to unravel which was the last tape order to be initiated. By leaving action following an error at the discretion of the programmer, the way is left open for changes in after-error action, and possibly for large scale record-keeping by the computer on the frequency and nature of tape reading and recording errors.

Reliability and Built-in Checks

It is difficult to develop a rational approach to the problem of how much checking should be built into a computer. What appears to occur in practice is that each design group adopts a different attitude to the matter, and goes ahead with the design of its machine. When the machine is finally installed and tried out in practice an assessment can begin to be made on the degree of checking that must be built into the programmes and into the organization external to the machine.

The less reliable the machine, the greater the trouble and money put into the external checking, but however the balance lies, reliable computers by present standards can be successfully applied to commercial problems. Pegasus has shown a high standard of reliability, and the criterion adopted for the tape store was that this standard should be more than maintained.

Annex No 7 Braunholtz & Hogg on magnetic tape system

We are cautious about any claims of perfect reliability in any machine which is not checked throughout by duplication of components or equivalent devices. A claim that no undetected error has been known to occur is different from a claim that it is known that no undetected error has occurred. Errors undetected (in the sense of not detected until after the results have been removed from the computer) should be so rare that there is always doubt whether it was the computer's fault or not. In the case of Pegasus, as with most commercial systems, some programmed limit and sum check tests on the numerical part of commercial output may be required to achieve such a standard of accuracy.

There is one feature which magnetic tape has in common with some other input/output media, and which is not common to the internal part of a computer: errors in recording or reading off will from time to time occur, and are not to be treated as indicating that the system is in a faulty or marginal state and requires maintenance, nor is any doubt thrown upon the preceding calculations. Therefore far more errors will actually occur in transferring information to and from the tape than internally, and thus far more opportunity for compensating errors passing the checking system. In addition, the storage of tape has a very low usage rate compared with the interior of a computer, and so it is not subjected to continuous testing by use. For these reasons a higher standard of checking is required on tape than, for instance, on internal storage.

The checking arrangements built into the Pegasus tape store will now be described.

(1) In write orders, as explained above, the information is read back by a reading head one inch behind the write head, and check sums are compared. This checks almost all of the reading circuits and writing circuits against each other. In this comparison three check sums are compared: the check sum formed in the logic as the information ran out of the buffer store to be written on tape; the check sum formed while reading the section off tape; and the check sum read off tape. Any difference sets the error staticizor. This comparison of three check-sums makes sure that writing has in fact occurred, so that, for instance, failure of the h.t. supply to the write circuits will be detected at once.

(2) The parity check digit in each word of the computing store is made full use of. It is retained on transfer to the buffer store, from the buffer store to tape, from tape to the buffer store and from the buffer store to the computing store. When being written on tape each word has its parity digit checked, as also when being transferred from the buffer store to the computing store, and a failure stops the machine.

(3) The check-sum mentioned in (1) above is formed as follows: There is a check-sum register, which is empty at the start of a write order. As each 6-bit character is written on tape it is added to the check-sum character with end around carry. (End around carry means that carry off the most-significant bit position is added into the least-significant bit position.) A check-sum has the advantage over a parity check that two errors in the same sense on one track cause a compensating error on a parity system, but not on a check-sum system. The end around carry of the check-sum is necessary to avoid the most significant channel having only its parity checked. The frequency of errors obtained so far is in the region of one per 3 000 to 15 000 sections. Without having recorded any figures, there is nevertheless good theoretical reason to suppose that errors tend to be in the same sense at any one time. Also, errors which do occur consist usually only of one or a few digits. Thus the probability of a compensating error on the check-sum seems to be pretty remote.

(4) Another form of fault which would not affect the check-sum is the case when, due to distortion of tape or misalignment of heads, digits are read as being in the wrong character, either in front of or behind where they should have been. A check has been put in to prevent this happening. The device detects any signal arriving on

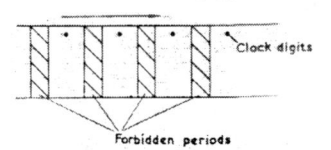

Fig. 5. Detection of faults due to distortion of tape & misalignment of heads

the information channels during a $30\mu sec$ gap between characters (Fig. 5).

(5) A count is kept of the number of information clock digits received during reading. If there should be a gap of 0.5 msec during which no clock digit arrives before the full number of clock digits have been received, the error staticizor is set. This will detect drop-out on clock digits.

(6) On the address track a parity count is kept of the address itself and a count of the clock digits is kept also. The form of addresses on tape is as shown,

$$1\delta 1\delta 1\delta 1 \ldots 1\delta 1 p 1$$

where the '1's are clocking digits and the δ the address digits (of which there are 14) and the p is the address parity digit. The parity on addresses would not appear to be so safe as the check-sum on information, but the following facts render the degree of safety great. Several successive drop-outs would include a clock digit, in which case the clock count would detect a fault; an error cannot do any harm unless the error turns the address into the address being searched for; in large scale working the next section forward will almost always be the section referred to, and a compensating error could do no harm.

(7) A buzzer on the tape control will ring for half a second whenever an error is detected. This will keep the operator and maintenance engineer informed of the state of the tape mechanisms; otherwise they would have very little knowledge of when the performance of a tape or mechanism was deteriorating.

REFERENCES

1. BRAUNHOLTZ, T. G. H., EMERY, G. The Design of the Pegasus Computer. *Electronic Engng.* 29, 358 & 420 (1957).
2. ROBINSON, A. A., MCAULAY, F., BANKS, A. H., HOGG, D. A Magnetic Tape Digital-Recording Equipment. *Proc. Instn. Elect. Engrs. 103B*, Suppl. No. 2, 337 (1956).

Acknowledgments

Our thanks are due to ElectroData Division of Burroughs Corporation for the ElectroData tape mechanisms and advice on their use; to Epsylon Sound Accessories Ltd, for the manufacture of the special heads used; to the Minnesota Mining & Manufacturing Co. Ltd (whose tape we use), for their assistance and co-operation.

This work would have been impossible without the knowledge and experience gained from the development of the 35mm tape store for the Ferranti Mark 1* computor.

Our thanks are also due to Mr. J. R. Travis, Dr. J. M. Bennett, Mr. J. F. Davison, Mr. G. E. Felton and Mr. P. M. Hunt for their invaluable contributions to the project, and to Mr. C. Strachey of N.R.D.C.P., to whom the form taken by the Pegasus computer is largely due.

Finally, thanks are due to the Directors of Ferranti Ltd. for permission to publish this article.

WIRE-TYPE ACOUSTIC DELAY LINES FOR DIGITAL STORAGE

By G. G. SCARROTT, Associate Member, and R. NAYLOR, M.Sc., Graduate.

(*The paper was first received 29th October, and in revised form 31st December, 1955. It was published in March, 1956, and was read at the* CONVENTION ON DIGITAL-COMPUTER TECHNIQUES, *12th April, 1956.*)

SUMMARY

The paper describes the design of acoustic delay lines using wire as the transmission medium. Delays of 3 millisec or more are possible with resolution adequate to permit a pulse repetition rate of 500 kc/s.

The acoustic signal is propagated in the torsional mode in wire of a material chosen for its low loss and negligible delay/temperature coefficient. The torsional mode is used, since thereby a longer delay can be made without intolerable distortion.

LIST OF SYMBOLS

A = Cross-sectional area of tape, cm².
c_L = Longitudinal phase velocity of sound in an infinitely thin straight wire, cm/sec.
c_T = Torsional phase velocity of sound in a straight wire, cm/sec.
E = Young's Modulus, dynes/cm².
E_s = Shear modulus of elasticity, dynes/cm².
H = Magnetic field, oersteds.
I = Moment of inertia per unit length, g-cm.
k = Radius of gyration, cm.
M = Bending moment, dyne-cm.
m = Mass per unit length, g/cm.
N = Number of digits in a store.
n = Number of tapes on a longitudinal-torsional mode transformer.
R = Radius of curvature of wire, cm.
R_n = Natural radius of curvature of wire, cm.
r = Radius of wire, cm.
S = Cross-sectional area, cm².
T = Temperature, deg C.
t = Time, sec.
v_L = Phase velocity of longitudinal stress waves, cm/sec.
v_T = Phase velocity of torsional stress waves, cm/sec.
x, y, l = Length, cm.
Z = Impedance (C.G.S. units).
θ = Angle of twist, rad.
λ = Wavelength, cm.
ρ = Density, g/cm³.
σ = Poisson's ratio.
τ = Time delay, sec.
ω = $2\pi f$.

(1) INTRODUCTION

Acoustic delay lines can be used for digital storage because the propagation of sound in solid and liquid media occurs at a low velocity compared with that of light and with a very small attenuation per unit wavelength.

The energy in the delay medium can be propagated as longitudinal, shear or torsional waves. When longitudinal waves are used the delay medium must be made with transverse dimensions either large or small compared with the wavelength, since at wavelengths comparable with the diameter severe dispersion occurs, owing to inter-mode coupling via Poisson contraction

effects. When shear waves are used the transverse dimension must be large compared with the wavelength. With torsional waves in a medium of circular cross-section, no dispersion occurs with any diameter. However, it is difficult to devise torsional transducers which can launch and detect plane waves over a diameter larger than the wavelength, and hence torsional delay lines cannot easily be made with large cross-section.

It follows that acoustic delay lines fall into two main classes, which may be called wide and narrow, distinguished by the ratio between transverse dimensions and wavelength. Wide delay lines are usually made using piezo-electric crystals as electromechanical transducers and mercury or quartz as the transmission medium. In this case, because of the large transverse dimensions the transducers can be made very thin in the direction of sound propagation without incurring prohibitive handling difficulties. Such delay lines can therefore be made to handle bandwidths of about 5 Mc/s without undue difficulty, since the length of the transducer in the direction of sound propagation determines the shortest sound wavelength which can be used effectively.

For narrow delay lines using wire as the transmission medium the transverse dimensions of the mechanical part of the transducer are smaller than the wavelength, and it is therefore impracticable to use such short waves. It follows that transducers for narrow-type delay lines cannot easily be made to handle bandwidths exceeding 1 Mc/s. However, since the length of the transducer is not less than the diameter of the wire, it is quite practicable to make the transducer by exploiting the magnetostriction effect in the wire itself. In spite of the inherently low efficiency of magnetostriction transducers, this arrangement is very convenient, since the problem of attaching small piezo-electric transducers to wire is thereby avoided. The use of wire as the delay medium confers the advantages that it can easily be drawn free from flaws, and by appropriate choice of material it can be obtained with negligible delay/temperature coefficient. A useful list of references for acoustical delay lines has been issued.[1]

(2) THE BASIC STORAGE SYSTEM

The schematic drawing of the basic storage unit is shown in Fig. 1. By means of the magnetostriction effect the transmitting

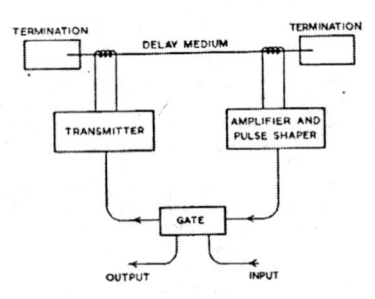

Fig. 1.—The basic unit.

Mr. Scarrott and Mr. Naylor are with Ferranti Ltd.

(2.1) Magnetostriction Transducers

It is well known that when a material is magnetized its linear dimensions are changed.[2] Fig. 2 shows a graph of the change

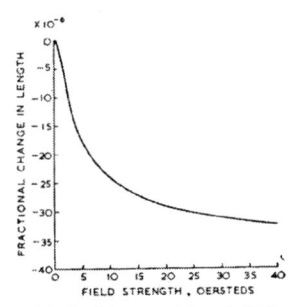

Fig. 2.—Magnetostriction of nickel.
Reproduced with permission from Reference 2.

in length per unit length along the direction of magnetization of a sample of nickel as a function of the applied magnetic field. Thus, when the transmitter valve permits current to flow in the transmitting coil, the wire becomes magnetized, causing the stress and particle-velocity waveforms to be as shown in Fig. 3. Particle velocity cannot be generated in zero time, and it is therefore convenient to describe the magnetized state as two equal stress waves of the same sign travelling in opposite directions, since the two waves superpose to cause stress but no particle velocity in the magnetized region.

One of these waves is absorbed in the termination, and the other travels along the wire to the receiving transducer and then to the other termination. The wire inside the receiving coil is magnetized by a biasing magnet so that the passing strain wave causes a change in the flux linking the coil. An output voltage pulse is therefore generated [Fig. 3(f)]. Thus a current step in the transmitter coil yields an anti-symmetric voltage signal (a di-pulse) in the receiver coil with a time interval t between the positive and negative peaks. When the current is turned off again another di-pulse of opposite sign results. If the time interval between turning on and turning off is made t, a symmetrical voltage signal is received which gives the best compromise between received signal amplitude and resolution time [Figs. 3(g) and 3(h)].

The upper limit of efficiency of the transducer action which has just been described is determined by the electro-mechanical coupling factor. This factor may be defined as the ratio between the energy density stored mechanically and that stored magnetically when a small change of magnetization occurs at constant length. The most efficient transducer action results if the magnetic circuit of the coil is made so that, when some electrical energy is supplied to the coil terminals, as much as possible of it should be stored magnetically in the magnetostrictive material. This occurs if the permeability of the material is high compared with that of air, but a high absolute permeability is not necessarily profitable. The most useful figure of merit for the magnetostrictive material is the electro-mechanical coupling factor defined above, which can be deduced as a function of permeability and magnetostriction coefficient.

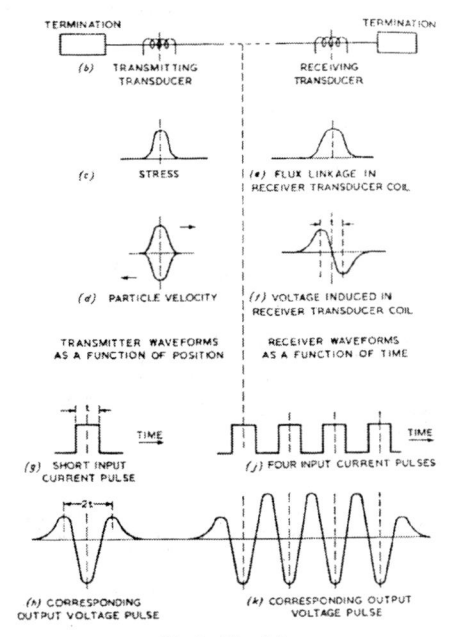

Fig. 3.—Waveforms.
(a)–(f) Due to a step function of current in the transmitting transducer.
(g), (h) Due to a short input pulse.
(j), (k) Due to four short input pulses.

Figs. 3(j) and 3(k) show the input current and corresponding output voltage waveforms for the system operating with the maximum digit rate at which the central peaks of neighbouring pulses do not interfere with one another.

The magnetostriction transducers are constructed by winding the coils as close as possible to the magnetostrictive material, the axial length of the coil being somewhat less than half a sound wavelength of the highest frequency which is required to be transmitted efficiently.

The upper limit to the number of turns on the coils is such that the resonant frequency of the coil together with stray capacitances is a little higher than the maximum frequency to be transmitted.

Ferroxcube cheeks are placed at the ends of the coils, since they reduce the length of the magnetostrictive material affected by the coil and thus increase the bandwidth of the system. Fig. 4 shows the amplitude/frequency response of a short delay line using receiver transducers with and without Ferroxcube cheeks, the separation of the cheeks being 0·2 cm. The transmitting transducers had Ferroxcube cheeks for both curves.

If the diameter of the wire inside the sending transducer is so great that the skin depth is small in comparison, eddy currents cause the total induction in the wire to be proportional to $1/\sqrt{\omega}$ with a phase lag of 45°. A similar effect occurs in the receiving transducer, so that the total effect is to modify the amplitude

Annex No 8 Scarrott & Naylor on enhanced delay-line store

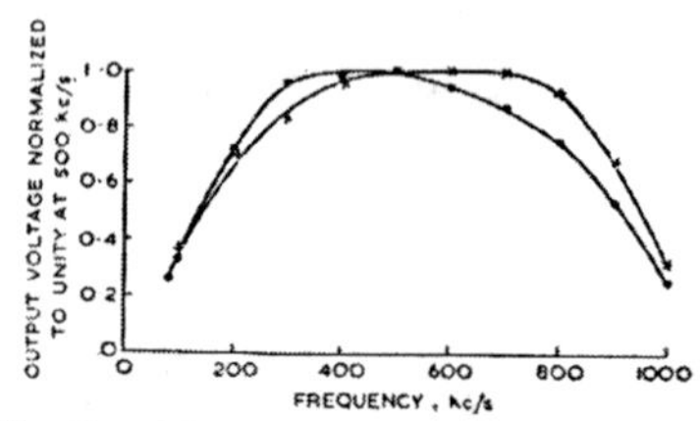

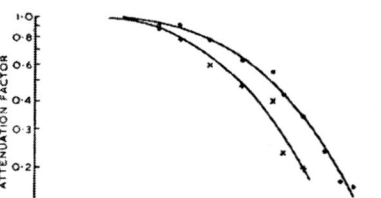

Fig. 4.—The effect of Ferroxcube cheeks on the amplitude response of the receiver transducer coils.
● Response without Ferroxcube cheeks.
× Response with Ferroxcube cheeks.

by a factor proportional to $1/\omega$ with a phase lag of 90°. This causes a distortion equivalent to an integration.

It was found experimentally that, for a 500 kc/s pulse repetition rate, 5-mil nickel tape gave the required output waveform with negligible distortion, but 40-mil tape caused the output waveshape to be completely integrated.

The performance of the transducers can be judged from the following figures: when using 20-mil × 5-mil annealed nickel tape, with transducers wound with 1 200 turns of 48 s.w.g. enamelled wire, a 17 mA input step results in a 0·2-volt peak-to-peak output transducer signal after 60 microsec delay. This delay is so short that negligible acoustic attenuation occurs.

(3) CHOICE OF MATERIALS

The ideal delay medium would be a loss-free substance which provides a delay and output waveshape independent of temperature changes. The material in the transducers should have a high electro-mechanical coupling.

Since these criteria cannot be satisfied by a single material, it was found convenient for long delays to weld two substances together, one having the high electro-mechanical coupling and the other having a low loss and negligible temperature coefficient of time delay.

(3.1) High Magnetostrictive Coefficient

The wire or tape inside the transducers is required to have a high electro-mechanical coupling in order to provide a high efficiency of power transfer. Annealed nickel was found to be a suitable material for this purpose, but other materials promise a better electro-mechanical coupling and are still under consideration.

(3.2) Low Loss for Transmission

The wire used as the delay medium should be made of a material which propagates sound waves with small loss, and experiments were carried out to obtain the amplitude/frequency responses of lines made of different materials (see Section 12.1).

Fig. 5 shows a typical result (nickel–iron–titanium alloy), from which it can be seen that the loss curve for a given time delay is substantially independent of the mode of transmission.

Fig. 6 shows the comparison of amplitude/frequency response of different materials normalized to 10 millisec delay from which the Q-factor can be obtained at a frequency f from

$$Q = -\frac{f\tau\pi}{\log_e A_f/A_0} \quad \quad (1)$$

where A_f/A_0 is the voltage loss at frequency f and τ is the time delay of 10 millisec.

Table 1 shows the values of Q-factor for different materials.

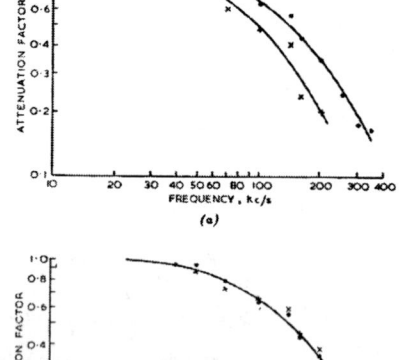

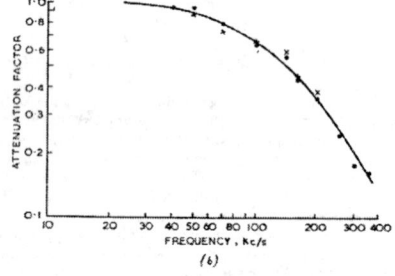

Fig. 5.—Amplitude/frequency responses for nickel–iron–titanium alloy.
(a) Attenuation factor for 28·6 m of wire.
(b) Attenuation factor for 5·7 millisec of delay.
● Longitudinal mode.
× Torsional mode.
The attenuation factor is measured as the output voltage normalized to unity at zero frequency.

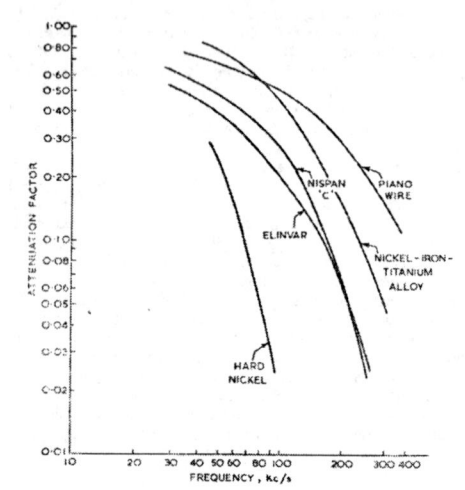

Fig. 6.—Comparison of amplitude/frequency responses of different materials normalized to a 10 millisec delay.
The attenuation factor is measured as the output voltage normalized to unity at zero frequency.

Annex No 8 Scarrott & Naylor on enhanced delay-line store

Table 1

COMPARISON OF Q-FACTORS FOR DIFFERENT MATERIALS AT 100 KC/S

Material	Q-factor
Piano wire	4 550
Nickel-iron-titanium alloy	4 030
Nispan C	2 500
Elinvar	2 300
Hard nickel	800

When the loss in the wire is of a hysteresis type, i.e. a constant loss per cycle, or the Q-factor is independent of frequency, the amplitude/frequency curves when plotted on a log-log scale should be exponential—as in the case of piano wire (see Fig. 6).

As might be expected, it was found that, in general, substances having a high Q-factor tend to have a low coefficient of magnetostriction, and vice versa.

The loss in nickel was found to increase as the wire was magnetized.

The above measurements were carried out on wire of 15 mils diameter.

(3.3) **Low Temperature Coefficient of Time Delay**

When using large-capacity stores it is essential that the time delay should not be dependent on temperature. The effect of temperature changes[3] can be seen by considering the following equation:

Since $$v_L = \sqrt{\frac{E}{\rho}}$$

the temperature coefficient of velocity is given by dv_L/v_L for a temperature change of 1°C.

Thus, $$\frac{dv_L}{v_L} = \frac{dE}{2E} - \frac{d\rho}{2\rho} \quad \ldots \ldots \quad (2)$$

but $$\frac{d\rho}{\rho} = -3\frac{dl}{l}$$

where l is the length of the line.

The relationship between the length of line, the time delay and the velocity of longitudinal waves is given by

$$\tau = l/v_L$$

and so $$\frac{d\tau}{\tau} = \frac{dl}{l} - \frac{dv_L}{v_L}$$

Thus, from eqn. (2)

$$\frac{d\tau}{\tau} = -\frac{1}{2}\left(\frac{dl}{l} + \frac{dE}{E}\right) \quad \ldots \ldots \quad (3)$$

Thus the material is required to have an elasticity/temperature coefficient equal and opposite to its linear expansion coefficient.

Since the shear elasticity/temperature coefficient is, in general, different from the Young's modulus temperature coefficient, slightly differing properties are required, depending on the mode of use.

Consider the maximum tolerance in the time delay to be $\pm 1/10$ digit period; then if the permitted temperature changes are within $\pm T^c$ the maximum number of digits that can be stored in a given line is

$$N = \frac{1}{10T\frac{d\tau}{\tau}} \quad \ldots \ldots \quad (4)$$

Experiments were carried out to measure the temperature coefficient of time delay of various materials using longitudinal waves (see Section 12.2). Table 2 shows a comparison of delay/temperature coefficients of the different materials, from which it can be seen that the nickel-iron-titanium alloy can be made to have a negligible value by carrying out the correct heat treatment.

Table 2

EXPERIMENTAL VALUES FOR TEMPERATURE COEFFICIENT OF TIME DELAY

Material	Temperature coefficient of time delay
	$\times 10^{-6}$
Hard nickel	+148
Piano wire	+136
Nispan C	+44
R31 steel	+6·7
Nickel-iron-titanium alloy from manufacturers	+28·8
The same after prolonged heat treatment	−45

A further list of temperature coefficients of time delay can be found elsewhere.[4]

(3.4) **Wire Supports**

It is difficult to make any theoretical predictions about the effect of specific support materials and devices. Experiment has shown that the blocks of synthetic sponge spaced at intervals of about 6 in circumferentially round the spiral provide adequate support and cause negligible acoustic effect.

(4) **CHOICE OF MODE**

In the preceding description of the operation of a magnetostriction transducer (see Section 2.1) it is clearly implied that the sound wave must be in the longitudinal mode in the portions of the wire in the transducers. However, since it is necessary to make the delay medium of different material (to reduce attenuation), the choice of mode in the delay medium can be considered to be still open. Longitudinal and torsional modes are the only ones free from gross distortion and will be considered in greater detail, under various headings.

(4.1) **Sound Velocity**

The velocity of propagation of longitudinal waves is given by

$$v_L = \sqrt{\frac{E}{\rho}}$$

and for torsional waves $$v_T = \sqrt{\frac{E_s}{\rho}}$$

where $$E_s = \frac{E}{2(1 + \sigma)}$$

Hence $$\frac{v_T}{v_L} = \sqrt{\left[\frac{1}{2(1+\sigma)}\right]} \simeq 0\cdot 6 \quad \ldots \quad (5)$$

since $\sigma \simeq 0\cdot 3$

Therefore a shorter length of wire is required for a given delay using torsional waves.

Annex No 8 Scarrott & Naylor on enhanced delay-line store

(4.2) Dispersion due to Finite Diameter of Wire

If the diameter of the wire is small, but not negligibly so compared with the sound wavelength, the phase velocity of longitudinal waves becomes dependent on the frequency according to the relation

$$v_L \simeq c_L\left(1 - \frac{2\pi^2 \sigma^2 k^2}{\lambda^2}\right) \quad \ldots \quad (6)$$

where $k^2 = r^2/2$ (see Section 12.3).

The dispersion due to this effect causes serious distortion, which can be minimized only by using very thin wire.

Since torsional strain in a circular wire is not accompanied by any other strain, no analogous dispersion occurs when using the torsional mode in the delay medium. It follows that a delay line employing the torsional mode can be made thicker than one employing the longitudinal mode.

(4.3) Curvature Dispersion

Since the velocity of sound in suitable materials is about 5 m/millisec for longitudinal waves, or 3 m/millisec for torsional waves, and the delay required may be several milliseconds, the wire must be coiled if it is to occupy a reasonable space. The curvature affects the phase velocity of both longitudinal and torsional waves by an amount which is a function of frequency, and therefore causes dispersion.

The phase velocity of longitudinal waves in a uniformly curved wire is given by

$$v_L \simeq c_L\left(1 + \frac{\lambda^2}{8\pi^2 R^2}\right) \quad \ldots \quad (7)$$

(see Section 12.4).

The dispersion due to this cause is serious with long delays and cannot be avoided without making the store of a clumsy size (with a large radius of curvature).

The phase velocity of torsional waves is also affected by the curvature of the wire according to the equation

$$v_T \simeq c_T\left[1 + \frac{\lambda_T^2(1+\sigma)}{8\pi^2 R_n R}\right] \quad \ldots \quad (8)$$

where R_n is the natural, and R the forced, radius of curvature (see Section 12.5). In this case the dispersion can be avoided by making $R_n = \infty$, i.e. by using wire which is naturally straight, coiled to a forced radius, R, which is too large to cause plastic deformation.

(4.4) Parasitic Transverse Motion

When waves which are principally of a longitudinal mode are propagated along a curved wire, they are accompanied by a parasitic transverse motion in the plane of curvature. A similar effect occurs when torsional waves are propagated in curved wire, when the parasitic transverse motion is normal to the plane of curvature.

The wire supports interfere with the transverse motion and lead to a form of dispersion.

It can be shown that for a given amount of wave power the parasitic motion is less in the torsional case than in the longitudinal case (see Section 12.6).

It is clear from the above arguments that it is advantageous to use the torsional mode of propagation in the delay medium.

(5) GENERATION OF TORSIONAL STRESS WAVES

Torsional waves may be efficiently launched and detected by the use of the mode transformer shown in Fig. 7. The two

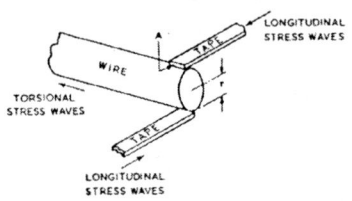

Fig. 7.—Mode transformer.

magnetostriction transducers launch longitudinal stress waves in the tape at equal distances from the wire, and these in turn cause torsional stress waves to be launched along the wire.

Section 12.7 gives the condition for matching the tape to the wire as

$$A = \frac{\pi r^2 \times 0 \cdot 3}{n} \quad \ldots \quad (9)$$

In general, two tapes are used (see Fig. 7). It should be noted that the transducers still launch longitudinal waves in the tapes, and so the physical dimensions of the transducer coils do not have to be reduced when using the torsional mode of propagation.

The diameter of the wire used for the torsional waves, 28 mils, is such that the peripheral distance between the welds is small compared with the wavelength of longitudinal waves.

The above theory considers the tape to be joined to the wire by perfect hinges. However, if a weld is used, the twisting of the wire tends to launch transverse waves back along the tape. Section 12.8 shows that, when using thin tape, the effect is negligible.

(6) METHODS OF PHASE ADJUSTMENT

As shown in Section 4.3, the use of the torsional mode in the delay wire renders phase distortion negligible. In the course of the development work, however, a rather powerful method of phase correction was devised. If the receiver transducer coil is long and such that the turns per unit length, n, are some function of distance x along the coil, say $n = f(x)$, the received waveshape is modified by convolution with a waveshape $f(x/v_L)$. It is clear that, if phase distortion is present (say due to supports or any other effect), there will always be some function which will correct this phase distortion and even slightly modify the pass band, if so desired.

Such a receiver coil has been called a correcting transducer coil.

(6.1) Low-Frequency Correction

To obtain the coil distribution, f(x), required to correct phase distortion in a given delay line it is first necessary to record the received waveshape due to a short transmitted pulse. The Fourier transform, $G(\omega)$, of this waveshape is a complex function of frequency. To correct a phase distortion only, the function $f(x/v_L)$ must have a Fourier transform $C(\omega)$ such that

$$\text{Arg } G(\omega) = -\text{Arg } C(\omega)$$

and $|C(\omega)| = \text{Constant over the pass band}$

Within limits, $|C(\omega)|$ can be chosen to be a function of ω which effects amplitude correction as well. Hence, knowing Arg $C(\omega)$ (from experiment) and $|C(\omega)|$ (from the known desired form of the received signal), a function $f(x/v_L)$ can be synthesized as the Fourier transform of $C(\omega)$.

The phase intercept of the whole system can be altered by an angle ϕ if desired by putting

Annex No 8 Scarrott & Naylor on enhanced delay-line store

$$\text{Arg } G(\omega) + \text{Arg } C(\omega) = \phi$$

The correcting function $f(x/v_L)$ can be checked by convolution with the original waveshape.

(6.2) High-Frequency Phase Modification

The alteration of the phase characteristic at high frequencies is best carried out by using lattice-type filters, the method being analogous to the delay equalization of television cables.[5]

(7) OPTIMUM USE OF BANDWIDTH

A complete delay-line system designed in the way described can be thought of as a communication channel of delay time τ and useful bandwidth f_b, which may be loosely defined[6] such that $\int_0^\infty A(f)df = A_{max} f_b$, where $A(f)$ is the amplitude at frequency f. This communication channel can be made into a store by regeneration in the well-known manner. The most efficient use of the channel would entail transmission at the maximum possible information rate through the channel. It is well known that in a positive bandwidth f_b cycles per second, $2f_b$ independent pulses per second can be sent. (If the response curve is rectangular, trapezoidal, or of certain other forms, this statement is exactly true with the above definition of bandwidth; in other cases it gives a good indication of the digit frequency which one may expect to achieve.) Hence if we accept the usual "all or nothing" mode of operating digital stores, $2f_b\tau$ digits can be stored. The usual methods of use as described in Section 2.1, give only half this capacity, and it is therefore profitable to consider ways of achieving the full capacity.

Although the conventional use of wire delay lines does not involve generation and modulation of a carrier wave, the loss of storage capacity is due to a mechanism similar to that which requires the doubled bandwidth in a double-sideband carrier system. It follows that in the general case, where the pass band is centred on an arbitrary frequency f, information can be sent along the channel at the full rate by using a single-sideband carrier system. This requires a low-pass filter and a frequency-changing modulator at each end of the system. A communication channel used in this way to transmit discrete pulses at the maximum rate has the curious property that, although pulses entering and leaving the complete system are all identical, pulses inside the channel are not, in general, identical, as their form depends on the phase of the carrier with respect to the pulses. Such parts of the channel would have to be strictly linear, otherwise pulses would suffer unequal distortion.

The single-sideband system requires elaborate equipment at each end, and it is thus of only theoretical interest in the present context. In some special cases, where f is an odd multiple of $\frac{1}{2}f_b$ and there is zero phase intercept, i.e. the output waveform is symmetrical for pulse input, it is immediately possible to achieve the full information rate. The delta-function response of such a system has zeros at times (after subtracting the overall delay τ) $\pm 1/2f$, $\pm 3/2f$, $\pm 5/2f$, etc., from the transmission time, which include the times $\pm 1/2f_b$, $\pm 3/2f_b$, $\pm 5/2f_b$, etc., in this case. The delta-function response of a pass band of width f_b has zeros at times $\pm 2/2f_b$, $\pm 4/2f_b$, etc., so that in this case the delta-function response has zeros at times $\pm 1/2f_b$, $\pm 2/2f_b$, $\pm 3/2f_b$, etc. Thus, independent pulses can be sent at intervals of $1/2f_b$, and the maximum output from any one pulse will coincide with zero output from each other, so that the pulses can be received without interference. It is also possible in certain other cases to achieve the full transmission rate without using single-sideband transmission. Thus if $f = f_b$ and there is no intercept, the delta-function response has zeros at times $\pm(1/2)/2f_b$, $\pm(3/2)/2f_b$, $\pm(5/2)/2f_b$, etc., since the centre frequency of the pass band is f_b, and at times $\pm 2/2f_b$, $\pm 4/2f_b$, etc., since the width of the pass band is f_b. Thus if pulses are transmitted at times 0, $1/4f_b$, $4/4f_b$, $5/4f_b$, $8/4f_b$, $9/4f_b$, etc., the maximum output from any one pulse coincides with zero output from each other.[7]

The response of a practical delay system is such that no energy is transmitted at zero or very low frequencies, but the ratio of frequencies passed by the system is fairly large, so that f is not much greater than $\frac{1}{2}f_b$. A method of exploiting such a pass band is to use a system which would, for theoretically perfect operation, require a low-frequency response proportional to frequency, and which is therefore such that a low-frequency cut-off removes only a very small amount of energy and does not affect the operation to any great extent. This requires that the output from each input pulse should be balanced about zero.

A method of achieving this would be to design the system to have an overall intercept of an odd number of right angles, so that an edge of current input yields a symmetrical output voltage. This could be achieved by suitable design of correcting transducer coil.

Fig. 8(a) shows a typical input signal from which the current drive to the transducer coil is as shown in Fig. 8(b). The output of the receiver, Fig. 8(c), at strobe time may have one of three values $+V$, $-V$ or 0, corresponding to a positive step, negative step or no change in the transmitter current.

The receiver output is compared at each strobe time with a comparator voltage derived from the result of the previous comparison [see Fig. 8(c)]. The effect is to make the strobed comparator treat the absence of any received signal as a signal of the same sign as that last received. Then a suitable output from the strobed comparator is a true copy of the input digit pattern.

At first sight the system appears to be ternary, depending on the recognition of three different levels of output. However, since only two different signals are transmitted, namely current or no current, it is a true binary system. At the receiving end, only two levels are to be recognized at any instant, since the output is either zero or an output opposite to that last received.

It should be emphasized that the non-return-to-zero method of working outlined above has not yet been put into operation.

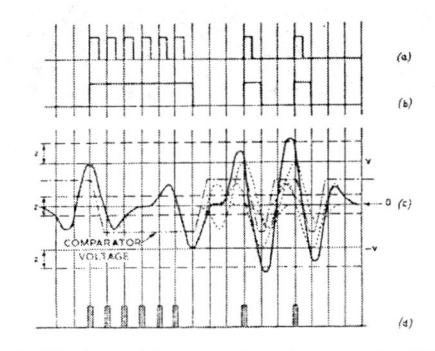

Fig. 8.—Waveforms of the system when using a non-return-to-zero method of operation.

(a) Input signal.
(b) Transmitter current.
(c) Receiver output.
(d) Delayed output signal.

The zones (z) in Fig. 8(c) are due to imperfections in the receiver waveshape.

Annex No 8 Scarrott & Naylor on enhanced delay-line store

(8) A PRACTICAL DELAY UNIT

A delay line has been made with about 30 ft of 28-mil-diameter nickel–iron–titanium alloy wire spiralled with a mean diameter of about 16 in. The line provides a delay of 3·2 millisec, and thus, when operating at a repetition rate of 500 kc/s, is capable of storing 1 600 digits. The temperature coefficient of time delay of the line is 4×10^{-6} per degC.

The transducer coils are 2·5 mm long, wound on polythene tubing using 100 turns of 48 s.w.g. enamelled wire. Ferroxcube checks are used, and the coils are transformer coupled to the transmitter and amplifier valves.

Fig. 9 shows the receiver output waveforms of the system

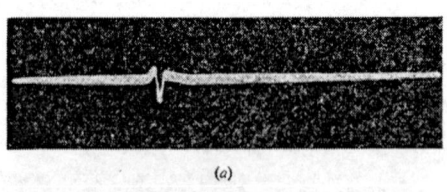

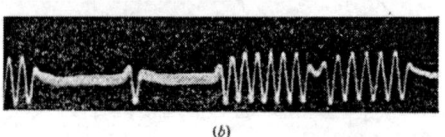

Fig. 9.—Output waveshapes of 3·2 millisec delay operating at 500 kc/s.
(a) Single pulse.
(b) Pulse pattern.

without any phase correction when operating at 2 microsec digit spacing.

(9) CONCLUSIONS

An acoustic delay system has been described which is cheap, reliable, robust and insensitive to temperature changes. This type of line is suitable for storage capacities up to 1 600 digits at digit rates up to 500 kc/s.

Since it is convenient to put more than one sending transducer on a single line, the wire-type delay line lends itself to multichannel working by a time-sharing method.

Fig. 10 shows a line used to provide two parallel channels in

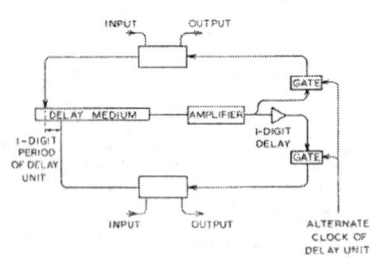

Fig. 10.—Delay line providing two channels by time sharing.

which the digit period of each channel is double that of the delay line.

The effective number of stores can, of course, be increased, depending on the number of transmitting transducers, even though only one piece of wire and one amplifier are required.

(10) ACKNOWLEDGMENTS

The authors wish to thank Ferranti Limited for permission to publish the paper, Mr. B. W. Pollard for his interest and encouragement, and Dr. G. Bradfield, Messrs. K. C. Johnson and J. Leech for their valuable discussions.

(11) REFERENCES

(1) FAGEN, M. D.: "Bibliography of Ultrasonic Delay Lines," Bell Telephone System Monograph No. 2317.
(2) BOZORTH, R. M.: "Ferromagnetism" (Van Nostrand, New York, 1951), pp. 11, 595 and 627.
(3) IDE, J. McDONALD: "Magnetostrictive Alloys with Low Temperature Coefficients of Frequency," *Proceedings of the Institute of Radio Engineers*, 1934, **22**, p. 177.
(4) CHANCE, B.: "Waveforms," Massachusetts Institute of Technology, Radiation Laboratory Series No. 19, 1949, p. 756.
(5) ALLNATT, J. W.: "The Delay Equalization of the London-Birmingham Television Cable System," *Proceedings I.E.E.*, Paper No. 1248 R, April, 1952 (**99**, IIIA, p. 338).
(6) STARR, A. T.: "Electric Circuits and Wave Filters" (Pitman, London), 2nd Edition (1940), p. 345.
(7) SUNDE, E. D.: "Theoretical Fundamentals of Pulse Transmission," *Bell System Technical Journal*, 1954, **33**, pp. 721 and 987.

(12) APPENDICES

(12.1) Measurement of Mechanical Losses in Various Materials

The schematic of the system used is shown in Fig. 11. Pulses

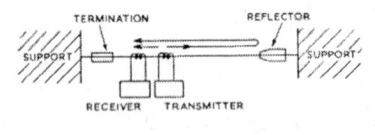

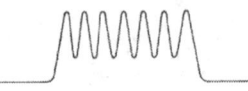

Fig. 11.—System used to measure the losses in the delay media.

of current as shown were transmitted, and the relative amplitudes of the direct and reflected signals were measured as the frequency of oscillations was varied. The results obtained gave the amplitude/frequency response of the delay media, as the paths from the transmitter to the output pass through the same transducers and amplifier.

In order to be able to measure the amplitude response of materials having a low magnetostriction coefficient, a relatively short length of nickel was butt-welded on to the material under test.

The attenuation/frequency responses for the torsional mode of propagation were obtained by twisting the annealed nickel under the transducers beyond the elastic limit, and since the longitudinal and torsional stress waves travel at different velocities, readings were easily taken. The generation of torsional waves is made possible because the lowest magnetic reluctance path is spiral.

(12.2) Measurement of Temperature Coefficient of Time Delay

The temperature coefficient of time delay of samples of wire was measured by using the wire as a resonant element and

Annex No 8 Scarrott & Naylor on enhanced delay-line store

observing the frequency changes, relative to a crystal oscillator, as the temperature was varied.

Specimens of wire were cut to about 10 cm length, i.e. two wavelengths of the longitudinal mode of 100 kc/s oscillations, and were held by paper supports at the displacement nodes (see Fig. 12). The transmitting and receiving transducers were placed as shown in the diagram, and the system was connected to form a magnetostriction oscillator. The resonant element and the transducers were mounted in a metal box, which was heated by an external electric lamp.

Fig. 13 shows the circuit of the oscillator. The output signal

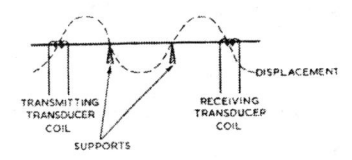

Fig. 12.—Resonant line used to measure the temperature coefficient of time delay of longitudinal waves.
The supports are at displacement nodes or stress antinodes.

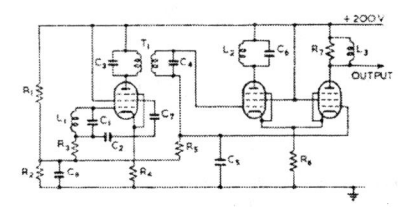

Fig. 13.—Magnetostriction oscillator.

R_1, 33 kΩ C_1, 22 μμF
R_2, R_4, 10 kΩ C_2, 0·02 μF
R_3, R_5, 39 kΩ C_3, C_4, 680 μμF
R_6, 6·8 kΩ C_5, 0·02 μF
R_7, 150 Ω C_6, 220 μμF
C_7, C_8, 0·02 μF
L_1, Receiving transducer coil.
L_2, Transmitting transducer coil.
L_3, 1 mH.
T_1, Dust-core transformer.
Valves, EF91.

is a differential square-wave, the time-constant of differentiation being long relative to the oscillation period. The output of the crystal oscillator was differentiated with a time-constant short relative to the oscillation period.

The two differentiated signals were then added, rectified filtered and fed to the plates of an oscillograph (see Fig. 14); the

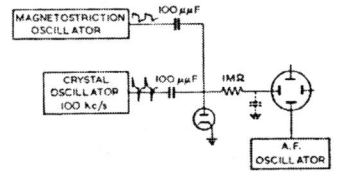

Fig. 14.—Block diagram of the apparatus used to measure the temperature coefficient of time delay.

resultant waveform formed a Lissajous figure with the output of an a.f. oscillator.

The length of the resonant element was adjusted by grinding so that the difference between the high frequencies was comparable with the audio frequency. The change of frequency with temperature was obtained from the readings of the a.f. oscillator, which gave stationary Lissajous figures.

The differentiation of the square waves enabled one to determine whether the magnetostriction oscillator frequency was above or below that of the crystal oscillator.

(12.3) Dispersion of Longitudinal Waves in a Straight Wire

Consider a length, $2l$, of straight wire with finite dimensions oscillating as shown in Fig. 15.

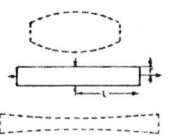

Fig. 15.—Longitudinal resonance in a segment of wire of finite transverse dimensions.

Divide the wire into filaments parallel to the axis and postulate that the wire executes oscillations at an angular frequency ω, so that the longitudinal displacement is given by

$$y = y_0 \sin \frac{\pi x}{2l} \sin \omega t$$

Hence, the longitudinal strain, $\partial y/\partial x$ is given by

$$\frac{\partial y}{\partial x} = y_0 \frac{\pi}{2l} \cos \frac{\pi x}{2l} \sin \omega t \quad \ldots \quad (10)$$

and thus the lateral strain is

$$\frac{\sigma y_0 \pi}{2l} \cos \frac{\pi x}{2l} \sin \omega t \quad \ldots \quad (11)$$

Consider a filament at a distance q from the axis of symmetry to be of length $2l$ and have an area dS; the potential energy at peak extension is then given by

$$dS 2l E \frac{1}{2} \frac{1}{2} \left(\frac{y_0 \pi}{2l}\right)^2 \quad \ldots \quad (12)$$

Since the peak longitudinal velocity is ωy_0, the longitudinal kinetic energy at zero extension is given by

$$\tfrac{1}{2} dS 2l \rho \times \tfrac{1}{2}(\omega y_0)^2 \quad \ldots \quad (13)$$

Expression (11) gives the lateral strain:

$$\frac{\sigma y_0 \pi}{2l} \cos \frac{\pi x}{2l} \sin \omega t$$

so that the lateral displacement of the filament at a distance q from the axis of symmetry is

$$\frac{q \sigma y_0 \pi}{2l} \cos \frac{\pi x}{2l} \sin \omega t$$

Thus, the lateral velocity is

$$\frac{\omega q \sigma y_0 \pi}{2l} \cos \frac{\pi x}{2l} \cos \omega t$$

and the peak lateral velocity is

$$\frac{\omega q \sigma y_0 \pi}{2l}$$

Annex No 8 Scarrott & Naylor on enhanced delay-line store

Thus, the transverse kinetic energy at zero extension is

$$\tfrac{1}{2}dS2l\rho\tfrac{1}{2}\left(\frac{\omega q\sigma y_0 \pi}{2l}\right)^2 \quad \ldots \ldots \quad (14)$$

Equating potential and kinetic energies from expressions (12)–(14) gives

$$E\left(\frac{\pi}{2l}\right)^2 dS = \rho\left(\omega^2 + \frac{\omega^2 q^2 \pi^2 \sigma^2}{4l^2}\right) dS$$

Integrating for all the filaments in the wire gives

$$SE\left(\frac{\pi}{2l}\right)^2 = \rho\omega^2\left(S + \frac{\sigma^2 \pi^2 S k^2}{4l^2}\right)$$

since
$$\int q^2 dS = k^2 S$$

Thus,
$$\frac{E}{\rho} = \left(\frac{2\omega l}{\pi}\right)^2 + \omega^2 \sigma^2 k^2$$

or
$$c_L^2 = v_L^2 + \omega^2 \sigma^2 k^2$$

Therefore
$$v_L \simeq c_L\left(1 - \tfrac{1}{2}\frac{\omega^2 \sigma^2 k^2}{c_L^2}\right) \quad \ldots \quad (15)$$

provided that $\left(\frac{\omega^2 \sigma^2 k^2}{c_L^2}\right)^2$ is negligible,

or
$$v_L \simeq c_L\left(1 - \frac{2\pi^2 \sigma^2 k^2}{\lambda^2}\right)$$

This result is given in Love's "Mathematical Theory of Elasticity" (4th Edition, 1927, p. 290).

The above method of proof illustrates the procedure followed in analysing the more complex cases given in Sections 12.4 and 12.5.

(12.4) Dispersion of Longitudinal Waves in a Wire Possessing Curvature

Consider a segment of wire, with a radius of curvature as shown in Fig. 16(a), oscillating longitudinally. In order to con-

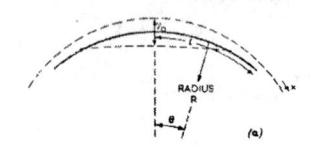

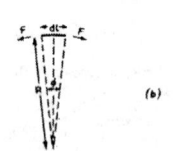

Fig. 16.—Curved segment in longitudinal resonance.
(a) Complete segment.
(b) An element thereof.

serve transverse momentum the longitudinal motion must give rise to a transverse motion in its plane of curvature; at the peak extension the energy is stored entirely as elastic energy, the longitudinal velocity at the ends is zero and the transverse velocity at the centre is zero.

Let the maximum strain at the centre be δ; then the stored potential energy is given by

$$\tfrac{1}{2}2lSE\tfrac{1}{2}\delta^2 \quad \ldots \ldots \quad (16)$$

$\tfrac{1}{2}\delta^2$ being the mean square strain, since the strain is sinusoidally distributed.

When the element is in the centre position the energy is in a kinetic form and is given by

$$\tfrac{1}{2}2lS\rho\frac{(\hat{v}_l^2 + \hat{v}_t^2)}{2} \quad \ldots \ldots \quad (17)$$

since the longitudinal and transverse velocities (v_l and v_t) are sinusoidally distributed.

In the extreme position the element of wire is lengthened by the longitudinal motion, x_0, at the ends and the transverse motion, y_0, at the middle. To determine the latter, consider the transverse motion at an angle θ from the perpendicular bisector to be given by

$$y = y_0 \cos\frac{\pi R\theta}{2l}$$

Then, since the extension is $yd\theta$, the total extension is

$$\int_{-l/R}^{l/R} y d\theta = \frac{4ly_0}{\pi R}$$

Thus, the mean strain due to the transverse motion y is given by $2y_0/\pi R$, and the total mean strain is given by

$$\frac{2y_0}{\pi R} + \frac{x_0}{l} = \frac{2\delta}{\pi} \quad \ldots \ldots \quad (18)$$

Consider now a small length dl at the centre of the wire; the transverse acceleration of this segment is the peak acceleration and is caused by the peak strain. Therefore the restoring force is $F\phi$ [see Fig. 16(b)] (ϕ small), and since $E = F/\delta S$ the restoring force is given by

$$F\phi = ES\delta\phi = ES\delta dl/R$$

Thus, the equation of motion is

$$dlS\rho\omega^2 y_0 = ES\delta dl/R$$

Therefore
$$y_0 = \frac{E\delta}{\omega^2 R\rho} \quad \ldots \ldots \quad (19)$$

Thus, the peak velocity, $\hat{v}_t$ is given by

$$\hat{v}_t = \omega y_0 = \frac{E\delta}{\omega R\rho} \quad \ldots \ldots \quad (20)$$

Substituting the value y_0 from eqn. (19) into eqn. (18) gives

$$x_0 = \frac{2l\delta}{\pi}\left(1 - \frac{E}{\rho R^2 \omega^2}\right) \quad \ldots \ldots \quad (21)$$

The peak longitudinal velocity, $\hat{v}_l$, is given by

$$\hat{v}_l = \omega x_0$$

and substitution for x_0 from eqn. (21) yields

$$\left.\begin{array}{l} \hat{v}_l = \dfrac{2\omega l\delta}{\pi}\left(1 - \dfrac{E}{\rho R^2 \omega^2}\right) \\[4pt] \text{or} \quad \hat{v}_l = \dfrac{2\omega l\delta}{\pi}\left(1 - \dfrac{c_L^2}{R^2 \omega^2}\right) \end{array}\right\} \quad (22)$$

since
$$c_L^2 = E/\rho$$

Annex No 8 Scarrott & Naylor on enhanced delay-line store

Equating energies, neglecting bending strains, i.e. eqns. (16) and (17) and substituting for $\hat{v}_l$ and $\hat{v}_t$ from eqns. (20) and (22) gives

$$E = \rho\left\{\frac{c_L^4}{\omega^2 R^2} + \left[\frac{2\omega l}{\pi}\left(1 - \frac{c_L^2}{\omega^2 R^2}\right)\right]^2\right\}$$

but since $l = \lambda/4$, then $v_L = f\lambda = 2l\omega/\pi$ and so

$$c_L^2 = \left(\frac{c_L^2}{\omega R}\right)^2 + v_L^2\left(1 - \frac{c_L^2}{\omega^2 R^2}\right)^2$$

Rearranging gives

$$\left.\begin{array}{l} v_L = c_L\left[1 - \left(\frac{c_L}{\omega R}\right)^2\right]^{-1/2} \\ \text{or} \quad v_L \simeq c_L\left(1 + \frac{c_L^2}{2\omega^2 R^2}\right) \end{array}\right\} \quad \ldots \quad (23)$$

provided that $\quad c_L^4 \ll (2\omega^2 R^2)^2$

or $\quad v_L \simeq c_L\left(1 + \frac{\lambda^2}{8\pi^2 R^2}\right)$

(12.5) Dispersion of Torsional Waves in a Wire possessing Curvature

Fig. 17 shows a specimen of curved wire oscillating torsionally.

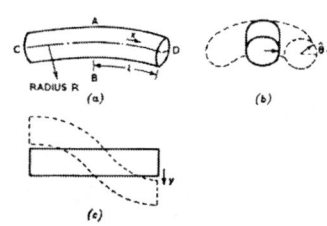

Fig. 17.—Curved segment in torsional resonance.
(b) View of (a) seen along DC.
(c) View of (a) seen along BA.

In order to conserve angular momentum about axis BA there must be a small transverse oscillation normal to the plane of curvature. Then consider the angle of twist, θ, to be given by

$$\theta = \hat{\theta}\sin\frac{\pi x}{2l}\sin\omega t$$

and the transverse displacement, y, to be given by

$$y = \hat{y}\sin\frac{\pi x}{2l}\sin\omega t$$

The axial angular momentum of an element dx of the wire is given by

$$I\omega dx\hat{\theta}\sin\frac{\pi x}{2l}\cos\omega t$$

Thus the angular moment resolved about an axis BA (Fig. 17) is

$$I\omega dx\hat{\theta}\sin\frac{\pi x}{2l}\cos\omega t\sin\left(\frac{x}{R}\right)$$

Therefore the total resolved angular momentum is

$$I\omega\hat{\theta}\cos\omega t\int_{-l}^{+l}\sin\frac{\pi x}{2l}\sin\left(\frac{x}{R}\right)dx$$

$$= I\omega\hat{\theta}\frac{8l^2}{\pi^2 R}\frac{\cos l/R}{1 - \frac{4l^2}{\pi^2 R^2}}\cos\omega t$$

$$\simeq I\omega\hat{\theta}\cos\omega t\frac{8l^2}{\pi^2 R} \quad \ldots \quad (24)$$

provided that $l \ll R$ and $4l^2/\pi^2 \ll R^2$

There is some additional angular momentum about the axis BA due to transverse motion, so that an element has angular momentum of

$$-xmdx\hat{y}\omega\sin\frac{\pi x}{2l}\cos\omega t$$

Thus the total angular momentum is

$$-m\omega\hat{y}\int_{-l}^{l}x\sin\frac{\pi x}{2l}\cos\omega t\,dx$$

$$= -m\omega\hat{y}\frac{8l^2}{\pi^2}\cos\omega t \quad \ldots \quad (25)$$

Since the total angular momentum must be zero, the sum of expressions (24) and (25) must be zero, i.e.

$$I\omega\hat{\theta}\frac{8l^2}{\pi^2 R}\cos\omega t = m\omega\hat{y}\cos\frac{8l^2}{\pi^2}\omega t$$

Therefore $\quad \hat{y} = \frac{I\hat{\theta}}{mR} = \frac{\hat{\theta}k^2}{R} \quad \ldots \quad (26)$

The method of determining dispersion of torsional waves in a wire possessing curvature can be found, as shown in Sections 12.3 and 12.4, by equating the total peak kinetic and peak potential energies of an oscillatory segment.

The rotational kinetic energy of an element is given by

$$\tfrac{1}{2}I dx\left(\hat{\theta}\omega\sin\frac{\pi x}{2l}\cos\omega t\right)^2$$

and thus the peak rotational kinetic energy is

$$\tfrac{1}{2}I\hat{\theta}^2\omega^2\int_{-l}^{l}\sin^2\left(\frac{\pi x}{2l}\right)dx$$

$$= \tfrac{1}{2}I\hat{\theta}^2\omega^2 l = \tfrac{1}{2}mk_0^2\hat{\theta}^2\omega^2 l \quad \ldots \quad (27)$$

The transverse kinetic energy of an element is

$$\tfrac{1}{2}mdx\left(\hat{y}\omega\sin\frac{\pi x}{2l}\cos\omega t\right)^2$$

and thus the peak transverse kinetic energy is

$$\tfrac{1}{2}m\hat{y}^2\omega^2 l \quad \ldots \quad (28)$$

Thus the total peak kinetic energy is given by the sum of expressions (27) and (28), i.e.

$$\tfrac{1}{2}ml\omega^2\left(k^2\hat{\theta}_0^2 + \hat{\theta}^2\frac{k^4}{R^2}\right)$$

$$= \tfrac{1}{2}\rho Sk^2l\omega^2\hat{\theta}_0^2\left(1 + \frac{k^2}{R^2}\right) \quad \ldots \quad (29)$$

To determine the peak potential energy, consider the twist, $d\theta/dx$, of a typical element due to the primary twist, i.e.

$$\frac{d\theta}{dx} = \hat{\theta}\frac{\pi}{2l}\sin\omega t\cos\frac{\pi x}{2l} \quad \ldots \quad (30)$$

Annex No 8 Scarrott & Naylor on enhanced delay-line store

Consider now an element of length dx and curvature $1/R$; the twist required to make it a portion of a helix at an angle ϕ to the original plane of curvature is ϕ/R. But, for a typical element,

$$\phi \simeq \frac{dy}{dx} = \hat{y}\frac{\pi}{2l} \sin \omega t \cos \frac{\pi x}{2l}$$

Therefore
$$\frac{\phi}{R} = \frac{\hat{y}\pi}{R2l} \sin \omega t \cos \frac{\pi x}{2l} \quad \ldots \quad (31)$$

Thus the total twist of a typical element is obtained from the sum of eqns. (30) and (31), and so the stored twist energy in the element is

$$\tfrac{1}{2}E_s k_t^2 \left[\frac{\pi}{2l}\left(\hat{\theta}+\frac{\hat{y}}{R}\right)\sin \omega t \cos \frac{\pi x}{2l}\right]^2 S dx$$

Substituting for $\hat{y}$ from eqn. (26) gives

$$\tfrac{1}{2}E_s k_t^2 \frac{\pi^2}{4l^2}\left(\hat{\theta}+\hat{\theta}\frac{k^2}{R^2}\right)^2 \left(\sin \omega t \cos \frac{\pi x}{2l}\right)^2 S dx$$

Thus, the total peak twist elastic energy is

$$\tfrac{1}{2}E_s k_t^2 S \hat{\theta}^2 \left(1+\frac{k^2}{R^2}\right)\frac{\pi^2}{4l} \quad \ldots \quad (32)$$

Consider now a filament of the wire at a distance q from the neutral axis bent with a curvature C; then the energy stored per unit length is

$$\tfrac{1}{2}E(qC)^2 dS$$

Thus, integrating over the cross-sectional area, S, of the bar gives the energy stored per unit length as

$$\tfrac{1}{2}EC^2 \int q^2 dS = \tfrac{1}{2}EC^2 k_t^2 S$$

where k_t is the transverse radius of gyration.
If a wire having a natural curvature $1/R_n$ and forced curvature $1/R$ in the same plane is twisted through an angle θ, it can be shown that the energy stored per unit length is

$$\frac{1}{2}\frac{E}{R_n R}\theta^2 k_t^2 S \quad \ldots \quad (33)$$

This same energy is released if the signs of one of the curvatures $1/R_n$ or $1/R$ is reversed. It should be noted that the support reactions of the wire are minimized when the natural and forced curvatures are in the same plane. Thus, the bending elastic energy of an element of length dx due to twisting through an angle θ is

$$\frac{1}{2}\frac{E}{R_n R}Sk_t^2\left(\hat{\theta}\sin\frac{\pi x}{2l}\sin \omega t\right)^2 dx$$

Hence the peak bending elastic energy is

$$\frac{1}{2}\frac{E}{R_n R}Sk_t^2 \hat{\theta}^2 l$$

$$= \frac{E_s(1+\sigma)}{R_n R}Sk_t^2 \hat{\theta}^2 l \quad \ldots \quad (34)$$

since $E = 2E_s(1+\sigma)$

Thus, by equating elastic and kinetic energies from expressions (29), (32) and (34), we obtain

$$\frac{4\omega^2 l^2}{\pi^2}\left(1+\frac{k^2}{R^2}\right) = \frac{E_s}{\rho}\left[\left(1+\frac{k^2}{R^2}\right)^2 + \frac{2k_t^2}{k^2}\frac{(1+\sigma)}{R_n R}\frac{4l^2}{\pi^2}\right]$$

But since $l = \lambda/4$ whence $4\omega^2 l^2/\pi^2 = v_T^2$ and $E_s/\rho = c_T^2$,

$$v_T^2 = c_T^2\left[1 + \frac{k^2}{R^2} + 2\left(\frac{k_t}{k}\right)^2 \frac{(1+\sigma)}{RR_n\left(1+\frac{k^2}{R^2}\right)}\frac{v_T^2}{\omega^2}\right]$$

But $\left(\frac{k_t}{k}\right)^2 = \frac{1}{2}$

Therefore
$$v_T^2 = \frac{c_T^2\left(1+\frac{k^2}{R^2}\right)}{1 - \frac{c_T^2}{\omega^2}\frac{(1+\sigma)}{RR_n\left(1+\frac{k^2}{R^2}\right)}}$$

Since $k^2/R^2 \ll 1$

$$v_t^2 = \frac{c_t^2}{1 - \frac{c_t^2(1+\sigma)}{\omega^2 R_n R}}$$

or
$$v_T \simeq c_T\left[1 + \frac{1}{2}\frac{c_T^2(1+\sigma)}{\omega^2 R_n R}\right] \quad \ldots \quad (35)$$

provided that $\left[\frac{c_T^2(1+\sigma)}{2\omega^2 R_n R}\right]^2$ is negligible

or
$$v_T \simeq c_T\left[1 + \frac{1}{8}\frac{\lambda_T^2}{\pi^2}\frac{(1+\sigma)}{R_n R}\right]$$

So that $v_T = c_T$ if either R or R_n becomes infinite.

(12.6) Comparison of Transverse Parasitic Motions due to Curvature

It is desired to compare the parasitic transverse motion when a given curved wire is propagating longitudinal waves with the transverse momentum caused in the same wire by an equal amount of torsional wave power.

Equating the peak kinetic energies per half wavelength in the two cases, from expressions (17) and (29), gives

$$\tfrac{1}{2}2l_L Sp\frac{(\hat{v}_t^2 + \hat{v}_r^2)}{2} = \tfrac{1}{4}\rho Sk^2 l_T \omega^2 \hat{\theta}^2\left(1+\frac{k^2}{R^2}\right) \quad \ldots \quad (36)$$

Substitution for $\hat{v}_t$ from eqn. (22), for $\hat{v}_r$ from eqn. (20), δ from eqn. (19) and $\hat{\theta}$ from eqn. (26) shows

$$\frac{y_T}{y_L} = \frac{\sqrt{(2\pi r)}}{\sqrt{(\lambda_T \lambda_L)}} \quad \ldots \quad (37)$$

if it is assumed that $(R/\lambda_L)^2 \gg 1$ and $(R/k)^2 \gg 1$, where λ_T and λ_L are the wavelengths of torsional and longitudinal waves respectively.

Since λ_T and λ_l are both large compared with the radius of the wire, it follows that the parasitic transvervse motion is less for torsional waves than for longitudinal waves.

(12.7) Mode Transformer

The acoustic impedance of a longitudinal wave travelling along tape is given by

$$Z_L = \sqrt{\left(\frac{\text{Mass}}{\text{Compliance}}\right)}$$

or
$$Z_L = A\sqrt{(\rho E)}$$

Annex No 8 Scarrott & Naylor on enhanced delay-line store

The acoustic impedance of the torsional wave in wire is

$$Z_T = \sqrt{\left(\frac{\text{Moment of inertia}}{\text{Angle per unit torque}}\right)}$$

or

$$Z_T = \frac{\pi r^4}{2}\sqrt{(E_s\rho)}$$

Since $Z_T = r^2 Z_L$, then with n tapes being matched to the wire,

$$Z_T = r^2 n Z_L \quad \ldots \ldots \quad (38)$$

and by substitution

$$A = \frac{\pi r^2}{2n}\sqrt{\frac{E_s}{E}}$$

assuming the density of tape and wire to be equal.
Since $\sqrt{(E_s/E)} \simeq 0{\cdot}6$, then with two tapes

$$A = 0{\cdot}15\pi r^2 \quad \ldots \ldots \quad (39)$$

(12.8) Parasitic Transverse Wave Motion in the Tapes due to Imperfect Mode Transformers

The following theory gives the torsional impedance due to the twisting of the wire at the mode transformer feeding transverse waves back along the tape, since the tape is joined to the wire by a weld and not a perfect hinge.

Consider the transverse deflection, y, of the tape at a distance x from the weld; the curvature is $\partial^2 y/\partial x^2$ and the bending moment, M, is given by

$$M = EAk_T^2 \frac{\partial^2 y}{\partial x^2} \quad \ldots \ldots \quad (40)$$

The shear force, F, on the tape due to this bending moment is

$$F = -\frac{\partial M}{\partial x} = -EAk_T^2 \frac{\partial^3 y}{\partial x^3}$$

and hence the transverse restoring force, dF, on the tape is obtained from $\partial F/\partial x$;

i.e.

$$dF = -EAk_T^2 \frac{\partial^4 y}{\partial x^4}dx$$

Thus, the acceleration is given by

$$-\frac{Ek_T^2}{\rho}\frac{\partial^4 y}{\partial x^4} = \frac{\partial^2 y}{\partial t^2}$$

Therefore

$$\frac{\partial^4 y}{\partial x^4} + \frac{1}{c_l^2 k_T^2}\frac{\partial^2 y}{\partial t^2} = 0 \quad \ldots \ldots \quad (41)$$

A solution for this equation must be selected which, at a fixed frequency, yields a travelling wave for large values of x but leaves $y = 0$ at $x = 0$ at all times; thus

$$y = \hat{y}\left[\sin\frac{2\pi}{\lambda}\left(x - \frac{2\pi k_T c_L t}{\lambda}\right) + \varepsilon^{-2\pi x/\lambda}\sin\frac{4\pi^2 k_T c_L t}{\lambda^2}\right] \quad (42)$$

so that

$$\frac{\partial^2 y}{\partial x^2} = \hat{y}\left(\frac{2\pi}{\lambda}\right)^2\left[-\sin\frac{2\pi}{\lambda}\left(x - \frac{2\pi k_T c_L t}{\lambda}\right) + \varepsilon^{-2\pi x/\lambda}\sin\frac{4\pi^2 k_T c_L t}{\lambda^2}\right]$$

$$= 2\hat{y}\left(\frac{2\pi}{\lambda}\right)^2 \sin\frac{4\pi^2}{\lambda}k_T c_L t \quad \text{if } x = 0$$

Substituting this equation into eqn. (40) gives

$$M = 2EAk_T^2\hat{y}\left(\frac{2\pi}{\lambda}\right)^2 \sin \omega t \quad \ldots \ldots \quad (43)$$

where

$$\omega = 4\pi^2 k_t c_L/\lambda^2 \quad \ldots \ldots \quad (44)$$

If Z_T is the impedance of each tape to the transverse mode in torsional form,

$$Z_T = \frac{M}{d\theta/dt} \quad \ldots \ldots \quad (45)$$

But since $\theta = dy/dx$, eqn. (42) gives

$$\theta = \hat{y}\frac{2\pi}{\lambda}\left[\cos\frac{2\pi}{\lambda}\left(x - \frac{2\pi k_t c_L t}{\lambda}\right) - \sin\frac{4\pi^2 k_t c_L t}{\lambda^2}\varepsilon^{-2\pi x/\lambda}\right]$$

$$= \hat{y}\frac{2\pi}{\lambda}(\cos\omega t - \sin\omega t) \quad \text{if } x = 0$$

$$= \hat{y}\frac{2\pi}{\lambda}\sqrt{(2)}\cos\left(\omega t + \frac{\pi}{4}\right)$$

Therefore

$$\frac{d\theta}{dt} = -\hat{y}\frac{2\pi\omega\sqrt{2}}{\lambda}\sin\left(\omega t + \frac{\pi}{4}\right) \quad \ldots \quad (46)$$

Substituting eqns. (43) and (46) in eqn. (45) gives

$$Z_T = -\frac{EAk_T^2 2\hat{y}}{\hat{y}2\frac{\sqrt{(2)}\pi}{\lambda}\omega}\left(\frac{2\pi}{\lambda}\right)^2 \Big/ -\frac{\pi}{4}$$

Substituting eqn. (44) in this gives

$$Z_T = -\frac{\sqrt{(2)}EAk_T^2}{\sqrt{(\omega k_T c_L)}} \Big/ -\frac{\pi}{4} \quad \ldots \ldots \quad (47)$$

Thus for two tapes the impedance is

$$Z_T = -\frac{2\sqrt{(2)}EAk_T^2}{\sqrt{(\omega k_T c_L)}} \Big/ -\frac{\pi}{4} \quad \ldots \ldots \quad (48)$$

Hence for two tapes the impedance mismatch ratio due to transverse waves in the tape is given by the ratio of eqns. (48) and (38):

$$\left(\frac{k_T}{r}\right)^2 \sqrt{\frac{\lambda_L}{\pi k_T}} \quad \ldots \ldots \quad (49)$$

Eqn. (49) shows that the tape must be thin to reduce the effect of these parasitic transverse waves, and substitution of numerical values indicates that the impedance for the transverse waves is about one-tenth that of the torsional waves at 500 kc/s when using 28-mil diameter wire and 5-mil × 20-mil tape.

Annex No 9 Common Input/Output Scheme

THE UNIVERSAL
INPUT/OUTPUT
SCHEME
AS APPLIED TO THE
MERCURY, PEGASUS II AND SIRIUS II
COMPUTERS.

February, 1961   EP.31

CONTENTS.

1   Introduction
2   General Description of the Scheme
3   Engineering Information
3.1   General
3.2   Computer Waveforms
      3.2.1   Levels and loading
      3.2.2   Select Signal
      3.2.3   Gate Signal
      3.2.4   Start Signal
      3.2.5   Information Signals
      3.2.6   Parity Digit
3.3   Ancillary Waveforms
      3.3.1   Levels and loading
      3.3.2   Ready Signal
      3.3.3   Information Signals
      3.3.4   Parity Information
3.4   Standard Plug Connections
3.5   Further selection within channels

Annex No 9 Common Input/Output Scheme

PART 1

Introduction

Peripheral equipment and ancillary input/output devices are being used in increasing numbers in conjunction with digital computers. Unnecessary expense and engineering effort can be saved if a standard system is adopted whereby ancillaries may be interchanged between one computer and another without the need for extensive modifications either to the ancillary or its associated electronics. The standardised or standardising circuits are colloquially known as "black boxes".

A further advantage offered by such a system is that quick and easy replacement, in the event of ancillary failure, can be effected resulting in a minimum of lost working time. Even if a direct replacement is not available it may be possible, on some programmes, to keep the computer in use, if only at reduced speed, whilst the defective equipment is serviced.

A scheme has been adopted by Ferranti Ltd., on the Mercury, Pegasus II and Sirius II computers such that ancillary input and output devices may be interchanged between any two of these three machines providing that the device is supplied by Ferranti Ltd., or designed to the given specification, for this purpose.

The application is not restricted to tape readers and punches and may be extended to include any equipment working on a character by character basis such as analogue to digital converters, graphical displays and process control equipment.

The object of this report is to detail engineering information required for the design of new equipment or any necessary 'black boxes'. A list of equipment already available to operate within the scheme is obtainable from Ferranti Ltd.

Annex No 9 Common Input/Output Scheme

PART 2

General Description of the Scheme

The Mercury, Pegasus II and Sirius II computers conform to certain standards with respect to the control waveforms that are passed to and from ancillary devices.

Ancillaries manufactured by Ferranti Ltd., to work within the scheme, are fitted with the necessary circuits enabling them to accept and produce these standard signals so that they may work with any one of these three machines. In some cases these circuits are built into the cabinet.

Other ancillaries produced by other manufacturers (Creed, Teletype etc) may be ordered from Ferranti Ltd., suitably modified, so that they also may be operated within the scheme.

In addition to the standardisation of waveforms standard plug connections are used throughout and the signals on individual pins are also standardised. In the event of an ancillary failure, therefore, replacement is simple and rapid and an exact replacement is not necessary to keep the computer working. For instance it is possible, on any output channel in the event of failure, to exchange a Creed 3000/Ferranti Punch for a Teletype/Ferranti Punch in order that the computer is kept in use although at reduced speed.

It should be noted that equipment supplied to operate within the scheme will not operate on the earlier Mercury computers which have not been modified to fall within the framework of the Universal Input/Output scheme: nor will ancillaries which were designed for the original Mercury input/output channels operate in this scheme.

Annex No 9 Common Input/Output Scheme

PART 3

Engineering Information

3.1 General

The control waveform which initiates the transfer or operation whether input or output, is always produced by the computer. In all cases the computer first tests for the 'not ready' condition and the ancillary devices must produce a control voltage which is indicative of this condition. These voltage levels are detailed in 3.3.2.

The sequence of operations within the ancillary device should be such that it is always in position to transmit or receive information, i.e. the information is transferred and the ancillary moves on ready for the next transfer. Whilst the device is moving on or setting up its information it must produce a 'not ready' condition. The 'ready' signal is gated, within the device, by the 'select' signal which is produced by the computer for each device. The 'ready' signal is utilised in the computer to prevent the production of a 'start' signal until the selected device shows the 'ready' condition.

Gates should be provided within the ancillary such that information is transferred when a 'start' signal is produced by the computer. The 'start' signal must also be gated with the 'select' signal, within the device, and used as a trigger to initiate the movement of the mechanism.

More detailed information with respect to the waveforms is now given under separate headings.

3.2 Computer Waveforms

    3.2.1 Levels and loading

    All computer produced waveforms are negative going between

Annex No 9 Common Input/Output Scheme

the following limits:-

(a) when absent, i.e. for zero, -5 volts to +1.7 volts

(b) when set, i.e. for a one, -20 volts to -0.8 volts.

In all cases the maximum current drawn must not exceed 1mA.

3.2.2. Select Signal

This is produced by decoding and gating within the computer and is used to select one of a number of channels or devices. It is possible in some cases to carry out further selection within a channel, or to select different modes of operation within a device, by decoding the n digits which are available at the same time as the 'select' signal. To make this facility available however extra equipment is required and this is dealt with separately.

3.2.3. Gate Signal

The 'gate' waveform is used to gate information into or out of the device. If an input device is concerned this 'gate' signal is used alone, but if an output device is concerned the information must be gated with 'gate' and 'start'. A schematic arrangement of the gates required is given as an example in Fig.1.

3.2.4. Start Signal.

This is used, in the case of output devices, in conjunction with the 'gate' signal to pass information to the ancillary. The 'start' signal should also be gated, within the device, by the 'select' signal to produce a 'go' signal for the device.

3.2.5. Information Signals

The information is set up on staticisers within the computer

Annex No 9 Common Input/Output Scheme

and presented in parallel form in all cases. The maximum number of binary digits per transfer is ten. The information must be gated within the device by 'gate' and 'start'.

3.2.6. Parity Digit

In some cases a parity digit is made available and may be stored with the output information. A system of even parity is used and the parity digit must be gated within the machine in the same manner as the information signals. The way in which this parity information is stored depends upon the type of device in use.

3.3. Ancillary Waveforms

3.3.1. Levels and loading

All waveforms produced by the ancillary device must be negative going and between the following limits:-

(a)   when absent, i.e. for zero, +5v to +8v.

(b)   when set, i.e. for a one, -20v to -16v, the current drain in every case does not exceed 2mA.

3.3.2. Ready Signal

The device must produce a 'ready' signal, if not engaged, which is gated by 'select' within the device. A 'not ready' condition must be produced not later than 10μs after the commencement of the 'start' signal. The 'not ready' condition is indicated by +8v and the 'ready' condition by -16v. The gating of the 'ready' signal by 'select' ensures that all unselected devices produce a 'not ready' condition, i.e. +8 volts. The computer is therefore controlled only by the selected device and a diode should be included in the 'ready' lead of all devices so that they may be 'or'ed together.
A typical schematic arrangement is shown in fig. 1.

- 5 -

Annex No 9 Common Input/Output Scheme

3.3.3.   Information Signals

The information must be fully set before a 'ready' condition is produced, and be in parallel form. A maximum of ten digits per transfer may be handled, as with output information, and must be gated within the device by the 'gate' signal. A diode should be included in each output lead so that devices may be 'or'ed together.

3.3.4.   Parity Information

In some cases a parity checking facility is provided and works on a system of even parity. The computer is stopped if the check fails. The stored parity digit must be presented at the same time as the information and gated by the 'gate' waveform within the device.

3.4 Standard Plug Connections

Unitor plugs and sockets are used as standard throughout the scheme at the ancillary end of computer/ancillary leads which have a standard length of thirty feet. The male portion of the plug is mounted on the ancillary with Pin 1 uppermost. The signals on each pin of the Unitor connectors are also standardised and are as given below:-

(a)   4-way Unitor

Pin 1   N
 " 2   115 v AC
 " 3   230 x AC
 " 4   EARTH

Annex No 9 Common Input/Output Scheme

```
(b)         8-way Unitor
Pin 1 ) L
 "  2 )
Pin 3 ) E
 "  4 )
Pin 5 ) N
 "  6 )
 "  7 )
 "  8 )

(c)         25-way Unitor
Pin  1  P0
 "   2  P1
 "   3  P2
 "   4  P3
 "   5  P4
 "   6  P5
 "   7  P6
 "   8  P7
 "   9  P8
 "  10  P9
 "  11  PARITY
 "  12  START
 "  13  GATE
 "  14  SELECT
 "  15  READY
 "  16  SPARE
 "  17   "
 "  18   "
 "  19   "
 "  20  EARTH
 "  21  0 Volts
 "  22  Reserved for special application on Sirius
 "  23    "     "    "        "          "    "
 "  24    "     "    "        "          "    "
 "  25    "     "    "        "          "    "
```

3.5 Further selection within channels

It was mentioned in 3.2.2. that it was possible to make further selection within a channel, in some cases, by decoding the n digits which are available at the same time as the 'select' signal. With

- 7 -

Annex No 9 Common Input/Output Scheme

Mercury, for instance, where ten binary digits are available, using a straight forward binary code, it is theoretically possible to have 1024 devices in each channel. Alternatively it is possible to have numerous modes of operation of a single device and select one of these modes.

If ancillary devices are designed to the specification detailed in the engineering information (Part 3) they will work on the input (or output) channels of any of the three computers. If however it is desired to operate more than one device, or a device with several modes of operation, in a particular channel then extra circuitry will be required between the computer and these devices. These circuits must be designed to operate with, and produce, the waveforms as laid down in the engineering information.

Further requirements of the extra 'black box' used in this case are that it should accept the Unitor plugs that are provided at the end of each channel lead and contain gates that provide a 'select' signal for the ancillary, or mode, according to the code of the n digits when gated by the computer 'select' signal.

If the 'black box' is designed to the above requirements, and with Unitor plugs terminating its output cables, any ancillaries designed to work within the scheme may be worked in conjunction with it. (Up to a maximum number of 1024 per channel is theoretically possible if all ten digits of the n information are utilised).

This facility of further selection within a channel is available on the Mercury and Sirius II computer but not on the Pegasus II computer. In the case of the latter machine only one ancillary device per channel is permissable.

Annex No 9 Common Input/Output Scheme

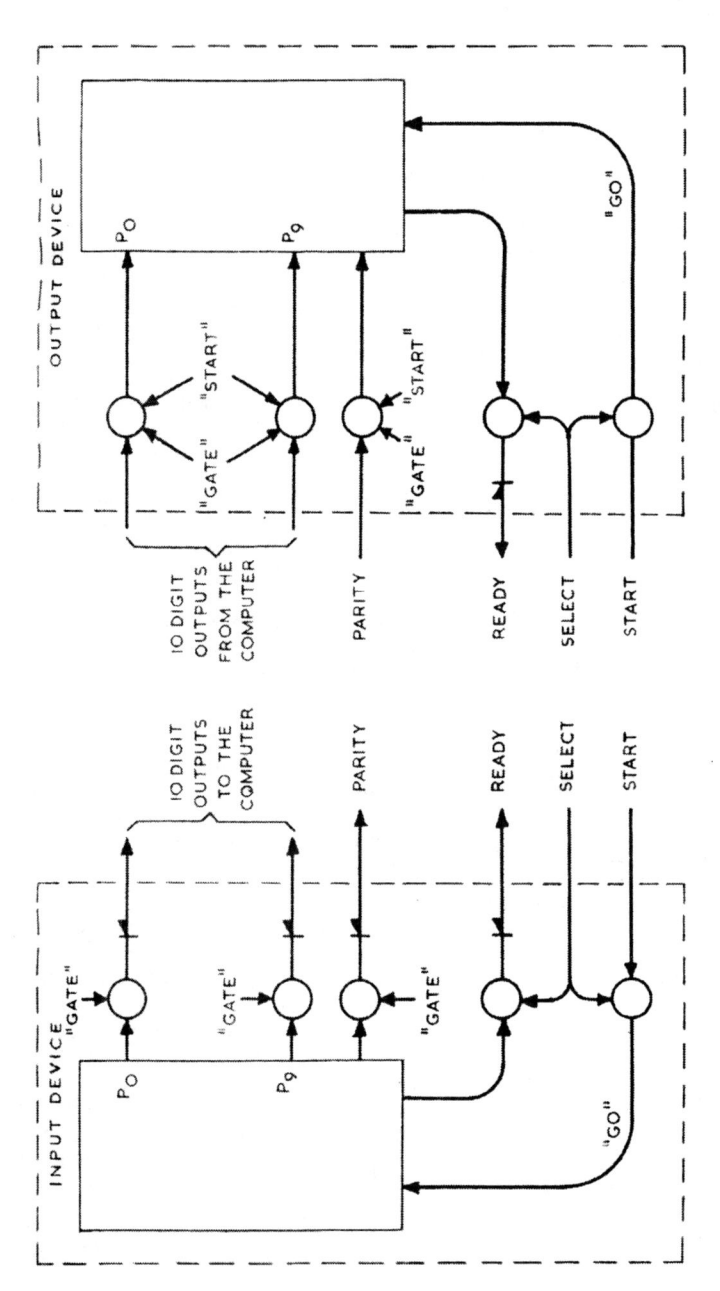

Annex 10 Merry extols the designers of Pegasus

The design of Pegasus

Ian Merry

I'm uncertain whether I welcome this opportunity to celebrate the engineering genius of Charles Owen and the conceptual brilliance of Christopher Strachey, or whether, like pious Aeneas before Queen Dido of Carthage, I've been asked to awaken ancient and unutterable feelings of regret. Regret that following the outstandingly successful development of Pegasus the design team was disbanded and, at least to my way of thinking, no worthy successor has ever been developed in Britain.

I'll identify a few of the individual characteristics of the members of the design team which had a significant influence on the design.

I learnt from my experience with Pegasus that good design requires the prejudices of a single design authority to be both articulated and respected. Problem definition is a vital precursor to problem solution.

Successful design depends on solutions with designabilty, amenable to design analysis and calculation, since design is constrained by the limitations of materials. Successful design goes, so to speak, with the grain. These were in effect the precepts on which both Owen and Strachey based their work; they were not however very typical of the world of electronics in the 1950s.

What was this world like? The impact of radar development during World War Two was still much in evidence. A major advance in glass technology, dating from about 1938 with the appearance of the Philips EF50 valve, had fostered a succession of high-gain miniature vacuum tubes only about an inch in diameter and no more than a few inches in length.

Point contact germanium diodes had been developed during the war as radar demodulators, based on little more than the kitchen science of crystal wireless sets of the 1920s. With the invention of Schockley's point contact transistor in 1947 a hesitant semiconductor industry had arisen concentrating on germanium semiconductor technology, hampered by the variability of point contact devices, and only marginally familiar with the technology of silicon and junction devices on which we all now depend.

Electronics was still mainly the concern of telecommunications and broadcasting, the former with its 22 inch wide racks of equipment 6-8 feet high, and the latter with racks as wide as 24 inches (at least in the BBC), bearing monolithic cadmium plated steel chassis, each weighing tens of pounds with a dozen or more valves and associated circuits.

Significantly, most of those involved in the wartime radar development had been graduates in physics, without academic engineering backgrounds, since in Britain at least electronic engineering was widely regarded as a dilettante not to say insecure profession until well into the 1950s.

This circumstance together with wartime pressures had confused the concept of design with the narrower field of circuit design, and established a widespread design tradition of suck-it-and-see whenever a problem arose outside the immediate experience of the designer. That's not to say that suck-it-and-see was how circuits were designed; that depended entirely on the intellectual probity of the designer. But suck-it-and-see was still very much the way of dealing with any problem that

Annex 10 Merry extols the designers of Pegasus

was not immediately in the competence of electronics.

Again, where the logical power of electronic digital computation had been clear since the early 1940s to the indoctrinated of Bletchley Park, it was the domain of the smallish band of mainly academic successors, among whom few had studied design as an engineer.

Even where, as in the BBC Engineering Department, numerically based design was given its full due, on the electronic front this was in the context of high quality analogue circuits made linear with a quasi-statuary 40 db of negative feedback!

Consequently there was no pressure at all on the makers of valves or semiconductor devices to publish the variances of their device parameter data. On the contrary it was rarely clear whether published data represented design targets or achieved median values!

Lastly, despite the marketing hype of the Festival of Britain in 1951 and the governmental initiative of NRDC, there was no longer the recognition of engineering as an important aspect of the British Raj, as had existed in the 19th and early 20th centuries.

Turning now to the major players in the design of Pegasus, there were four in number: Charles Owen, Christopher Strachey, Brian Maudesley and myself. I would like to pay tribute to Owen's engineering sagacity.

He had the essential vision of a successful engineer, which is to have formed an architectural concept of the finished work from the earliest possible moment. Changes to that concept could be made as the design progressed, but any change had to be demonstrably beneficial, and to meet Charles' exacting standards of acceptability.

Given the clear benefits and the conformity with the standards of acceptability, there was in my experience no need for further persuasion. It was stimulating to work with someone who had no need to reinforce his prejudices with anything but logic and good sense.

In addition Charles was very ready to pass on his own knowledge -- a characteristic which endeared him to me as I had no previous experience of digital techniques. With all of that, and though often doggishly witty, Charles was essentially a plain man for whom facts were facts and fancies were fancies.

Christopher Strachey on the other hand was a modern Renaissance man. Besides his achievements as a mathematical logician and systems conceptualizer, he was a most talented musician; he and I used to sing and play together. His skill in technical discussion or general conversation was such as to make everyone else present perform beyond their usual level, as a consequence of his own rather competitive verbal brilliance.

The third principal member of the design team, Brian Maudesley, was unusual in both background and personality. A mechanical engineer from Ferranti Edinburgh fallen among intellectuals, he held his own in consequence of a unique capacity for mechanical innovation, and for his mild manner, all supported by a physical stature of 6' 8".

As for myself, I joined Ferranti after four and a half years in the BBC Engineering Research Department where I had worked on a number of electronic and electromechanical projects connected with both disc and magnetic recording, and where I had encountered many of the problems which were still then at issue in the Pegasus project.

My only previous experience with digital circuits had involved telephone relays -- a brief encounter which left me with no yearning for further involvement with relay switching!

We come now to the principles on which the architecture and design of Pegasus was based. Strachey's major objective was to reduce the labour of the programmer, especially by providing efficient and consistent order code; by freeing the programmer from undue concern with machine architecture; by minimizing performance bottlenecks; and by maintaining an autonomous invigilation of all machine

Annex 10 Merry extols the designers of Pegasus

functions, using odd-parity checking throughout.

Owen for his part had an intense preoccupation with machine reliability and availability. His experience led him to believe that while this required conservative design, with care this did not get in the way of elegance and economy. Both he and Strachey aimed to build all of the complex control functions without recourse to special purpose circuits.

With both prudence and modesty Owen took the view that basic circuit elements used in the Elliott 401 represented the soundest basis for progress. Packages containing several OR configurations of point contact diode AND gates, logically ORed, followed by a cathode follower direct output or an inverter or a simple pulse amplifier retiming and delay circuit furnished the logical armoury of the bit-level logic, as in the 401, while single word packages using a nickel delay line as a serial storage medium provided immediate access memory for accumulators and registers.

Now it's fairly obvious that the more complex a logical function, the more numerous are likely to be the various inputs. So the number of inputs to individual AND gates should be as little restricted by circuit component deficiencies as is prudent.

To upgrade the Elliott logic circuits, Owen instituted a statistical analysis of the problem, and ascertained by experiment the variance of the germanium diode back leakage resistance. In this way he avoided on the one hand the Scylla of AND gates with the more leaky diodes exhibiting pattern sensitive failings, and on the other the Charybdis of oversensitive gate design.

In considering the remarkable success in achieving the design objectives, remember that Pegasus is a serial machine in which the 39 working bits of each word arrive sequentially at any point, or as we now say at every interface in the machine.

To maintain the economic advantages of this serial approach, interface width has to be kept to a minimum, nearly always only one bit wide. The parts of the machine where static registers hold a number of words concurrently are thus few in number.

The thinking required in the logical design, particularly of the control functions, therefore required the designer to envisage successive machine states represented by circuit states changing autonomously and quickly under the inexorable flow of serial data. This is a duality which it is difficult to represent conspicuously in any diagram form, and was quite beyond the descriptive mathematical techniques of the time.

In this regard I well remember the seminar when the logical designers first gave an explanation of the control architecture. By then Pegasus was in active use and the logical design seemed to be consistent, but for my part at least the description of the various control cycles was and remains baffling.

Coming now to the engineering problems which had to be solved, we can regard them arising against three design aims. These are reliability, economy and performance.

Past experience had shown that the major areas of transient unreliability were pattern sensitivity of individual logic or storage units, where correct operation continues until a particular sequence of binary digits occurs which evokes an incorrect output.

Secondly, on drum systems generally, think of a difficulty and they appear to have it. Thirdly we had to live with package, plug and socket electrical contact variability. Happily by this time other electrical component deficiencies did not present causes of transient problems, and were adequate in terms of operational life given that they were not sourced from suspect quarters such as Government surplus -- a false economy which bedevilled some other projects.

Now except to a mechanical engineer of particular discernment there is little intellectual

Annex 10 Merry extols the designers of Pegasus

stimulus in addressing the problem of erratic plug and socket behaviour, which is why, I think, the problem hung around for so long. In many ways this was the most dangerous of the package circuit problems since so many package interfaces were at risk.

Maudesley tackled and solved the problem with determination. To keep the contact resistance of each contact adequately low, he insisted that it was insufficient to rely on the comparative incorruptibility of noble metal surfaces; instead, on each insertion of a package every female contact should scrape its corresponding male and ensure a new metal to metal interface. Given an adequate thickness of noble metal plating of the male contacts, a quite adequate if limited number of insertions could be made.

It might have seemed a risky way of proceeding, as noble metal surfaces can get worn away very quickly. In fact we reckoned that we could do at least 50 insertions without trouble, and that was well beyond the number of insertions one would normally expect a package to receive.

The in-line multi-contact socket used was to have the necessary female geometry, and a concomitant to this solution was the provision of a robust and stable mounting for package board and socket. This was achieved most economically by the use of aluminium alloy diecastings for the package shelf mounting.

The robust behaviour of Pegasus after switch-on and throughout the life of the various machines has been very largely due to this solution to package structure and contact geometry.

Lastly of course the package board itself had to be of an adequate rigidity and stability. Attention to details of this sort had not distinguished previous computer projects.

The drum system appeared to present problems in every possible area. The geometry of the magnetic fields caused the head signal to be rapidly attenuated with an increase in the read head-to-recording medium gap. About half the signal is lost in geometrical progression for each extra tenth of a bit length gap.

With a drum diameter of 10 inches and 128 42-bit words per track, it turns out that an overall variation in signal of 2:1 ensues if the radial runout of the drum surface (due to machining tolerance, variations in coating thickness and bearing shake) is no more than about half a thou, and exponentially pro rata.

Owen had already decided this was too demanding by a factor of two. He had laid down that alternate bits would be recorded in pairs of tracks, so that we could have double the wavelength for each bit, with write and read head diplexing handled by machine logic. This was a strategy previously adopted at Elliotts.

I soon realized that not only the diplexing but also the actual phase encoded waveform could now come directly from the logic. This removed the need for a special purpose circuit, pleasing everybody especially me.

However even a total runout tolerance of half a thou appeared to have caused difficulties with previous bearing design and bearing life. And there was some disquiet in connection with the drum under development at Ferranti in Manchester for the forthcoming Mercury computer.

At the BBC, while studying the problems of television magnetic recording, I had tackled the problem in the lab by using a horizontally mounted narrow drum or disc with a little known 360 degree bearing design. This had however to be hand lapped to a radial consistency of about one tenth of a thou. The drum coating with its magnetic surface was then sapphire turned.

A 360 degree bearing is nominally permanently lubricated, and it works best with a lubricant with particular physical properties like sperm oil. I introduced this with an eye dropper to my own machines. Maudesley would have none of this quasi-magical 19th century engineering and quickly came up with a solution.

Annex 10 Merry extols the designers of Pegasus

He realized that precision boring spindles have to perform with a radial runout of better than one tenth of a thou without adjustment over a period of many months, so decided to approach the manufacturer of such machine tools and give him the problem.

Bill Burnham of Burnham and Turners in Mansfield cheerfully undertook to make a suitable drum mechanism if we provided him with outline design and details of the motor to be incorporated. Bill entertained no taboos or superstitions about putting three bearings on one shaft.

He assured constancy in bearing behaviour and bearing life by using twin sets of angular contact ball bearings under considerable axial pressure. As I recall it the original prototype which was used in the first Pegasus cost only £300, excluding the electric motor. The drum fitted to the CCS machine is a later and larger version although it's built on precisely the same principles.

Other Ferranti drums were run as slaves to the rest of the machine, synchronized in a phase-lock with crystal controlled logic circuits, requiring an elegant servo system, and culminating in a very hefty power amplifier. This was in my view to turn good design on its head, because you are making a cumbersome object (a rotating drum) slave to a more pliant system (a lot of digital circuits). Our drum needed over a quarter of a horse-power, making this scheme doubly unattractive.

I therefore got Owen to agree that the logic should be driven from a clock track recorded on the drum. The rotational speed of the drum would then be kept within the limits required by the delay lines, using quite a simple servo loop with a crystal reference.

As the drum drive had to be at 150 Hz for the 4000 rpm rotation speed, this loop included the motor excitation of the 150 Hz alternator set. That left us with a small problem: how do you record a clock track on the magnetic oxide, which is consistent, the right number of bits, and actually joins without any bumps?

We accomplished this by first recording an approximately correct, but incomplete clock track, which was then temporarily phase-locked by a hand adjustment of the servo. At the correct rotation speed, using a crystal controlled reference and using an expanded trace oscilloscope, the rotational inertia of the drum made this practically possible without any excessive manual dexterity on the part of the operator. At first a clock frequency of correct length to close on itself was then recorded.

Ferranti drums had previously been nickel coated because the low coercivity required little power output from the write amplifiers. However these coatings had occasional magnetic weak or dead spots, owing I believe to stresses in the plating.

Subsequently when I went to IBM I discovered they had similar problems at about the same time with their drums on the IBM 650. They eventually overcame them with weird chemicals in the plating baths. At the BBC however I'd found that Fe_2O_3 oxide dispersion used for coating magnetic tape was readily spray painted onto a drum, using just an ordinary spray gun, and so we abandoned nickel for red iron oxide.

Split rings of low loss ferrite also worked as well as read and write heads up to well over 0.5 MHz, needing only pairs of miniature power pentodes to drive the magnetic oxide into saturation. Better still, correctly formed ferrite recording head blanks were then becoming available. I was fortunate in finding a subcontractor, Epsilon Ltd, making multistack heads for tape recorders who were willing to package banks of ferrite heads with a low impedance to my requirements.

Drum system performance, reliability and usability was greatly increased by abandoning relay head switching and developing valve and germanium diode crossbar switches for writing and reading.

The read switch came before any amplification and was entirely novel. Charles Owen had to be convinced by a test lasting several months with a random batch of diodes that diode noise

Annex 10 Merry extols the designers of Pegasus

would not cause errors; however diode noise remained below 250 microvolts, and was quite harmless to the unamplified phase modulated signal of some 3-4 mV from the heads.

These switches meant that the relay switch settling times of 20 milliseconds, which is what you got in a Post Office relay, were totally avoided; in fact the read amplifier recovery after writing time of about 500 ms became a limiting factor, while track switching took only about half that time.

So we both improved the performance and enabled single word as well as eight word block transfers to be efficient. Lastly, block addresses in the drum address track were permutated to leave two blocks between blocks of successive block addresses within any block where the addresses remain in natural sequence.

This gave time for some computation between successive blocks without involving the programmer, and he didn't have to go in for fancy addressing of his data via optimum programming, which was in general use for other drum systems.

As a result of these innovations the drum system became in harmony with the general approach that distinguished the Strachey-Owen design.

I'll mention two other features of the logical design that contributed to overall performance. These were the provision of multiple accumulators and many more registers; and the incorporation in the order code of a comprehensive and logically regular method of handling address modification using some of these extra registers.

How much more effective would Pegasus' contemporary, the IBM 650, have been with these features, designed as it was for similar user areas? How sad that Pegasus could not have been equally widely exploited.

That concludes my survey of Pegasus development except to say as I wrote in the Computer Journal of June 1991, "It is a matter of record that all of these features were working in the Pegasus pilot by April 1956.

"Development begun in 1955 added card and tape peripherals in the subsequent years, leading to machine sales of nearly 40 machines overall. Regardless of these good beginnings an evident loss of focus on behalf of the Ferranti senior management, coupled with NRDC's short term financial preoccupations, fostered an atmosphere in which by 1956 the burden of continuing investment was only acceptable at a level requiring a fundamental choice between the Mercury team in Manchester and the Pegasus team in London.

"Except for the peripheral developments mentioned above the Pegasus team was largely disbanded, and staff were redirected to work on Ferranti contract and defence work, or in the case of some of the leading team members regrouped under American auspices in September 1956. This was a blow to the infant British computer industry at a most crucial time from which subsequent events have shown it never wholly recovered, exemplifying how inadequate investment ensures a net and enduring loss."

The history of Pegasus has always seemed to me to be a paradigm of the British industrial malady -- not just the shibboleth that Britain fails to market its wares, but more fundamentally that we no longer recognize or foster and therefore we cannot exploit our real strengths.

This article is based on a talk given by the author as part of the Elliott/Pegasus all-day seminar at the Science Museum on 21 May 1992.

Lightning Source UK Ltd.
Milton Keynes UK
UKOW032016030912

198319UK00008B/3/P